Using Cointegration Analysis in Econometric Modelling

Using Cointegration Analysis in Econometric Modelling

R. I. D. HARRIS
University of Portsmouth

PRENTICE HALL
HARVESTER WHEATSHEAF

London New York Toronto Sydney Tokyo Singapore Madrid Mexico City Munich

First published 1995 by
Prentice Hall/Harvester Wheatsheaf
Campus 400, Maylands Avenue
Hemel Hempstead
Hertfordshire, HP2 7EZ
A division of
Simon & Schuster International Group

Typeset in 10/12 Times
by Mathematical Composition Setters Ltd.

Printed and bound in Great Britain by
T. J. Press (Padstow) Ltd

Library of Congress Cataloging in Publication Data

Harris, Richard I. D., 1957-
Using cointegration analysis in econometric modelling/R.I.D. Harris.
p. cm.
Includes bibliographical references and index.
ISBN 0-13-355892-4
1. Econometric models. 2. Economics–Statisical methods.
I. Title
HB141.H373 1995 94–45273
330'.01'5195–dc20 CIP

British Library Cataloguing in Publication Data

A catalogue record for this book is available from
the British Library

ISBN 0-13-355892-4

3 4 5 99 98 97

To Suzette,
Jonathan, Benjamin
and Paul

Contents

Preface

Like many books, this one began with my attempts to teach students about unit roots and cointegration and then finding that there was no text available at a level that both they and I could understand. In fact, there was very little on the subject in the standard textbooks and even now most include one (or perhaps two) chapters when the topic deserves a more thorough treatment. The other problem that I (and it seemed to me the majority of my non-specialist colleagues) faced was the technical rigour associated with the subject. Unfortunately, I am not a highly trained econometrician, but like other applied economists I want to use the most appropriate (and often the latest) techniques in applied work. This meant a lot of hard work trying to understand techniques such as the Johansen procedure, and then more hard work trying to put them into practice. So this book is intended for students and others working in the field of economics who want to know the why and how, but do not have too much time to spend on updating their working knowledge of applied time series econometrics.

I have tried to incorporate into this book as many of the latest techniques in the area as possible, and to provide as many examples as necessary to illustrate these. To help the reader, one of the major data sets used is supplied in the statistical appendix, which also includes many of the key tables of critical values used for various tests involving unit roots and cointegration.

I have no doubt made some mistakes in interpreting the literature, and I would like to thank in advance those readers who might wish to point these out to me. I would also like to thank Jeremy Smith, who talked me through a few misconceptions, and to exonerate him from the remaining errors, and also Pradeep Jethi, the Commissioning Editor for Harvester Wheatsheaf, for his willingness to support this project. Finally, permission from the various authors and copyright holders to reproduce the statistical tables is gratefully acknowledged.

R.H.

1

Introduction and overview

Important terms and concepts

Differencing and levels Data generating processes Strong and weak exogeneity Autoregressive distributive lag (ADL) models Congruency 'White noise' error term Random (stochastic) variables Autoregressive (AR) processes Moving-average processes Polynomial lag operator

During the last decade applied economists attempting to estimate time series econometric models have been aware of certain difficulties that arise when unit roots are present in the data. To ignore this fact, and to proceed to estimate a regression model containing non-stationary variables at best ignores important information about the underlying (statistical and economic) processes generating the data, and at worst leads to nonsensical (or spurious) results. For this reason, it is incumbent on the applied researcher to test for the presence of unit roots and if they are present (and the evidence suggests that they generally are) to use appropriate modelling procedures. Detrending is not appropriate (Chapter 2) and simply differencing the data[1] to remove the non-stationary (stochastic) trend is only part of the answer. While the use of differenced variables will avoid the spurious regression problem, it will also remove any long-run information. In modelling time series data we need to retain this long-run information but to ensure that it reflects the co-movement of variables due to the underlying equilibrating tendencies of economic forces, rather than those due to common, but unrelated, time trends in the data.

Modelling the long-run when the variables are non-stationary is a new and expanding area of econometrics (both theoretical and applied). It is new in that while it is possible to find antecedents in the literature dating back to, for example, the seminal work of Sargan (1964) on early forms of the error-correction model, it was really only in 1986 (following the March special issue of the *Oxford Bulletin of*

Economics and Statistics) that cointegration became a familiar term in the literature.[2] It is also a rapidly expanding area, as witnessed by the number of articles that have been published since the mid-1980s. There have been, and continue to be, major new developments. However, cointegration analysis may have reached a (first) plateau, and initial concentration on the theoretical side has now probably been superseded (at least in the volume of new work published) by attempts to apply the theory.

The purpose of this book is to present to the reader those techniques that are gaining most acceptance, and to present them in as non-technical a way as possible while still retaining an understanding of what they are designed to do. Those who want a more rigorous treatment to supplement the current text are referred to Banerjee, Dolado, Galbraith and Hendry (1993) in the first instance, and then of course to the appropriate journals. It is useful to begin by covering some introductory concepts, leaving a full treatment of the standard econometric techniques relating to stationary data to other texts (see, for example, the contrasting approaches of Thomas, 1993, and Davidson and MacKinnon, 1993). This is followed by an overview of the remainder of the book, providing a route-map through the topics covered, starting with a simple discussion of long-run and short-run models (Chapter 2) and then proceeding through to estimating these models using multivariate techniques (Chapters 5 and 6).

Some initial concepts

This section will review some of the most important concepts and ideas in time series modelling, providing a reference point for later on in the book. A fuller treatment is available in a standard text such as that by Harvey (1990). We begin with the idea of a data generating process (hereafter d.g.p.), in terms of autoregressive and moving-average representations of dynamic processes. This will also necessitate some discussion of the properties of the error term in a regression model, and statistical inferences based on the assumption that such residuals are 'white noise'.

Data generating processes

As economists, we only have limited knowledge about the economic processes which determine the observed data. Thus, while models involving such data are formulated by economic theory, and then tested using econometric techniques, it has to be recognised that theory in itself is not enough. For instance, theory may provide little evidence about the processes of adjustment, which variables are exogenous and, indeed, which are irrelevant or constant for the particular model under investigation (Hendry, Pagan and Sargan, 1984). A contrasting approach is based on statistical theory, which involves trying to characterise the statistical processes whereby the data were generated.

We begin with a very simple stationary univariate model observed over the sequence of time $t = 1, \dots, T$:

$$y_t = \rho y_{t-1} + u_t \qquad |\rho| < 1$$

or

$$(1 - \rho L)\, y_t = u_t \tag{1.1}$$

where L is the lag operator such that $Ly_t = y_{t-1}$. This statistical model states that the variable y_t is generated by its own past together with a disturbance (or residual) term, u_t. The latter represents the influence of all other variables excluded from the model, which are presumed to be random (or unpredictable) such that u_t has the following statistical properties: its expected value (or mean) is zero ($E(u_t) = 0$); fluctuations around this mean value are not growing or declining over time (i.e., it has constant variance denoted $E(u_t^2) = \sigma^2$); and it is uncorrelated with its own past ($E(u_t\, u_{t-i}) = 0$). Having u_t in (1.1) allows y_t to also be treated as a random (stochastic) variable.[3]

This model can be described as a d.g.p. if the observed realisation of y_t over time is simply one of an infinite number of possible outcomes, each dependent on drawing a sequence of random numbers, u_t, from an appropriate (e.g., standard normal) distribution.[4] Despite the fact that in practice only a single sequence of y_t is observed, in theory any number of realisations is possible over the same time period. Statistical inferences with respect to this model are now possible based upon its underlying probability distribution.

The simple time series model (1.1) can be extended to let y_t depend on past values up to a lag length of p:

$$y_t = \rho_1 y_{t-1} + \rho_2 y_{t-2} + \dots + \rho_p y_{t-p} + u_t$$

or

$$A(L) y_t = u_t \tag{1.2}$$

where $A(L)$ is the polynomial lag operator $1 - \rho_1 L - \rho_2 L^2 - \dots \rho_p L^p$. The d.g.p. in (1.2) is described as a pth-order autoregressive (AR) model.[5] This is in contrast to specifying the dependence of y_t on its own past as a moving-average (MA) process, such as the following first-order MA model:

$$y_t = u_t + \theta u_{t-1} \qquad |\theta| < 1 \tag{1.3}$$

or a model with past values up to a lag-length of q:

$$y_t = u_t + \theta_1 u_{t-1} + \dots + \theta_q u_{t-q}$$

or

$$y_t = B(L) u_t \tag{1.4}$$

where $B(L)$ is the polynomial lag operator $\theta_0 + \theta_1 L + \theta_2 L^2 + \dots + \theta_q L^q$. Finally, it is possible to specify a mixed ARMA model:

$$A(L)y_t = B(L)u_t \tag{1.5}$$

which is the most flexible d.g.p. for a univariate series.

So far, the d.g.p. underlying the univariate time series y_t contains no economic information. That is, while it is valid to model y_t as a statistical process (cf. the Box–Jenkins approach), this is of little use if we are looking to establish (causal) linkages between variables. Thus, (1.1) can be generalised to include other variables (both stochastic, such as x_t, and deterministic, such as an intercept), for example:

$$y_t = \alpha_0 + \gamma_0 x_t + \alpha_1 y_{t-1} + u_t \tag{1.6}$$

Since x_t is stochastic, let its underlying d.g.p. be given by:

$$x_t = \xi x_{t-1} + \varepsilon_t \qquad |\xi| < 1 \text{ and } \varepsilon_t \sim IN(0, \sigma_\varepsilon^2) \qquad (1.7)^6$$

If u_t and ε_t are not correlated, we can state that $E(u_t\varepsilon_s) = 0$ for all t and s, and then it is possible to treat x_t *as if* it were fixed for the purposes of estimating (1.6). That is, x_t is independent of u_t (denoted $E(x_t u_t) = 0$) and we can treat it as (strongly) exogenous in terms of (1.6), with x_t being said to (Granger-) cause y_t. Equation (1.6) is called a conditional model in that y_t is conditional on x_t (with x_t determined by the marginal model given in (1.7)).

Note, if (1.7) is reformulated as:

$$x_t = \xi_1 x_{t-1} + \xi_2 y_{t-1} + \varepsilon_t \tag{1.8}$$

then $E(x_t u_t) = 0$ is retained but since past values of y_t now determine x_t, the latter can only be considered weakly exogenous in the conditional model (1.6).[7]

As with the univariate case, the d.g.p. denoted by (1.6) can be generalised to obtain what is known as an autoregressive distributed-lag (ADL) model:

$$A(L)\, y_t = B(L)x_t + u_t \tag{1.9}$$

where the polynomial lag operators $A(L)$ and $B(L)$ have already been defined.[8] Extending to the multivariate case is straightforward, replacing y_t and x_t by vectors of variables, $\mathbf{y}_t$ and $\mathbf{x}_t$.

The great strength of using an equation such as (1.9) as the basis for econometric modelling is that it provides a good first approximation to the (unknown) d.g.p. Recall the above arguments that theory usually has little to say about the form of the (dynamic) adjustment process (which (1.9) is flexible enough to capture), or about which variables are exogenous (this model can also be used as a basis for testing for exogeneity). In fact, Hendry, Pagan and Sargan (1984) argue that the process of econometric modelling is an attempt to match the unknown d.g.p. with a validly specified econometric model, and thus '... economic theory restrictions on the analysis are essential; and while the data are the result of economic behaviour, the actual statistical properties of the observables corresponding to y and z are also obviously relevant to correctly analysing their empirical relationship. In a nutshell, measurement without theory is as valueless as the converse is non-operational.' In practical terms, and according to the Hendry-type approach, the test of model adequacy is whether the model is *congruent* with the data evidence, which in a single equation model is defined in terms of the statistical properties of the model (e.g., a 'white noise' error term and parameters that are constant over time), and whether the model is consistent with the theory from which it is derived and with the data it admits. Finally, congruency requires the model to encompass rival models.[9]

Role of the error term, u_t, and statistical Inference

As stated above, the error term, u_t, represents the influence of all other variables excluded from the model, which are presumed to be random (or unpredictable) such that u_t has the following statistical properties: its mean is zero ($E(u_t) = 0$); it has constant variance ($E(u_t^2) = \sigma^2$); and it is uncorrelated with its own past ($E(u_t u_{t-i}) = 0$). To this we can add that the determining variable(s) in the model, assuming that they are stochastic, must be independent of the error term ($E(x_t u_t) = 0$).[10] If these assumptions hold, then it is shown in standard texts such as that by Johnston (1984) that estimators like the OLS estimator will lead to unbiased estimates of the parameter coefficients of the model (indeed, OLS is the best linear unbiased estimator). If it is further assumed that u_t is drawn from the (multivariate) normal distribution, then this suffices to establish inference procedures for testing hypotheses involving the parameters of the model, based on χ^2, t- and F-tests and their associated probability distributions.

Thus, testing to ensure that $u_t \sim IN(0, \sigma_u^2)$, that is an independently distributed random 'white noise' process drawn from the normal distribution, is an essential part of the modelling process. Its failure leads to invalid inference procedures unless alternative estimators (e.g., GLS or systems estimators) and/or alternative probability distributions (such as the Dickey–Fuller distribution) are invoked.

Outline of the book

The next chapter deals with short- and long-run models. Inherent in the distinction is the notion of equilibrium; that is, the long-run is a state of equilibrium where there is no inherent tendency to change since economic forces are in balance, while the short-run depicts the disequilibrium state. Long-run models are often termed 'static models', but there is no necessity actually to achieve equilibrium at any point in time, even as $t \to \infty$. All that is required is that economic forces move the system towards the equilibrium defined by the long-run relationship posited. Put another way, the static equilibrium needs to be reinterpreted empirically since most economic variables grow over time. Thus, what matters is the idea of a steady-state relationship between variables which are evolving over time. This is the way the term 'equilibrium' is used in this book.

When considering long-run relationships, it becomes necessary to consider the underlying properties of the processes that generate time series variables. That is, we must distinguish between stationary and non-stationary variables since failure to do so can lead to a problem of spurious regression whereby the results suggest that there are statistically significant long-run relationships between the variables in the regression model when in fact all that is being obtained is evidence of contemporaneous correlations rather than meaningful causal relations. Simple examples of stationary and non-stationary processes are provided, and it is shown that whether a variable is stationary depends on whether it has a unit root. Comparing stationary and non-stationary variables is also related to the different types of time trend that can be found in variables. Non-stationary variables are shown to contain stochastic (i.e., random) trends, while stationary variables contain deterministic (i.e., fixed) trends. Since random trends in the data can lead to spurious correlations, an example of a spurious regression is given together with some explanations of why this occurs.

This leads naturally to the question of when it is possible to infer a causal long-run relationship(s) between non-stationary time series. The simple answer is: when the variables are cointegrated. The Engle and Granger (1987) definition of cointegration is explained, alongside the economic interpretation of cointegration, which states that if two (or more) series are linked to form an equilibrium relationship spanning the long-run, then even though the series themselves may contain stochastic trends (i.e., be non-stationary) they will nevertheless move closely together over time and the difference between them will be stable (i.e., stationary). Thus the concept of cointegration mimics the existence of a long-run equilibrium to which an economic system converges over time. The absence of cointegration leads back to the problem of spurious regression.

Chapter 2 finally discusses short-run (dynamic) models. Simple examples of dynamic models are presented and linked to their long-run, steady-state (equilibrium) solutions. It is pointed out that estimating a dynamic equation in the levels of the variables is problematic, and differencing the variables is not a solution since this then removes any information about the long-run. The more suitable approach is to convert the dynamic model into an error-correction formulation (ECM), and it is shown that this contains information on both the short-run and long-run properties of the model, with disequilibrium as a process of adjustment to the long-run model. The relationship between ECMs and the concept of cointegration is also explored, to show that if two variables y_t and x_t are cointegrated, then there must exist an ECM (and conversely, that an ECM generates cointegrated series).

Having discussed the importance of unit roots, the next task (Chapter 3) is to test for their presence in time series data. This begins with a discussion of the Dickey–Fuller (DF) test for a unit root, showing that a t-test of the null hypothesis of non-stationarity is not based on the standard t-distribution but, rather, on the non-standard Dickey–Fuller distribution. Assumptions about what is the most appropriate d.g.p. for the variable being tested are found to be important when performing the test, that is should an intercept and trend (i.e., deterministic components) be included in the test equation? Not only does inclusion and exclusion lead to different critical values for the DF test, but it is also important to ensure that the test for a unit root nests both the null hypothesis and the alternative hypothesis. To do this it is necessary to have as many deterministic regressors in the equation used for testing as there are deterministic components in the assumed underlying d.g.p. In order to test what will probably be in practice the most common form of the null hypothesis (that the d.g.p. contains a stochastic trend against the alternative of trend-stationary), it is necessary to allow both an intercept and a time trend t to enter the regression model used to test for a unit root.

To overcome the problems associated with which (if any) deterministic components should enter the DF test (including problems associated with test power), the sequential testing procedure put forward by Perron (1988) is discussed. Then the DF test is extended to allow for situations when more complicated time series processes underlie the d.g.p. This results in the augmented-DF test, which entails adding lagged terms of the dependent variable to the test equation. A question that often arises in applied work is how many extra lagged terms should be added, and there is some discussion of this problem. This in turn leads to a consideration of the power and size properties of the augmented-DF test (i.e., the tendency to under-reject the null when it is false and over-reject the null when it is true, respectively). In finite samples it can be shown that any trend-stationary process can be approximated arbitrarily well by a unit root process and, similarly, any unit root process can be approximated by a trend-stationary process, especially for smaller sample sizes. That is, some unit root processes display finite sample behaviour closer to (stationary) 'white noise' than to a (non-stationary) random walk (while some trend-stationary processes behave more like random walks in finite samples). This implies that a unit root test '... with high power against *any* stationary alternative *necessarily* will have correspondingly high probability of false rejection of the unit root null when applied to near stationary processes' (Blough, 1992, p. 298). This follows from the closeness of the finite sample distribution of any statistic under a particular trend-stationary process and the finite sample distribution of the statistic under a difference-stationary process that approximates the trend-stationary process. Thus, Blough (op. cit., p. 299) states that there is a trade-off between size and power in that unit root tests must have either high probability of falsely rejecting the null of non-stationarity when the true d.g.p. is a nearly stationary process (poor size properties) or low power against any stationary alternative. This problem of the size and power properties of unit root tests means that any results obtained must be treated with some caution.

There are further 'problems' associated with testing for non-stationarity. A structural break in a series will have serious consequences for the power of the test, if it is ignored. Taking into account the possibility that the intercept and/or slope of the underlying d.g.p. has changed (at an unknown date or dates) can be handled using the sequential testing methods outlined in Banerjee, Lumsdaine and Stock (1992). Examples are provided and discussed. Chapter 3 finally discusses testing for seasonal unit roots. First of all, it is suggested, that where possible, seasonally *un*adjusted data should be used when testing for unit roots, since the filters used to adjust for seasonal patterns often distort the underlying properties of the data. In particular, there is a tendency for the Dickey–Fuller test to be biased towards rejecting the null hypothesis of non-stationarity substantially less often than it should when seasonally adjusted series are tested. However, using unadjusted data that exhibit strong seasonal patterns opens up the possibility that these series may contain seasonal unit roots (i.e., the seasonal processes themselves are non-stationary). Three different tests for seasonal unit roots are discussed based on Osborn (1990) and an example is presented using UK data on consumption, income and wealth.

After testing for unit roots in the data, and assuming that these are present, the next task is to estimate the long-run relationship(s). Chapter 4 deals with cointegration in single equations, while Chapter 5 considers the possibility of more than one cointegration relationship. The most common single equation approach to testing for cointegration is the Engle–Granger (EG) approach. This amounts to estimating the static OLS regression model in order to obtain an estimate of the cointegration vector (i.e., the estimate of β which establishes a long-run *stationary* relationship between the non-stationary variables in the model). Such a simple and popular approach, which of course ignores any short-run dynamic effects and the issue of endogeneity, is justified on the grounds of the 'superconsistency' of the OLS estimator. The latter states that the OLS estimator of β with non-stationary $I(1)$ variables converges to its true value at a much faster rate than does the usual OLS estimator with stationary $I(0)$ variables, assuming cointegration (Stock, 1987). The most common form of testing for cointegration is based on an ADF unit root test of the residuals from the OLS regression. The need to use the correct critical values for testing the null hypothesis of no cointegration is discussed and also its dependence on the presence or otherwise of $I(2)$ variables in the regression. A first potential problem with the test procedure is also discussed, namely the common factor restriction imposed on the long-run model by the ADF test for cointegration.

Despite the popularity of the EG approach, there are other serious problems such as small sample bias and the inability to test statistical hypotheses; hence, the advent of alternative testing procedures. Testing whether the speed-of-adjustment coefficient is significant in an error-correction model is one alternative and this is comparable to estimating a dynamic autoregressive distributed-lag (ADL) model and testing whether the model converges to a steady-state solution. The major advantage of the ADL approach is that it generally provides unbiased estimates of the long-run model and valid t-statistics (even, on the basis of Monte-Carlo evidence, when some of the regressors in the model are endogenous). The fully modified estimator is also discussed, but yields few advantages over the standard OLS estimator.

However, there still remain several disadvantages with a single equation approach. The major problem is that when there are more than two variables in the model, there can be more than one cointegration relationship among these variables. If there is, then adopting a single equation approach is inefficient in the sense that we can only obtain a linear combination of these vectors. However, the drawbacks of the single equation model extend beyond its inability to estimate all the long-run relationships between the variables validly; even if there is only one cointegration relationship, estimating a single equation is potentially inefficient (i.e., it does not lead to the smallest variance against alternative approaches). It is shown that this results from the fact that unless all the right-hand-side variables in the cointegration vector are weakly exogenous, information is lost by not estimating a system which allows each endogenous variable to appear on the left-hand side of the estimated equations in the multivariate model. Thus, it is only really applicable to use the single equation approach when there is a single unique cointegration vector and when all the right-hand-side variables are weakly exogenous. Before proceeding to the multivariate approach, Chapter 4 considers the short-run (EC) model based on a single equation, and in particular gives an example of Hendry's general-to-specific modelling approach using *PcGive*. The last topic covered in the chapter is seasonal cointegration.

Chapter 5 is given over entirely to the Johansen procedure. Starting with a *vector* error-correction model (VECM), it is shown that this contains information on both the short- and long-run adjustments to changes in the variables in the model. In particular, the problem faced is to decompose the long-run relationships into those which are stationary (and thus comprise the cointegration vectors) and those which are non-stationary (and thus comprise the 'common trends'). To do this, Johansen specifies a method based on reduced rank regressions, which is discussed in one of the 'technical boxes' used throughout the book to present the more difficult material. Before using Johansen's approach, it is important to consider whether the multivariate model contains $I(0)$ and $I(1)$ variables alone, in which case the modelling procedure is much simpler, or whether $I(2)$ variables are also present (i.e., variables that need to be differenced twice to achieve stationarity). If the latter, then the situation becomes far more complicated and Johansen has developed a procedure to handle the $I(2)$ model, although (at the time of writing) this is not available in any software package. Instead, current practice is to test for the presence of $I(2)$ variables and if they are present to seek to replace them through some form of differencing (e.g., if money supply and prices are $I(2)$, we could reformulate the model to consider real money, $m_t - p_t$).[11]

Since the Johansen approach requires a correctly specified VECM, it is necessary to ensure that the residuals in the model are 'white noise'. This, *inter alia*, involves setting the appropriate lag-length in the model and including (usually dummy) variables that only affect the short-run behaviour of the model. It is pointed out that residual misspecification can arise as a consequence of omitting these important conditioning variables, and increasing the lag-length is often not the solution (as it usually is, for example, when autocorrelation is present). The procedures for testing the properties of the residuals are discussed and illustrated through examples. We then consider the method of testing for 'reduced rank', that is, testing how many cointegration vectors are present in the model. This involves a discussion of Johansen's trace and maximal-eigenvalue tests, and consideration of the small sample reliability of these statistics (at the same time an example of a likely $I(2)$ system is considered and the testing procedure for $I(2)$ variables is discussed). At this stage a major issue is confronted which presents considerable difficulty in applied work, namely that the reduced rank regression procedure provides information on how many unique cointegration vectors span the cointegration space, while any linear combination of the stationary vectors is itself also a stationary vector and thus the estimates produced for any particular vector in $\boldsymbol{\beta}$ are not necessarily unique. To overcome this 'problem' will involve testing the validity of linear restrictions on $\boldsymbol{\beta}$. Before this, it is necessary to turn to the question of whether an intercept and trend should enter the short- and/or long-run model. Various models are presented and discussed along with the testing procedure for deciding which should be used in empirical work. An example of the use of the so-called Pantula principle is provided.

Weak exogeneity is considered next. This amounts to testing whether rows of the speed-of-adjustment matrix, $\boldsymbol{\alpha}$, are zero and if such hypotheses are accepted the VECM can be respecified by conditioning on the weakly exogenous variables. The reasons for doing this, as well as a discussion of conditional and marginal models, are presented, while the concept of 'weak exogeneity' and how it is defined in various contexts is also discussed. The actual procedures that are used to perform tests of the null hypothesis that elements of $\boldsymbol{\alpha}$ are zero are discussed together with examples that use the *Cats* and *PcFiml* software packages. This then leads on to testing hypotheses about the cointegration relations involving $\boldsymbol{\beta}$, which involves imposing restrictions motivated by economic arguments (e.g., that some of the β_{ij} are zero, or that homogeneity restrictions are needed such as $\beta_{1j} = -\beta_{2j}$) and then testing whether the columns of $\boldsymbol{\beta}$ are identified. The form of the linear restrictions is discussed in some detail, along with various examples. Before proceeding to tests for unique cointegration vectors (i.e., restrictions on each of the vectors in $\boldsymbol{\beta}$) the more general tests developed by Johansen and Juselius (1992) are discussed and illustrated. These general tests have become quite common in applied work, with the first (depicted $\mathcal{H}_4$) amounting to a test of the same restrictions placed on all the cointegration vectors spanning $\boldsymbol{\beta}$. If r_1 cointegration vectors are assumed to be known, while the remaining r_2 vectors are unrestricted, then we have the second general test, labelled $\mathcal{H}_5$, while the $\mathcal{H}_6$ general test is that the same k restrictions are placed on r_1 of the cointegration vectors spanning $\boldsymbol{\beta}$, and the remaining r_2 vectors are unrestricted.

Lastly, the discussion moves on to testing for unique cointegration vectors (and hence structural long-run relationships). This involves testing that the restrictions placed on each of the cointegration vectors (the columns of $\boldsymbol{\beta}$) in fact lead to an identified system, that is, a model where any one cointegration vector cannot be represented by a linear combination of the other vectors. Johansen's method for identification is carefully discussed and illustrated by several examples. The importance of this approach is stressed, since the unrestricted estimates of $\boldsymbol{\beta}$ are often difficult to interpret in terms of their economic information.

Finally, Chapter 6 considers modelling the short-run multivariate system and other extensions that seem likely to gain importance as the cointegration approach develops. First of all, it is stressed that obtaining long-run estimates of the cointegration relationships is only a first step to estimating the complete model. The short-run structure of the model is also important in terms of the information it conveys on the short-run adjustment behaviour of economic variables, and this is likely to be at least as interesting from a policy viewpoint as estimates of the long-run. Another important aspect of modelling both the short- and long-run structures of the system is that we can attempt to model the contemporaneous interactions between variables, that is, we can estimate a simultaneous system, and this then provides an additional layer of valuable information. Based on the example of a small monetary model for the UK developed in Hendry and Mizon (1993) and Hendry and Doornik (1994), the following steps are illustrated: (i) use the Johansen approach to obtain the long-run cointegration relationships between the variables in the system; (ii) estimate the short-run vector autoregression (VAR) in error-correction form (hence VECM) with the cointegration relationships explicitly included and obtain a parsimonious representation of the system; (iii) condition on any (weakly) exogenous variables thus obtaining a conditional PVAR model; and (iv) model any simultaneous effects between the variables in the (conditional) model and test to ensure that the resulting restricted model encompasses the PVAR parsimoniously.

One final point that is worth emphasising, and which should be fairly obvious from the above overview of the book, is that an applied economist should really begin his or her analysis by using a multivariate framework and not by using a single equation approach. The exception will obviously be when only two variables are involved. The main reason for taking a systems approach from the outset is that to do otherwise restricts the practitioner to considering only one cointegration relationship when there may in fact be more, and even if (s)he is only interested in one vector, it is probable that (s)he will not obtain consistent and efficient estimates without allowing for the possibility of other cointegration vectors. Of course, where tests for weak exogeneity permit, moving down to the single equation approach can be justified after using the Johansen procedure.

Notes

1. That is converting x_t to Δx_t, where $\Delta x_t = x_t - x_{t-1}$, will remove the non-stationary trend from the variable (and if it does not, because the trend is increasing over time, then x_t will need to be differenced twice, etc.).
2. Work on testing for unit roots developed a little earlier (e.g., the PhD work of Dickey, 1976, and Fuller, 1976).
3. In contrast, y_t would be a deterministic (or fixed) process if it were characterised as $y_t = \rho y_{t-1}$ which, given an initial starting value of y_0, results in y_t being known with complete certainty at each time period. Note also, deterministic variables (such as an intercept or time trend) can also be introduced into (1.1).
4. The standard normal distribution is of course appropriate in the sense that it has a zero mean and constant variance and each observation is uncorrelated with any other.
5. Hence, (1.1) was a first-order AR process.
6. Note, $\varepsilon_t \sim IN(0, \sigma_\varepsilon^2)$ is to state that the residual term is independently and normally distributed with zero mean and constant variance, σ_ε^2. The fact that σ_ε^2 is multiplied by a (not shown) value of 1 means that ε_t is not autocorrelated with its own past.

7. That is, x_t still causes y_t but not in the Granger sense because of the lagged values of y_t determining x_t. For a review of these concepts of weak and strong exogeneity, together with their full properties, see Engle, Hendry and Richard (1983).
8. While we could further extend this to allow for an MA error-process, it can be shown that a relatively simple form of the MA error-process can be approximated by sufficiently large values of p and q in (1.9).
9. A good discussion of congruency and modelling procedures is given in Doornik and Hendry (1992).
10. Although not considered above, clearly this condition is not met in (1.1), and similar dynamic models, where y_{t-1} is a predetermined explanatory variable, since $E(y_t u_{t-i}) \neq 0$ for $i \geq 1$. However, it is possible to show by applying the Mann–Wald theorem (Johnston, p. 362) that with a sufficiently large sample size this will not lead to bias when estimating the parameter coefficients of the regression model.
11. Note, $m_t - p_t$ will only be $I(1)$ if m_t and p_t cointegrate. That is, subtracting an $I(2)$ variable from another $I(2)$ variable does not necessarily result in an $I(1)$ variable.

2

Short- and long-run models

Important terms and concepts

Static (long-run) models Equilibrium Stationary and non-stationary variables
Spurious regression Unit roots Difference-stationary Trend-stationary
Monte Carlo experimentation Cointegration Dynamic (short-run) models
Error-correction model

Long-run models

One particular example that will be used throughout the book is the UK demand for money function, especially since this model features extensively in the literature on cointegration. The static (or long-run) demand for money can either be derived from Keynesian theoretical models relating to the transactions demand theory (e.g. Baumol, 1952; Tobin, 1956; Laidler, 1984), or to the portfolio balance approach (e.g. Tobin, 1958), or from Monetarist models based on the quantity theory of money (e.g., Friedman and Schwartz, 1982). Apart from deciding whether income or wealth (or both) should enter, a common empirical specification typically has the demand for money as positively determined by the price level, P, and income (and/or wealth), Y, and negatively related to its opportunity cost, the interest rate(s), R:

$$m^{\mathrm{d}} = \beta_0 + \beta_1 p + \beta_2 y - \beta_3 R \tag{2.1}$$

where (here and elsewhere) variables in lower case are in logarithms. This model depicts an equilibrium relationship such that for given values of the right-hand-side variables and their long-run impact on money demand (i.e., the β_i), there is no reason for money demand to be at any other value than m^{d}.

Although (2.1) is frequently used, it is often found in empirical work that $\beta_1 = 1$, and therefore price homogeneity is imposed so that the model becomes the demand for *real* money balances (i.e., p is subtracted from both sides of the equation). In addition, when interest rates are subject to regulation by policy makers (i.e., they are a policy instrument), then they are no longer a good proxy for the actual costs of holding money but, rather, tend to indicate the restrictiveness of monetary policy. In such instances, it is usual practice to supplement (or even replace) R in the model by including the inflation rate, Δp, as a proxy for the opportunity cost of $(m^d - p)$. Thus, an alternative empirical specification is:

$$m^d - p = \gamma_0 - \gamma_1 \Delta p + \gamma_2 y - \gamma_3 R \tag{2.2}$$

It is worth noting at this early stage that we have not made any assumptions about whether changes in any of the right-hand-side variables in (2.1) *cause* changes in the demand for money balances. In fact, this is a crucial issue in econometric modelling (including the issue of cointegration) and one which distinguishes whether we can estimate a model using a single equation approach (Chapter 4) or whether a system of equations need to be estimated (Chapter 5). Since (2.1) depicts an equilibrium, then by definition the demand for money equates in the long-run to its supply (with variables, such as interest rates, adjusting to bring about market clearing).[1] If we were to assume that the money stock is under the control of policy makers, then with $m^d \equiv m^s$ it is possible to rearrange (2.1) to obtain a new equation with, *inter alia*, the money supply determining prices (or interest rates, or income). Thus, if one or more of the right-hand-side variables in (2.1) is contemporaneously influenced by changes in money supply, we need to consider whether a system of equations should be estimated in order to determine all the endogenous variables in the model. That is, the variables in (2.1) may feature as part of several equilibrium relationships governing the joint evolution of the variables. More generally, if there are n variables in the equation, then there can exist up to $n - 1$ linearly independent combinations, each corresponding to a unique equilibrium relationship.

Stationary and non-stationary time series

In addition to the question of whether the model should be estimated using a single equation approach (e.g., OLS) or a systems estimator, it is necessary also to consider the underlying properties of the processes that generate time series variables. That is, we can show that models containing non-stationary variables will often lead to a problem of spurious regression, whereby the results obtained suggest that there are statistically significant relationships between the variables in the regression model when in fact all that is obtained is evidence of contemporaneous correlations rather than meaningful causal relations.

Starting with a very simple data generating process (d.g.p.), suppose that a variable y_t is generated by the following (first-order autoregressive) process:

$$y_t = \rho y_{t-1} + u_t \tag{2.3}$$

Box 2.1 Stationary and non-stationary variables

In (2.3), if $\rho = 1$ then y_t will be non-stationary and it is possible to rearrange and accumulate y_t for different periods, starting with an initial value of y_{t-n}, to obtain:

$$y_t = y_{t-n} + \sum_{j=0}^{n-1} u_{t-j} \tag{2.1.1}$$

That is, the current value of y_t depends on its initial value and all disturbances accruing between $t - n + 1$ and t, while the variance of y_t is $t\sigma^2$ and this increases to become infinitely large as $t \rightarrow \infty$. In fact y_t does not converge to a mean value in any normal sense since if at some point $y_t = c$ then the expected time until y_t again returns to c is infinite (see Figure 2.1).

However, if $|\rho| < 1$ then y_t will be stationary and it is possible rearrange and accumulate y_t for different periods, starting with an initial value of y_{t-n}, to obtain:

$$y_t = \rho^n y_{t-n} + \sum_{j=0}^{n-1} \rho^j u_{t-j} \tag{2.1.2}$$

Since $|\rho| < 1$, as $n \rightarrow \infty$ (2.1.2) reduces to y_t being determined solely by a finite moving average (MA) process of order n with most weight being placed on the first elements of the disturbance term (i.e., $u_t + \rho u_{t-1} + \rho^2 u_{t-2} \ldots$). Thus, when y_t is stationary, it has a constant mean and variance (and indeed covariance) which are independent of time. In this simple example where y_t is determined by (2.3), y_t has a mean of 0 and a variance of $(\sigma^2 / 1 - \rho^2)$. Thus, it is possible to conclude that a stochastic process is (weakly) stationary if:

1. $E[y_t]$ = constant for all t;
2. Var $[y_t]$ = constant for all t; and
3. Covar $[y_t, y_{t+n}]$ = constant for all t.

Lastly, Figure 2.1 plots the non-stationary y_t together with a second variable $\Delta y_t (= y_t - y_{t-1})$, which is stationary since $\Delta y_t = u_t$ and u_t is stationary (given (1–3) above). In fact, the series y_t does not return to c because it is the sum of the past disturbance terms, that is, it is the cumulative sum of the y_t series given in (2.1.1).

Thus, current values of the variable, y_t, depend on last period's value, y_{t-1}, plus a disturbance term, u_t, the latter encapsulating all other random (i.e., stochastic) influences. It is assumed that this disturbance term comprises n random numbers drawn from a normal distribution with mean equal to 0 and variance σ^2. (Note, in later examples of stationary and non-stationary variables, σ^2 will be set equal to 1.) The variable y_t will be stationary if $|\rho| < 1$. If $\rho = 1$ then y_t will be non-stationary.[2] A stationary series tends to return to its mean value and fluctuate around it within a more-or-less constant range (i.e., it has a finite variance), while a non-stationary series has a different mean at different points in time (and thus the concept of the mean is not really applicable) and its variance increases with the sample size (for more technical details see Box 2.1).

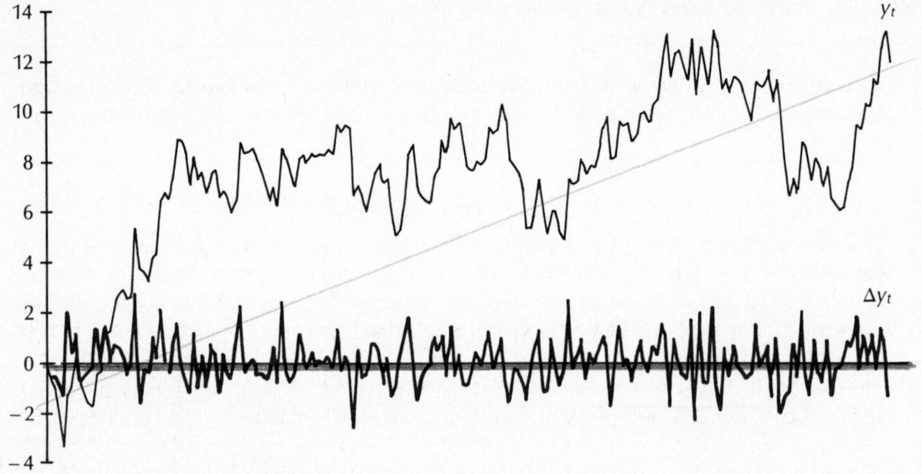

Figure 2.1   Non-stationary series $y_t = y_{t-1} + u_t$, $u_t \sim IN(0, 1)$

$$\Delta y_t = y_t - y_{t-1} = u_t$$

Figure 2.1 plots a non-stationary series based on a starting value of $y_0 = 0$. As can be seen, the variance of y_t is increasing with time and there is no tendency for the series to revert to any mean value. This contrasts both with $\Delta y_t (= y_t - y_{t-1})$, the stationary first difference of y_t, which is also plotted in Figure 2.1, and with the stationary version of y_t appearing in Figure 2.2.[3] Stationary variables can be seen to fluctuate around their mean (equal to 0 here), and to have a finite variance. It is also apparent from Figure 2.1 that a non-stationary variable becomes stationary after it is differenced (although not necessarily just by *first*-differencing – it will be shown that

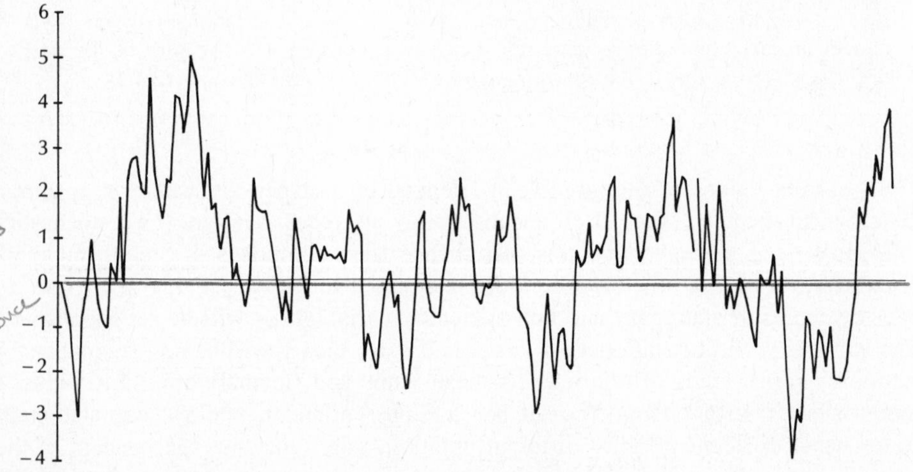

Figure 2.2   Stationary series $y_t = 0.9y_{t-1} + u_t$, $u_t \sim IN(0, 1)$

Box 2.2 Unit roots and stationarity

Consider the general *n*th order autoregressive (AR) process (of which (2.3) is a special case):

$$y_t = \psi_1 y_{t-1} + \psi_2 y_{t-2} + \ldots + \psi_p y_{t-p} + u_t \tag{2.2.1}$$

To simplify the notation, all the y_{t-i} can be collected on the left-hand side in a single term:

$$\Psi(L)y_t = u_t \tag{2.2.2}$$

where $\Psi(L)$ is the polynomial lag operator $1 - \psi_1 L - \psi_2 L^2 - \ldots - \psi_p L^p$. Forming the characteristic $(1 - \psi_1 L - \psi_2 L^2 - \ldots - \psi_p L^p = 0)$, if the roots of this equation are all greater than unity in absolute value (noting that some roots might be complex and thus their moduli must be greater than $|1|$),[4] then y_t is stationary. For the simple AR(1) case, if the root of $(1 - \psi_1 L = 0)$ is greater than unity in absolute value then y_t will be stationary. Thus, the AR(1) model is stationary provided $|\psi_1| < 1$, since the root is simply $L = 1/\psi_1$.

In the case of an AR(3) process:

$$(1 - \psi_1 L - \psi_2 L^2 - \psi_3 L^3)\, y_t = u_t \tag{2.2.3}$$

and if a unit root exists then it must be possible to factorise (2.2.3) into:

$$(1 + \alpha L + \beta L^2)(1 - L)y_t = u_t \tag{2.2.4}$$

where α and β depend on the ψs. If there is only one unit root then the roots of $(1 + \alpha L + \beta L^2 = 0)$ must both be greater than unity in absolute value. If this is so, then $(1 - L)y_t = \Delta y_t$ must be a stationary process, although, because of the unit root, y_t is non-stationary. If there are two unit roots we can further factorise (2.2.4) into:

$$(1 - \gamma L)(1 - L)(1 - L)y_t = u_t \tag{2.2.5}$$

where γ depends on α and β. If $|\gamma| < 1$ then the second difference of y_t (i.e., $(1 - L)(1 - L)y_t = \Delta^2 y_t$) will be stationary. Thus, when two unit roots are present, twice differencing a variable ensures that a stationary series is obtained. This principle applies when there are any number of unit roots.

Lastly, since a particular data series may be approximated by an unknown AR(p) process, involving up to p unit roots, it is useful to reformulate (2.2.1) as:

$$\Delta y_t = \psi^* y_{t-1} + \psi_1^* \Delta y_{t-1} + \psi_2^* \Delta y_{t-2} + \ldots \psi_{p-1}^* \Delta y_{t-p} + u_t \tag{2.2.6}$$

where $\psi^* = \psi_1 + \psi_2 + \ldots + \psi_p - 1$. In the AR(3) case where there is at least one unit root, we can rewrite the left-hand-side of (2.2.4) as $(1 + \alpha L + \beta L^2)\Delta y_t$ and rearrange to obtain:

$$\Delta y_t = -\alpha \Delta y_{t-1} - \beta \Delta y_{t-2} + u_t \tag{2.2.7}$$

Comparing an AR(3) version of (2.2.6) with (2.2.7) indicates that $\psi^* = 0$ if there is a unit root (and consequently $\psi_1 + \psi_2 + \psi_3 = 1$). If $\psi^* < 0$, then $\psi_1 + \psi_2 + \psi_3 < 1$, and y_t must be stationary. In fact this result can be generalised to cover any AR(p) process, such that in any test for stationarity we need only consider the hypothesis that $\psi^* = 0$ against $\psi^* < 0$ based on (2.2.6).

the number of times a variable needs to be differenced in order to induce stationarity depends on the number of unit roots it contains).

The question of whether a variable is stationary depends on whether it has a unit root. To see this, rewrite (2.3) as:

$$(1 - \rho L)y_t = u_t \tag{2.4}$$

where L is the lag operator (i.e., $Ly_t = y_{t-1}$, while $L^2y_t = y_{t-2}$, etc.). Forming a characteristic equation (i.e., $(1 - \rho L) = 0$); if the roots of this equation are all greater than unity in absolute value then y_t is stationary. In our example, there is only one root ($L = 1/\rho$), thus stationarity requires that $|\rho| < 1$ (for more complicated examples, including more than one unit root, see Box 2.2).

Another way to consider stationarity is to look at the different types of time trend that can be found in variables. If we allow (2.3) to have a non-zero intercept:

$$y_t = \beta + \rho y_{t-1} + u_t \tag{2.5}$$

and if $\rho = 1$, then by rearranging and accumulating y_t for different periods, starting with an initial value of y_0, the non-stationary series y_t can be rewritten as:

$$y_t = y_0 + \beta t + \sum_{j=1}^{t} u_j \tag{2.6}$$

(see also Box 2.1 and equation (2.1.1)), where it can be seen that y_t does not return to a fixed deterministic trend ($y_0 + \beta t$) because of the accumulation of the random error terms.[5] In fact, when $\rho = 1$, y_t will follow a stochastic trend, that is, it will drift upwards or downwards depending on the sign of β (as shown in Figure 2.3). This can be seen by taking the first difference of y_t, giving $\Delta y_t = \beta + u_t$, with the expected (i.e., mean) value of Δy_t being equal to β, the growth rate of y_t (assuming the variable is in

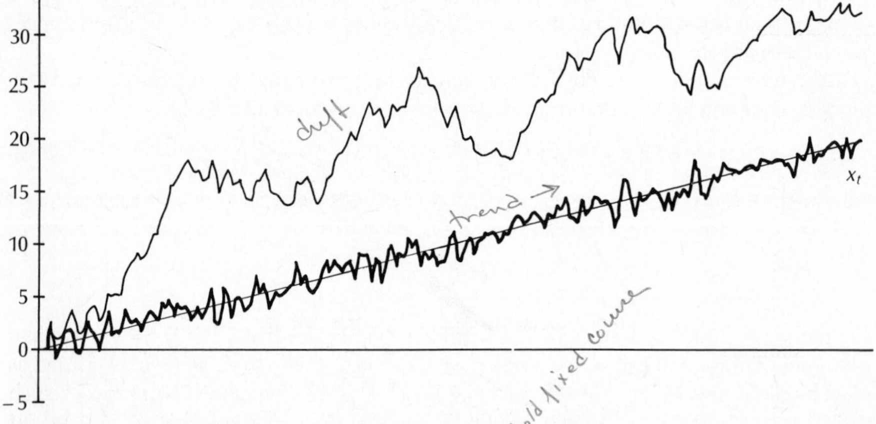

$y_t = y_{t-1} + 0.1 + u_t$; $x_t = 0.1t + u_t$ $u_t \sim IN(0, 1)$

Figure 2.3 Non-stationary series with drift, y_t, and trend-stationary series, x_t

logs). Since the first difference of y_t is stationary (Δy_t fluctuates around its mean of β and has a finite variance), then y_t itself is referred to as difference-stationary since it is stationary after differencing.

In contrast, consider the following d.g.p.:

$$x_t = \alpha + \beta t + u_t \tag{2.7}$$

where $\alpha + \beta t$ is a deterministic trend and the disturbance, u_t, is the non-trend (stochastic) component. Since u_t is stationary (e.g., $u_t \sim IN(0, 1)$), x_t is said to be trend-stationary, that is, it may trend but deviations from the deterministic trend are stationary (see Figure 2.3). Note, equations (2.6) and (2.7) have the same form (they both exhibit a linear trend), except that the disturbance term in (2.6) is non-stationary.

Thus, considering the two types of trend, it has been possible to contrast difference-stationary and trend-stationary variables, and in passing to note that the presence of a stochastic trend (which is non-stationary) as opposed to a deterministic trend (which is stationary) can make testing for unit roots complicated.

Spurious regressions

Trends in the data can lead to spurious correlations that imply relationships between the variables in a regression equation, when all that is present are correlated time trends. The time trend in a trend-stationary variable can either be removed by regressing the variable on time (with the residuals from such a regression forming a new variable which is trend-free and stationary) or nullified by including a deterministic time trend as one of the regressors in the model. In such circumstances,

Box 2.3 An example of a spurious regression

Figure 2.4 plots the UK money supply, m_t, for the period 1963(i)-1989(ii) together with a non-stationary random series with drift, x_t, the latter defined as:

$$x_t = 0.1 + x_{t-1} + \varepsilon_t \qquad \varepsilon_t \sim IN(0, 1) \tag{2.3.1}$$

with $x_0 = 0$.

Although no formal testing has been undertaken yet, it is likely that m_t is non-stationary (although the possibility still exists that it is stationary around a deterministic trend). In any event, both series contain trends leading to the following spurious regression result:

$$\underset{(30.3)}{m_t = 6.633} + \underset{(15.4)}{0.879}\, x_t + u_t \tag{2.3.2}$$

where the t-value decidedly rejects the null of no association between the two series. The R^2 obtained is 0.70 and the Durbin–Watson statistic equals 0.01. The residuals from the regression are also plotted, with u_t also seeming to be non-stationary (which should be the case if both m_t and x_t are non-stationary and there is no meaningful relationship between the two series).

the standard regression model is operating with stationary series which have constant means and finite variances, and thus statistical inferences (based on t- and F-tests) are valid.

Regressing a non-stationary variable on a deterministic trend generally does not yield a stationary variable (instead the series needs to be differenced prior to processing). Thus, using standard regression techniques with non-stationary data can lead to the problem of spurious regressions involving invalid inferences based on t- and F-tests. For instance, consider the following d.g.p.:

$$y_t = y_{t-1} + u_t \qquad u_t \sim IN(0, 1) \tag{2.8}$$

$$x_t = x_{t-1} + v_t \qquad v_t \sim IN(0, 1) \tag{2.9}$$

That is, both x and y are uncorrelated non-stationary variables such that when the following regression model is estimated:

$$y_t = \beta_0 + \beta_1 x_t + \varepsilon_t \tag{2.10}$$

it should generally be possible to accept the null $H_0{:}\beta_1 = 0$ (while the coefficient of determination, R^2, should also tend towards zero). However, because of the non-stationary nature of the data, implying that ε_t is also non-stationary, any tendency for both time series to be growing (e.g., see y_t in Figure 2.1) leads to correlation which is picked up by the regression model, even though each is growing for very different reasons and at rates which are uncorrelated (i.e., δ_1 converges in probability to zero in the regression ($\Delta y_t = \delta_0 + \delta_1 \Delta x_t + \eta_t$)). Thus, correlation between non-stationary series does not imply the kind of causal relationship that might be inferred from stationary series.[6]

The problem of spurious correlation, resulting in a non-zero estimate of β_1, is compounded by the fact that t- and F-statistics do not have the standard distributions generated by stationary series; with non-stationary series, there is a tendency to reject the null in both cases, and this tendency in fact increases with the sample size. In a Monte Carlo experiment reported in Banerjee *et al.* (1993, pp. 73–5), equation (2.10) was estimated 10 000 times, with x and y as defined in ((2.8) and (2.9)), resulting in an estimated mean value for β_1 of −0.012, and an associated standard error of 0.006 (given a sample size of $T = 100$), thus rejecting the null that $E[\beta_1] = 0$. Based on the 10 000 replications, the probability of rejecting the null of no association at the conventional significance level of 0.05 was found to be 0.753 (i.e., in 75.3 per cent of the regressions, values of $|t| > 1.96$ were obtained[7]). This was due to the fact that the mean t-statistic obtained from the experiment was −0.12 instead of zero, with an associated standard deviation of 7.3. The non-standard distribution of the t-statistic accounts for the very high rejection rate of the null. (See also Box 2.3.)

In summary, there is often a problem of falsely concluding that a relationship exists between two unrelated non-stationary series. This problem generally increases with the sample size and it cannot be solved by attempting to detrend the underlying series as would be possible with trend-stationary data. This leads to the question of

Box 2.4 Orders of integration and cointegration

For series to be cointegrated, they must have comparable long-run properties. That is, suppose a series must be differenced d times before it becomes stationary; it is said to be integrated of order d, denoted $I(d)$. If a linear combination of any two time series y_t and x_t is formed, and each is integrated of a different order, then the resulting series will be integrated at the highest of the two orders of integration. Thus if $y_t \sim I(1)$ and x_t $I(0)$, then these two series cannot possibly be cointegrated as the $I(0)$ series has a constant mean while the $I(1)$ series tends to drift over time, and consequently the error $(u_t = (y_t - \alpha x_t) \sim I(1))$ between them would not be a stable over time. Cointegration requires that if y_t on x_t are both $I(d)$, and if there exists a vector β, such that the disturbance term from the regression $(u_t = y_t - \beta x_t)$ is of a lower order of integration, $I(d - b)$, where $b > 0$, then y_t and x_t are cointegrated of order (d, b).

However, it is possible to have a mixture of different order series when there are three or more series in the model. As Pagan and Wickens (1989) point out, in this instance a subset of the higher-order series must cointegrate to the order of the lower-order series. So, if $y_t \sim I(1)$, $x_t \sim I(2)$, and $z_t \sim I(2)$ then as long as we can find a cointegration relationship between x_t and z_t such that $v_t(= x_t - \lambda z_t) \sim I(1)$, then v_t can potentially cointegrate with y_t to obtain $w_t(= y_t - \xi v_t) \sim I(0)$.

Lastly, and again if there are $n > 2$ variables in the model, there can be more than one cointegration vector. It is possible for up to $n - 1$ linearly independent cointegration vectors to exist, and this has implications for testing and estimating cointegration relationships (Chapter 4). Only when $n = 2$ is it possible to show that the cointegration vector is unique.

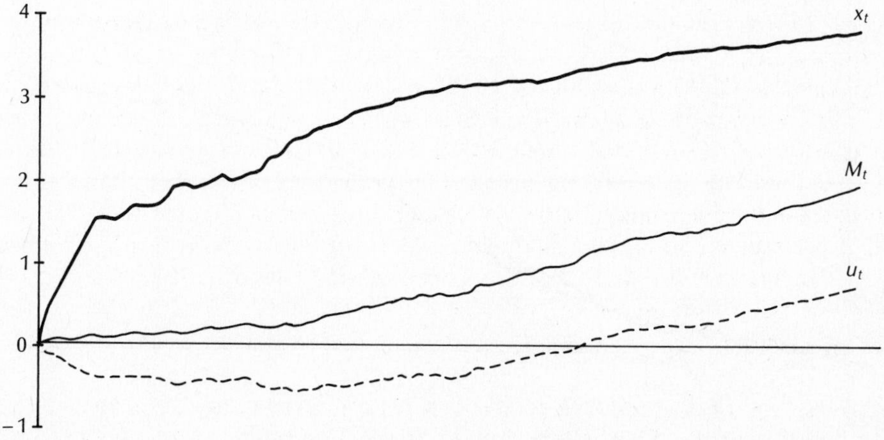

$x_t = x_{t-1} + 0.1 + \varepsilon_t \quad \varepsilon_t \sim IN(0, 1)$ Note, all variables are in logs and $u_t = m_t - 0.879. \quad x_t - 6.633$.

Figure 2.4 UK money supply, m_t, 1963–89, and non-stationary series with drift, x_t

when it is possible to infer a causal long-run relationship(s) between non-stationary time series, based on estimating a standard regression such as (2.10).

Cointegration

If a series must be differenced d times before it becomes stationary, then it contains d unit roots (see Box 2.2) and is said to be integrated of order d, denoted $I(d)$. Consider two time series y_t and x_t, which are both $I(d)$. In general, any linear combination of the two series will also be $I(d)$; for example, the residuals obtained from regressing y_t on x_t are $I(d)$. If, however, there exists a vector β, such that the disturbance term from the regression ($u_t = y_t - \beta x_t$) is of a lower order of integration, $I(d - b)$, where $b > 0$, then Engle and Granger (1987) define y_t and x_t as cointegrated of order (d, b). Thus, if y_t and x_t were both $I(1)$, and $u_t \sim I(0)$, then the two series would be cointegrated of order $CI(1, 1)$.

The economic interpretation of cointegration is that if two (or more) series are linked to form an equilibrium relationship spanning the long-run, then even though the series themselves may contain stochastic trends (i.e., be non-stationary) they will nevertheless move closely together over time and the difference between them will be stable (i.e., stationary). Thus the concept of cointegration mimics the existence of a long-run equilibrium to which an economic system converges over time, and u_t defined above can be interpreted as the disequilibrium error (i.e., the distance that the system is away from equilibrium at time t).

Figure 2.5 shows the UK money supply (based on the narrow measure M1) and aggregate price level for the period 1963(i) – 1989(ii). Both series exhibit trends,

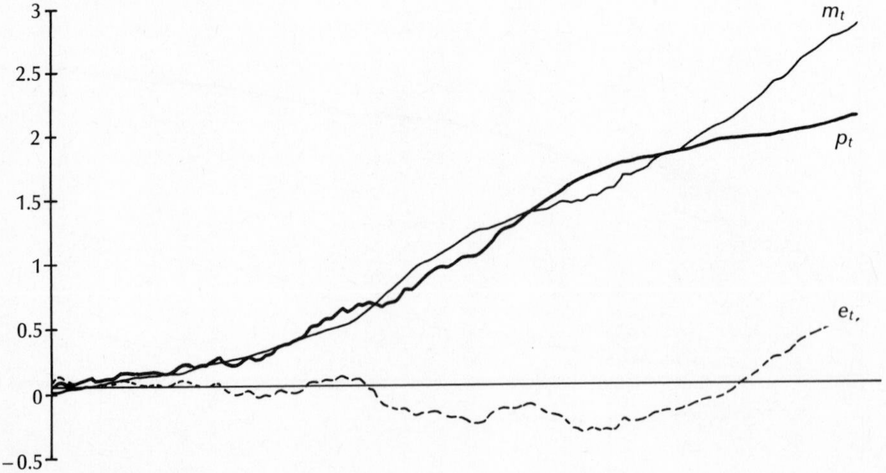

$e_t = m_t - 1.1085p_t - 11.166$

Figure 2.5 UK money supply, m_t, and price level, p_t, 1963–89

although until formally tested (see Chapter 3) both could be stationary variables around a deterministic trend, rather than difference-stationary (the latter implying that they contain one or more unit roots). Assuming for now that m_t and p_t are non-stationary (and possibly $I(1)$), it can be seen that both series generally appear to move together over time, suggesting that there exists an equilibrium relationship (cf. the demand for money relationship discussed earlier). The outcome of regressing m_t on p_t (plus a constant) is to obtain the residual series e_t, which on visual inspection might be $I(0)$ stationary. This suggests that there possibly exists a cointegration vector (for the data used here $\beta = 1.1085$, with a t-value of 41.92) which defines a stable (equilibrium) relationship between money and prices.

Thus, following directly from the identification of cointegration with equilibrium, it is possible to make sense of regressions involving non-stationary variables. If these are cointegrated then regression analysis imparts meaningful information about long-run relationships, whereas if cointegration is not established we return to the problem of spurious correlation.

Short-run models

Equation (2.1) sets out the equilibrium relationship governing the demand for money. However, even assuming that it is possible to estimate this long-run model *directly* (an issue discussed in some detail in Chapter 4), it is also of interest to consider the short-run evolution of the variables under consideration, especially since equilibrium (i.e., the steady-state) may rarely be observed. This is important from a forecasting perspective, as is the economic information that can be obtained from considering the dynamics of adjustment.

The major reason why relationships are not always in equilibrium centres on the inability of economic agents to adjust to new information instantaneously.[8] There are often substantial costs of adjustment (both pecuniary and non-pecuniary) which result in the current value of the dependent variable, Y, being determined not only by the current value of some explanatory variable, X, but also by past values of X. In addition, as Y evolves through time in reaction to current and previous values of X, past (i.e., lagged) values of itself will also enter the short-run (dynamic) model. This inclusion of lagged values of the dependent variable as regressors is a means of simplifying the form of the dynamic model (which would otherwise tend to have a large number of highly correlated lagged values of X); by placing restrictions on how current Y_t adjusts to the lagged values of X_{t-i} $(i = 0, \ldots, q)$ it is possible to reduce the number of such terms entering the estimated equation at the cost of some extra lagged terms involving Y_{t-i} $(i = 1, \ldots, p)$.[9] A very simple dynamic model (with lags $p = q = 1$) of short-run adjustment is:

$$y_t = \alpha_0 + \gamma_0 x_t + \gamma_1 x_{t-1} + \alpha_1 y_{t-1} + u_t \tag{2.11}$$

where the white noise residual is $u_t \sim IN(0, \sigma^2)$. Clearly, the parameter coefficient γ_0

denotes the short-run reaction of y_t to a change in x_t, and not the long-run effect that would occur if the model were in equilibrium. That latter is defined as:

$$y_t = \beta_0 + \beta_1 x_t \qquad (2.12)$$

So in the long-run, the elasticity between Y and X is $\beta_1 = (\gamma_0 + \gamma_1)/(1 - \alpha_1)$, assuming that $\alpha_1 < 1$ (which is necessary if the short-run model is to converge to a long-run solution).

The dynamic model represented by (2.11) is easily generalised to allow for more complicated, and often more realistic, adjustment processes (by increasing the lag-lengths p and q). However, there are several potential problems with this form of the dynamic model. The first has already been mentioned and concerns the likely high level of correlation between current and lagged values of a variable, which will therefore result in problems of multicollinearity (high R^2 but imprecise parameter estimates and low t-values, even though the model may be correctly specified). Using the Hendry-type 'general-to-specific' approach, which would involve eliminating insignificant variables from the estimated model, might therefore result in misspecification (especially if **X** is in fact a vector of variables). Also, some (if not all) of the variables in a dynamic model of this kind are likely to be non-stationary, since they enter in levels. As explained earlier, this leads to the potential problem of common trends and thus spurious regression, while t- and F-statistics do not have standard distributions and the usual statistical inference is invalid.[10] A solution might be to respecify the dynamic model in (first) differences. However, this then removes any information about the long-run from the model and consequently is unlikely to be useful for forecasting purposes.

A more suitable approach is to adopt the error-correction (ECM) formulation of the dynamic model. Rearranging and reparameterising (2.11) gives:

$$\Delta y_t = \gamma_0 \Delta x_t - (1 - \alpha_1)\,[y_{t-1} - \hat{\beta}_0 - \hat{\beta}_1 x_{t-1}] + u_t \qquad (2.13)$$

where $\hat{\beta}_0 = \hat{\alpha}_0/1 - \hat{\alpha}_1$. Equations (2.11) and (2.13) are equivalent, but the ECM has several distinct advantages. First, and assuming that X and Y are cointegrated, the ECM incorporates both short-run and long-run effects. This can be seen by the fact that the long-run equilibrium, (2.12), is incorporated into the model. Thus, if at any time the equilibrium holds then $[y_{t-1} - \hat{\beta}_0 - \hat{\beta}_1 x_{t-1}] = 0$. During periods of disequilibrium, this term is non-zero and measures the distance the system is away from equilibrium during time t. Thus, an estimate of $(1 - \alpha_1)$ will provide information on the speed of adjustment, that is, how the variable y_t changes in response to disequilibrium.[11] For instance, suppose that y_t starts to increase less rapidly than is consistent with (2.12), perhaps because of a series of large negative random shocks (captured by u_t). The net result is that $[y_{t-1} - \hat{\beta}_0 - \hat{\beta}_1 x_{t-1}] < 0$, since y_{t-1} has moved below the steady-state growth path, but since $-(1 - \alpha_1)$ is negative, the overall effect is to boost Δy_t, thereby forcing y_t back towards its long-run growth path as determined by x_t (in equation (2.12)).

A second feature of the ECM is that all the terms in the model are stationary so standard regression techniques are valid, assuming cointegration and that we have estimates of β_0 and β_1. There is clearly a problem if these need to be estimated at the same time in the ECM. Often, β_1 is set equal to one (and β_0 is set equal to zero), and justified on the basis that the theory imposes such a long-run elasticity. This can be tested by including x_{t-1} as an additional regressor, since it should have an estimated coefficient value of zero, if in fact $[\hat{\beta}_0, \hat{\beta}_1]' = [0, 1]'$. However, including the potentially non-stationary variable x_{t-1} is itself problematic, since the t-statistic of the coefficient of x_{t-1} does not have a standard normal distribution, thereby invalidating the usual testing procedure. The issues of testing for cointegration and estimating the ECM are considered in Chapter 4.

Third, as should be obvious from equations (2.12) and (2.13), the ECM is closely bound up with the concept of cointegration. In fact, Engle and Granger (1987) show that if y_t and x_t are cointegrated $CI(1, 1)$, then there must exist an ECM (and conversely, that an ECM generates cointegrated series). The practical implication of Granger's representation theorem for dynamic modelling is that it provides the ECM with immunity from the spurious regression problem, provided that the terms in levels cointegrate.

The simple ECM depicted in (2.13) can be generalised to capture more complicated dynamic processes. Increasing the lag-length p and/or q in (2.11) results in additional lagged first differences entering (2.13). In general, we can reformulate the ECM as:

$$A(L)\,\Delta y_t = B(L)\,\Delta x_t - (1-\pi)[y_{t-p} - \hat{\beta}_0 - \hat{\beta}_1 x_{t-p}] + u_t \tag{2.14}$$

where $A(L)$ is the polynomial lag operator $1 - \alpha_1 L - \alpha_2 L^2 - \ldots - \alpha_p L^p$; $B(L)$ is the polynomial lag operator $\gamma_0 + \gamma_1 L + \gamma_2 L^2 + \ldots + \gamma_q L^q$; and $\pi = (\alpha_1 + \alpha_2 + \ldots + \alpha_p)$. Lastly, it is also possible to specify the ECM in multivariate form, explicitly allowing for a set of cointegration vectors. This will be explored more fully in Chapter 5.

Conclusion

This chapter has considered short- and long-run models. Inherent in the distinction is the notion of equilibrium; that is, the long-run is a state of equilibrium where economic forces are in balance and there is no tendency to change, while the short-run depicts the disequilibrium state where adjustment to the equilibrium is occurring. When dealing with non-stationary data, equilibrium is synonymous with the concept of cointegration. Failure to establish cointegration often leads to spurious regressions which do not reflect long-run economic relationships but, rather, reflect the 'common trends' contained in most non-stationary time series. Cointegration is also linked very closely to the use of short-run error-correction models, thus providing a useful and meaningful link between the long- and short-run approach to econometric modelling.

Notes

1. There is no necessity actually to achieve equilibrium at any point in time, even as $t \to \infty$. All that is required is that economic forces are prevalent to move the system towards the equilibrium defined by the long-run relationship posited. Put another way, the static equilibrium presented in (2.1) needs to be reinterpreted empirically since most economic variables grow over time. Thus, of more importance is the idea of a steady-state relationship between variables which are evolving over time. This is the way the term 'equilibrium' is used here. For a more detailed discussion of the definition of equilibrium used see Banerjee *et al.* 1993, Chapter 1).
2. If $|\rho| > 1$, then y_t will be non-stationary and explosive (i.e., it will tend to either $\pm\infty$).
3. Note, u_t was the same for all the series in Figures 2.1–2.3.
4. Note, the roots of the characteristic equation can be complex (i.e., contain a real and imaginary part, $h \pm vi$, where h and v are two real numbers and i is an imaginary number), and the modulus is the absolute value of the complex root and is calculated as $\sqrt{(h^2 + v^2)}$.
5. Note, the linear trend, βt, in (2.6) reflects the accumulation of the successive β intercepts when rearranging (2.5) for different periods.
6. In fact, this correlation occurs because x and y share a 'common trend'. Hence, relationships between non-stationary variables that seem to be significant but are in fact spurious are termed 'common trends' in the integration and cointegration literature.
7. For stationary series, the probability of $|t| > 1.96$ is 5 per cent.
8. Even if expectations were fully efficient, and agents could anticipate and therefore react contemporaneously to changes in determinants, there are likely to be (non-linear) adjustment costs that make it uneconomic to move instantaneously to a new equilibrium.
9. For instance, if the effects of the X_{t-i} are restricted to decline in a geometric progression $(1 + \varphi + \varphi^2 + \varphi^3 \ldots)$ so that more distant lags have little impact on current Y, then we end up with the Koyck-lag model: $y_t = \alpha_0(1 - \varphi) + \gamma_0 x_t + \varphi y_{t-1} + e_t$, which is equivalent to $y_t = \alpha_0 + \gamma_0(x_t + \varphi x_{t-1} + \varphi^2 x_{t-2} \ldots) + u_t$ where $e_t = u_t - \varphi u_{t-1}$.
10. However, as will be discussed in Chapter 4, if the right-hand-side variables in the model are weakly exogenous, invalid inference and potential bias will not be a problem.
11. Large values (tending to −1) of $-(1 - \alpha_1)$ indicate that economic agents remove a large percentage (since the model is in logs) of the resulting disequilibrium each period. Small values (tending towards 0) suggest that adjustment to the long-run steady-state is slow, perhaps because of the large costs of adjustment (pecuniary and non-pecuniary).

3

Testing for unit roots

Important terms and concepts

Dickey–Fuller test   Augmented Dickey–Fuller test   Phillips and Perron test   Asymptotic   Size and power properties of tests   Structural breaks and unit root tests   Seasonal unit roots   Seasonal differencing   Multiple unit roots

When discussing stationary and non-stationary time series, the need to test for the presence of unit roots in order to avoid the problem of spurious regression was stressed. If a variable contains a unit root then it is non-stationary and unless it combines with other non-stationary series to form a stationary cointegration relationship, then regressions involving the series can falsely imply the existence of a meaningful economic relationship.

In principle it is important to test the order of integration of each variable in a model, to establish whether it is non-stationary and how many times the variable needs to be differenced to result in a stationary series. Also, as will be seen, testing for stationarity for a single variable is very similar to testing whether a linear combination of variables cointegrate to form a stationary, equilibrium relationship. Testing for the presence of unit roots is not straightforward. Some of the issues which arise are as follows:

- It is necessary to take account of the possibility that the underlying (but, of course, unknown) d.g.p. may, *inter alia*, include a time trend (stochastic or deterministic).
- The d.g.p. may be more complicated than a simple AR(1) process (e.g., (2.3)), and indeed may involve moving-average (MA) terms.
- It is known that when dealing with finite samples (and especially small numbers of observations) the standard tests for unit roots are biased towards accepting the null hypothesis of non-stationarity when the true d.g.p. is in fact stationary but close to having a unit root (i.e., there is a problem with the power of the test).

- There is concern that an undetected structural break in the series may lead to under-rejecting of the null.
- Quarterly data might also be tested for seasonal unit roots in addition to the usual test for unit roots at the zero frequency level.

The Dickey-Fuller test

There are several ways of testing for the presence of a unit root. The emphasis here will be on using the Dickey–Fuller (DF) approach (cf. Dickey and Fuller, 1979) to testing the null hypothesis that a series does contain a unit root (i.e., it is non-stationary) against the alternative of stationarity. There are other tests of this null (e.g., the Sargan–Bhargava (1983) CRDW-test, based on the usual Durbin–Watson statistic; and the non-parametric tests developed by Phillips and Perron, based on the Phillips (1987) Z-test, which involve transforming the test statistic to eliminate any autocorrelation in the model), but DF tests tend to be more popular either because of their simplicity or their more general nature. There are also more recent tests that take as the null the hypothesis that a series is stationary, against the alternative of non-stationarity (e.g., see Kahn and Ogaki (1992)). These have yet to achieve widespread usage, and since the consequences of non-stationarity are so important, it is probably better to take a conservative approach with non-stationarity as the maintained hypothesis.[1]

The simplest form of the DF test amounts to estimating:

$$y_t = \rho_a y_{t-1} + u_t \tag{3.1a}$$

or

$$(1 - L)y_t = \Delta y_t = (\rho_a - 1)y_{t-1} + u_t \qquad u_t \sim IID(0, \sigma^2) \qquad (3.1b)^{2}$$

Either variant of the test is applicable, with the null being $H_0\colon \rho_a = 1$ against the alternative $H_1\colon \rho_a < 1$. The advantage of (3.1b) is that this is equivalent to testing

Table 3.1 Critical values for the DF-test

Sample size	Critical values for τ level of significance			Critical values for τ_μ level of significance			Critical values for τ_τ level of significance		
	0.01	0.05	0.10	0.01	0.05	0.10	0.01	0.05	0.10
Dickey–Fuller distribution									
25	−2.66	−1.95	−1.60	−3.75	−3.00	−2.63	−4.38	−3.60	−3.24
50	−2.62	−1.95	−1.61	−3.58	−2.93	−2.60	−4.15	−3.50	−3.18
100	−2.60	−1.95	−1.61	−3.51	−2.89	−2.58	−4.04	−3.45	−3.15
t−distribution									
∞	−2.33	−1.65	−1.28	−2.33	−1.65	−1.28	−2.33	−1.65	−1.28

Source: Fuller (1976)

$(\rho_a - 1) = \rho_a^* = 0$ against $\rho_a^* < 0$; more importantly, though, it also simplifies matters to use this second form of the test when a more complicated AR(p) process is considered (cf. Box 2.2 in the last chapter).[3] The standard approach to testing such a hypothesis is to construct a t-test; however, under non-stationarity, the statistic computed does not follow a standard t-distribution but, rather, a Dickey–Fuller distribution. The latter has been computed using Monte Carlo techniques, which involves taking (3.1) as the underlying d.g.p., imposing the null hypothesis by fixing $\rho_a = 1$, and randomly drawing samples of the u_t from the normal distribution; this then generates thousands of samples of y_t, all of which are consistent with the d.g.p: $y_t = y_{t-1} + u_t$. Then for each of the y_t a regression based on (3.1) is undertaken, with ρ_a *now free to vary*, in order to compute (on the basis of thousands of replications) the percentage of times the model will reject the null hypothesis of a unit root when the null is true. These are the critical values for rejecting the null of a unit root at various significance levels (e.g., 10 per cent, 5 per cent and 1 per cent) based on the DF distribution of $[(\hat{\rho}_a - 1)/se(\hat{\rho}_a)]$.[4]

It is informative to compare the critical values for the DF and standard t-distributions. Assume that model (3.1b) has been estimated for some series y_t, resulting in a t-ratio of -1.82 attached to the coefficient of y_{t-1}. Looking at the first set of critical values in Table 3.1, it is clear that for different sample sizes it would be necessary to accept the null of non-stationarity at the 5 per cent significance level using the values of the DF τ-distribution. However, using the comparable critical values for the standard t-distribution (the final row), the null could be rejected at this significance level. Thus, failure to use the DF (τ-distribution would lead on average to over-rejection of the null.

Testing for a unit root using (3.1) involves making the prior assumption that the underlying d.g.p. for y_t is a simple first-order autoregressive process with a zero mean and no trend component (i.e., no deterministic variables). However, it also assumes that in the d.g.p. at time $t = 0$, y_t also equals zero, since in a model with no deterministic variables the mean of the series is determined by the initial observation under the hypothesis of a unit root. *So, using regression equation (3.1) is only valid when the overall mean of the series is zero.* Alternatively, if the 'true' mean of the d.g.p. were known, it could be subtracted from each observation and (3.1) could then be used to test for a unit root; but this is unlikely to happen in practice.[5] Thus, when the underlying d.g.p. is given by (3.1) but it is not known whether y_0 in the d.g.p. equals zero, then it is better to allow a constant μ_b to enter the regression model when testing for a unit root:

$$\Delta y_t = \mu_b + (\rho_b - 1)\, y_{t-1} + u_t \qquad u_t \sim IID(0, \sigma^2) \tag{3.2}$$

The appropriate critical values to be used in this case are given by the DF distribution relating to τ_μ since the latter was generated assuming that the underlying d.g.p. is given by (3.1) but the model used for testing is (3.2).[6] Note, ρ_b and τ_μ are both invariant with respect to y_0, that is, whatever the unknown starting value of the series, the distribution of the test statistic τ_μ is not affected. This is an important property since in its absence critical values would depend on some unknown value of y_0, and we would therefore need to know both the value of y_0 and its associated DF distribution before we could undertake any test for a unit root.

However, (3.2) cannot validly be used to test for a unit root when the underlying d.g.p. is also given by (3.2). In this instance, if the null hypothesis is true $\rho_b = 1$, and y_t will follow a stochastic trend, that is, it will drift upwards or downwards depending on the sign of μ_b (see the discussion of equations (2.5) and (2.6) in the last chapter). Under the alternative hypothesis that $\rho_b < 1$, then y_t is stationary around a constant mean of $\mu_b/(1-\rho_b)$, *but it has no trend.* Thus, using (3.2) to test for a unit root does not nest both the null hypothesis and the alternative hypothesis. Put another way, suppose the true d.g.p. is a stationary process around a deterministic trend (e.g., $y_t = \alpha + \beta t + u_t$), and (3.2) is used to test whether this series has a unit root. Since the d.g.p. contains a trend component (albeit deterministic), the only way to fit this trend is for the regression equation to set $\hat{\rho}_b = 1$, in which case $\hat{\mu}_b$ becomes the coefficient $\hat{\beta}$ on the trend (cf. equations (2.6) and (2.7)). This would be equivalent to accepting the null that there is a stochastic (i.e., non-stationary) trend, when in fact the true d.g.p. has a deterministic (i.e., stationary) trend. What this example illustrates is that in order to test what will probably be in practice the most common form of the null hypothesis (that the d.g.p. contains a stochastic trend against the alternative of trend-stationary), it is necessary to have as many deterministic regressors as there are deterministic components in the d.g.p., and thus we must allow a time trend t to enter the regression model used to test for a unit root:

$$\Delta y_t = \mu_c + \gamma_c t + (\rho_c - 1) y_{t-1} + u_t \qquad u_t \sim IID(0, \sigma^2) \tag{3.3}$$

The appropriate critical values are given by the DF distribution relating to τ_τ (see Table 3.1); it is interesting to note that $\tau_\tau < \tau_\mu < \tau$ and then to make comparisons with the standard t-values. Clearly, inappropriate use of the latter would lead to over-rejection of the null hypothesis, and this problem becomes larger as more deterministic components are added to the regression model used for testing. Note also that ρ_c and τ_τ are both invariant with respect to y_0 and μ_c so neither the starting value of the series nor the value of the drift term have any affect on the test statistic τ_τ.

It is possible that the underlying d.g.p. is given by (3.3), which would mean that y_t has both a stochastic and a deterministic trend. In this event, one would need a regression model which included an additional term (such as t^2) in order to be able to test for a unit root, necessitating an additional block of critical values in Table 3.1. In practice, this is unlikely to be a problem since the hypothesis of a unit root with a deterministic trend is usually precluded *a priori*, because it implies an implausible ever-increasing (or decreasing) rate of change (if y_t is in logarithmic form).[7]

Before discussing the testing procedure that should be adopted when using the DF test, it is worth noting that tests of the joint hypothesis that $\gamma_c = 0$ and $\rho_c = 1$ can also be undertaken, using the non-standard F-statistic Φ_3 reported in Dickey and Fuller (1981).[8] In (3.3), if the DF t-test of the null hypothesis $H_0: \rho_c = 1$ is not rejected, but the joint hypothesis $H_0: (\rho_c - 1) = \gamma_c = 0$ is, then this implies that the trend is significant under the null of a unit root and *asymptotic* normality of the t-statistic

$((\hat{\rho}_c - 1)/se(\hat{\rho}_c))$ follows. Thus, instead of using the critical values from the DF type distribution, the standard t-statistic (for $n = \infty$) should be used to test $H_0{:}(\rho_c - 1) = 0$. This result follows from West (1988) and occurs when a stochastic trend is present in the regression but it is *dominated* by a deterministic trend component. This form of dominance is also present when testing the joint hypothesis that $\mu_b = 0$ and $\rho_b = 1$, using (3.2) and the F-statistic Φ_1 (given in Dickey and Fuller, op. cit.).[9] If one fails to reject $H_0{:}\rho_b = 1$, but can reject the joint hypothesis $H_0{:}(\rho_b - 1) = \mu_b = 0$, then the constant is significant under the null of a unit root and *asymptotic* normality of the t-statistic $((\hat{\rho}_b - 1)/se(\hat{\rho}_b))$ follows. Note, rejection of either of the above joint hypotheses, using the appropriate F-test, results in both the d.g.p. and the regression model used to test for a unit root having the same form (unlike the tests outlined above involving the DF distribution). This is known as an exact test, while the tests based on the DF distribution are called similar tests.[10] However, there are two reasons to be cautious about conducting unit root tests using exact tests: first, asymptotic normality of the t-statistic *only* occurs when the non-zero constant (and trend) in the d.g.p. is (are) matched by a constant (and trend) in the model used for testing. So, for example, including a trend in the model when the d.g.p. does not have a trend means that we have to use the DF distribution to obtain valid critical values. Since it is unlikely that we will be sufficiently confident about the correct specification of the d.g.p., it is probably safer to use the DF distribution. Second, it has been suggested (Banerjee *et al.*, 1993) that in finite samples, the DF distribution may be a better approximation than the normal distribution, even though asymptotically (i.e., $n \to \infty$) the latter is to be preferred.

One last item of information that will help in deciding a possible testing strategy is that the inclusion of additional deterministic components in the regression model used for testing, beyond those included in the (unknown) d.g.p., results in an increased probability that the null hypothesis of non-stationarity will be accepted when in fact the true d.g.p. is stationary (i.e., the power of the test of the unit root hypothesis decreases against stationary alternatives).[11] This problem was mentioned when comparing the values in Table 3.1, since critical values for rejecting the null are ordered as follows: $\tau_\tau < \tau_\mu < \tau$. That is, adding a constant and then a trend to the model increases (in absolute value) the critical values, making it more difficult to reject the null hypothesis, even when it should be rejected.[12]

Table 3.2 Testing procedure using the DF test (unknown d.g.p.)

Step and model	Null hypothesis	Test statistic	Critical values[1]
(1) $\Delta y_t = \mu_c + \gamma_c t + (\rho_c - 1)y_{t-1} + u_t$	$(\rho_c - 1) = 0$	τ_τ	Fuller, Table 8.5.2, block 3
(2) $\Delta y_t = \mu_c + \gamma_c t + (\rho_c - 1)y_{t-1} + u_t$	$(\rho_c - 1) = \gamma_c = 0$	Φ_3	Dickey and Fuller, Table VI
(2a) $\Delta y_t = \mu_c + \gamma_c t + (\rho_c - 1)y_{t-1} + u_t$	$(\rho_c - 1) = 0$	t	Standard normal
(3) $\Delta y_t = \mu_b + (\rho_b - 1)y_{t-1} + u_t$	$(\rho_b - 1) = 0$	τ_μ	Fuller, Table 8.5.2, block 2
(4) $\Delta y_t = \mu_b + (\rho_b - 1)y_{t-1} + u_t$	$(\rho_b - 1) = \mu_b = 0$	Φ_1	Dickey and Fuller, Table IV
(4a) $\Delta y_t = \mu_b + (\rho_b - 1)y_{t-1} + u_t$	$(\rho_b - 1) = 0$	t	Standard normal
(5) $\Delta y_t = (\rho_a - 1)y_{t-1} + u_t$	$(\rho_a - 1) = 0$	τ	Fuller, Table 8.5.2, block 1

[1] Fuller (1976) and Dickey and Fuller (1981).

To summarise the issues discussed so far, t-tests of the null hypothesis of a unit root must use critical values from the DF distribution and not the standard t-distribution. Similarly, F-tests of joint hypotheses concerning the unit root and the significance of constant or trend terms must also use the critical values of the appropriate DF distribution (obtained from Dickey and Fuller, 1981). It is necessary to ensure that the regression model used for testing has more deterministic components than the hypothesised d.g.p., otherwise the test will not nest the null and alternative hypotheses. In general, since the underlying d.g.p. is unknown, this suggests using (3.3) for testing the unit root hypothesis. However, having unnecessary nuisance parameters (constant and trend terms) will lower the power of the test against stationary alternatives. Thus, Perron (1988) has put forward the sequential testing procedure outlined in Table 3.2, which starts with the use of (3.3) and then eliminates unnecessary nuisance parameters. If we fail to reject the null using the most general specification (perhaps because of the low power of the test), testing continues on down to more restricted specifications. The testing stops as soon as we are able to reject the null hypothesis of a unit root. Note, steps (2a) and (4a) are only undertaken if we are able to reject the joint hypotheses in (2) and (4) respectively. Even in these situations, tests based on the DF distributions may be preferable, in which case the results obtained from steps (2a) and (4a) should be treated with some caution.

There are several econometric packages available that will allow the user to go through this testing strategy fairly easily and they usually provide the appropriate critical values.[13] However, all the tests can be carried out by running OLS regressions and by referring to the Dickey and Fuller tables referenced in Table 3.2 (and which are also reproduced in the Statistical Appendix).

Augmented Dickey–Fuller test

If a simple AR(1) DF model is used when in fact y_t follows an AR(p) process, then the error term will be autocorrelated to compensate for the misspecification of the dynamic structure of y_t. Autocorrelated errors will invalidate the use of the DF distributions, which are based on the assumption that u_t is 'white-noise'. Thus, assuming that y_t follows a pth order autoregressive process:

$$y_t = \psi_1 y_{t-1} + \psi_2 y_{t-2} + \ldots \psi_p y_{t-p} + u_t$$

or

$$\Delta y_t = \psi^* y_{t-1} + \psi_1^* \Delta y_{t-1} + \psi_2^* \Delta y_{t-2} + \ldots \psi_{p-1}^* \Delta y_{t-p+1} + u_t \qquad u_t \sim IID(0, \sigma^2) \qquad (3.4)$$

where $\psi^* = (\psi_1 + \psi_2 + \ldots + \psi_p) - 1$. If $\psi^* = 0$, against the alternative $\psi^* < 0$, then y_t contains a unit root. To test the null hypothesis, we again calculate the DF t-statistic $(\hat{\psi}^*/se(\hat{\psi}^*))$, which can be compared against the critical values in Table 3.1 (for τ). Note that this is only strictly valid in large samples, since in small samples percentage points of the augmented Dickey–Fuller (ADF) distribution are generally

Box 3.1 Phillips–Perron-type tests for unit roots

The ADF-type test includes additional higher-order lagged terms to account for the fact that the underlying d.g.p. is more complicated than a simple AR(1) process. The extra terms, involving lags of the dependent variable, 'whiten' the error term in the regression equation used for testing, since autocorrelated errors (due to the misspecification of the dynamic structure of y_t) will invalidate the use of the DF distributions.

An alternative approach is that suggested by Phillips (1987) and extended by Perron (1988) and Phillips and Perron (1988). Rather than taking account of extra terms in the d.g.p. by adding them to the regression model, a non-parametric correction to the t-test statistic is undertaken to account for the autocorrelation that will be present (when the underlying d.g.p. is not AR(1)). Thus, DF-type equations (cf. (3.1)–(3.3)) are estimated, in line with Perrons (1988) testing strategy, and then the t-test statistic (of the null hypothesis of non-stationarity) is amended to take account of any bias due to autocorrelation in the error term of the DF-type regression model. This bias results when the variance of the 'true' population

$$\sigma^2 = \lim_{T\to\infty} E(T^{-1} S_T^2)$$

differs from the variance of the residuals in the regression equation:

$$\sigma_u^2 = \lim_{T\to\infty} T^{-1} \sum_{t=1}^{T} E(u_t^2)$$

Consistent estimators of σ_u^2 and σ^2 are:

$$S_u^2 = T^{-1}\sum_{t=1}^{T} (u_t^2); \qquad S_{T\ell}^2 = T^{-1} \sum_{t=1}^{T} (u_t^2) + 2T^{-1} \sum_{t=1}^{\ell} \sum_{t=j+1}^{T} u_t u_{t-j} \tag{3.1.1}$$

where ℓ is the lag truncation parameter used to ensure that the autocorrelation of the residuals is fully captured. In practice, the estimate for $S_{T\ell}^2$ is not guaranteed to be non-negative in finite samples and therefore the formula is modified in practice to include a term that ensures non-negativity.[14] It can be seen from (3.1.1) that when there is no autocorrelation the last term in the formula defining $S_{T\ell}^2$ is zero and $\sigma_u^2 = \sigma^2$.

Based on (3.1.1), an asymptotically valid test that $\rho_b = 1$ in (3.2), when the underlying d.g.p. is not necessarily an AR(1) process, is given by the Phillips Z-test:

$$Z(\tau_\mu) = (S_u/S_{T\ell})\tau_\mu - \frac{1}{2}(S_{T\ell}^2 - S_u^2)\left\{S_{T\ell}\left[T^2 \sum_{t=2}^{T} (y_{t-1} - \bar{y}_{-1})^2\right]^{1/2}\right\}^{-1} \tag{3.1.2}$$

where τ_μ is the t-statistic associated with testing the null hypothesis $\rho_b = 1$ in (3.2). The critical values for this test statistic are the same as those for τ_μ (cf. Table 3.1) and $Z(\tau_\mu)$ reduces to the DF test statistic τ_μ when autocorrelation is not present (since $S_u = S_{T\ell}$). Other Z-tests corresponding to tests involving trend and no constant or trend terms (and joint tests of hypotheses) are provided in Table 1 of Perron (1988).

Monte Carlo work (most notably by Schwert, 1989) suggests that the Phillips-type test has poor size properties (i.e., the tendency to over-reject the null when it is true) when the underlying d.g.p. has large negative moving-average components, and MA terms are

→

present in many macroeconomic time series. Banerjee *et. al* (1993) also state: '... one might suspect as well that the power of the Said–Dickey procedure would be higher for processes involving AR errors, because the test regression captures AR terms precisely' (p. 113). Note, however, that a recent attempt to improve the performance of the Phillips-type test has been made through prewhitening of the residual term in the regression model (see Maekawa, 1994, for details).

not the same as those applicable under the strong assumptions of the simple Dickey–Fuller model (Banerjee, *et al.*, 1993, p. 106).

As with the simple DF test, the above model needs to be extended to allow for the possibility that the d.g.p. contains deterministic components (constant and trend). As the model is extended the appropriate large sample critical values are those given in Table 3.1. The model needed to test for the null hypothesis of a stochastic trend (non-stationary) against the alternative of a deterministic trend (stationary) is as follows:

$$\Delta y_t = \psi^* y_{t-1} + \sum_{i=1}^{p-1} \psi_i^* \Delta y_{t-i} + \mu + \gamma t + u_t \qquad u_t \sim IID(0, \sigma^2) \tag{3.5}$$

The augmented model can be extended even further to allow for moving-average (MA) parts in the u_t.[15] It is generally believed that MA terms are present in many macroeconomic time series after first differencing (e.g., time average data, an index of stock prices with infrequent trading for a subset of the index, the presence of errors in the data, etc.). Said and Dickey (1984) developed an approach in which the orders of the AR and MA components in the error term are unknown, but can be approximated by an AR(k) process where k is large enough to allow a good approximation to the unknown ARMA(p, q) process, so ensuring that u_t is approximately 'white noise'. In terms of the augmented model the Said-Dickey approach can be approximated by replacing the lag-length of $(p - 1)$ with k, with the technical condition that k increases at a suitable rate as the sample size increases.[16]

Thus, the ADF test is comparable to the simple DF test but it involves adding an unknown number of lagged first differences of the dependent variable to capture autocorrelated omitted variables that would otherwise, by default, enter the error term, u_t (an alternative approach to adding lagged first differences of the dependent variable is to apply a non-parametric correction to take account of any possible autocorrelation; this is the Phillips and Perron approach, and it is discussed in Box 3.1). In this way, we can validly apply unit root tests when the underlying d.g.p. is quite general. However, it is also very important to select the appropriate lag-length; too few lags may result in over-rejecting the null when it is true (i.e., adversely affecting the size of the test), while too many lags may reduce the power of the test (since unnecessary nuisance parameters reduce the effective number of observations available). Banerjee *et al.* (1993) favour a generous parameterisation, since '... if too many lags are present ... the regression is free to set them to zero at the cost of some

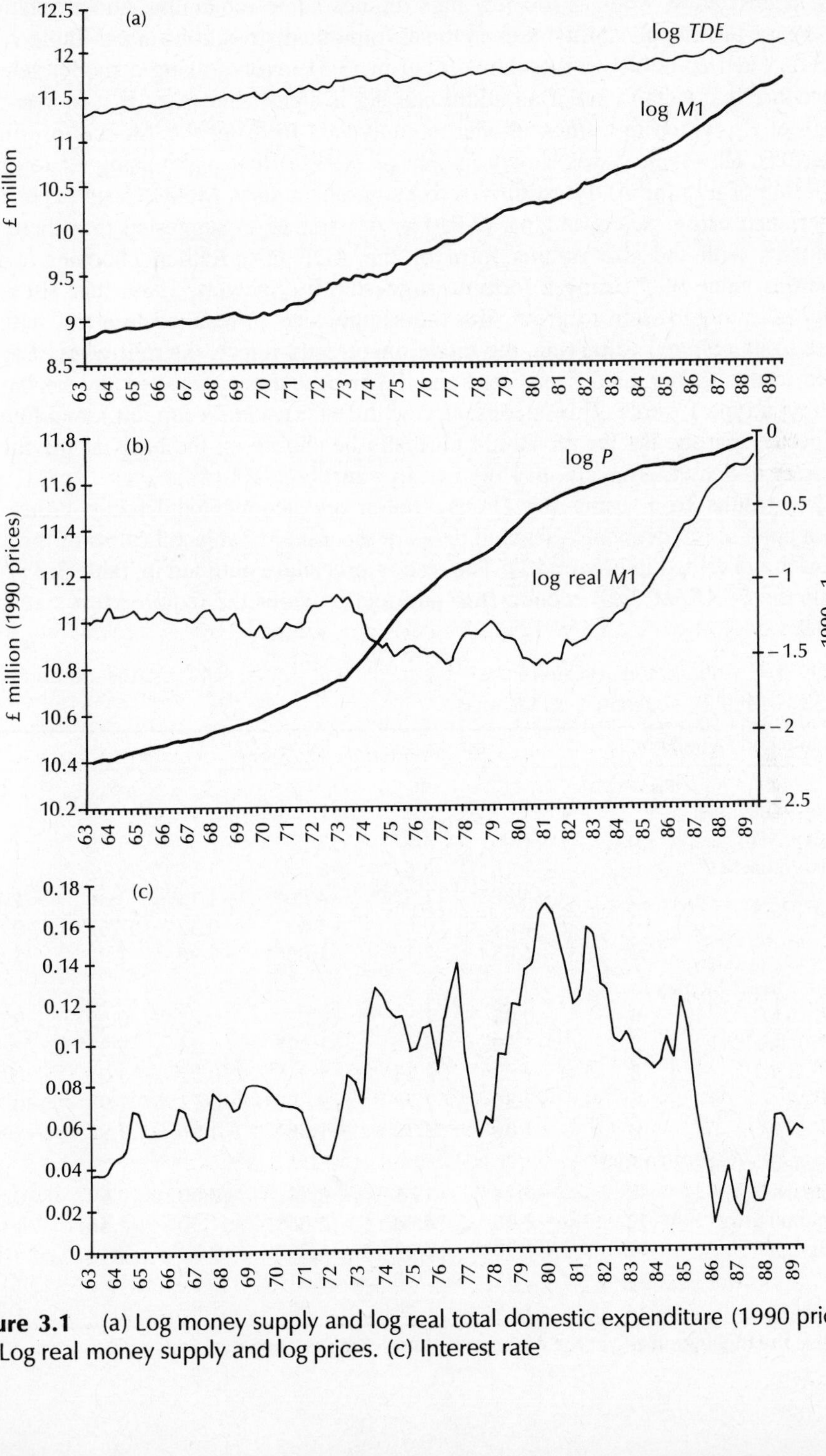

Figure 3.1 (a) Log money supply and log real total domestic expenditure (1990 prices). (b) Log real money supply and log prices. (c) Interest rate

loss in efficiency, whereas too few lags implies some remaining autocorrelation ... and hence the inapplicability of even the asymptotic distributions in ...,' Table 3.1.

Suggested solutions to the choice of p in (3.5) involve using a model selection procedure that tests to see if an additional lag is significant (e.g., if it increases the value of $\bar{R}^2$, which in a linear model is equivalent to using the Akaike information criterion). However, it was shown in Harris (1992a) that maximising $\bar{R}^2$ to choose the value of p in the ADF test proved to be unsatisfactory; Monte Carlo experiments undertaken using various d.g.p.s (ARMA, AR and MA) suggested that there were problems with the size of this form of the ADF test. Rather, choosing a fairly generous value of p (using a formula suggested by Schwert, 1989, that allows the order of autoregression to grow with the sample size T) resulted in a test with size close to its nominal value (i.e., the model incorrectly rejects the null when it is true, close to the 10 per cent, 5 per cent and 1 per cent times expected on the basis of making a type 1 error). This is consistent with Banerjee *et al.* (op. cit.), and thus it is suggested that the lag-length should normally be chosen on the basis of the formula reported in Schwert (op. cit., p. 151): i.e., $l_{12} = \text{int}\{12(T/100)^{1/4}\}$.

The results from using the Dickey–Fuller and augmented Dickey–Fuller tests when applied to UK money-demand data are reported in Table 3.3 (plots of the actual series are provided in Figure 3.1). The testing procedure outlined in Table 3.2 is used, while the *SHAZAM* (7.0) econometric package provides the required test statistics.[17]

Table 3.3 Augmented Dickey–Fuller tests of unit roots: UK money–demand data (1963:1–1989:2); seasonally unadjusted

Variable and lag-length		Test statistic (see Table 3.2)					
	lag length	τ_τ	Φ_3	t	τ_μ	Φ_1	t
Dickey–Fuller test							
log Real *M*1	0	1.05	5.67*	1.05	2.35	5.10**	2.35
log Nominal *M*1	0	−1.18	8.64**	−1.18	3.66	59.02**	3.66
log *TDE*	0	−4.80**	11.58**	−4.80**	−1.16	3.34	−1.16
log *P*	0	−1.02	0.65	−1.02	0.32	107.67**	0.32
R	0	−1.85	2.17	−1.85**	−1.96	1.92	−1.96**
Lag-length set by max $\bar{R}^2$							
log Real *M*1	8	−0.05	1.58	−0.05	−0.01	0.55	−0.01
log Nominal *M*1	8	−1.59	5.16	−1.59*	2.24	5.39**	2.24
log *TDE*	8	−1.91	2.05	−1.91**	0.32	3.02	0.32
log *P*	6	−2.30	2.72	−2.30**	−0.71	1.98	−0.71
R	0	−1.86	2.18	−1.86**	−1.96	1.92	−1.96**
Lag-length = int{12 $(T/100)^{1/4}$}							
log Real *M*1	12	−0.24	1.86	−0.24	−0.60	0.54	−0.60
log Nominal *M*1	12	−2.06	4.48	−2.06**	1.50	2.46	1.50
log *TDE*	12	−1.50	1.29	−1.50*	0.33	3.31	0.33
log *P*	12	−2.51	3.40	−2.51**	−1.00	1.82	−1.00
R	12	−1.58	1.88	−1.58*	−1.89	1.79	−1.89**

Rejects the null hypothesis at the **5 per cent and *10 per cent levels respectively.

Box 3.2 Multiple unit root tests

In Box 2.4 it was stated that if a series must be differenced *d* times before it becomes stationary, it is said to be integrated of order *d*, denoted $I(d)$. That is, the series contains *d* unit roots. Suppose y_t is found to be non-stationary based on the ADF test using the test procedure outlined in Table 3.2. It has been suggested that rather than assume that the first difference (Δy_t) is stationary, implying that $y_t \sim I(1)$, it is necessary to apply the ADF test to the new variable, Δy_t. Failure to reject the null that this new variable is non-stationary would imply that in fact y_t is at least $I(2)$.This procedure of testing from lower to higher orders of integration should continue until the hypothesis of non-stationarity is rejected.

However, Dickey and Pantula (1987) argue that this is an invalid testing procedure since if $y_t \sim I(2)$ applying the ADF test using (3.5) takes as the alternative hypothesis that y_t is stationary. What needs to be tested first in this instance is whether the variable Δy_t is non-stationary against the alternative that Δy_t is stationary. That is, they suggest that the correct sequential testing procedure is to take the largest number of unit roots likely as the maintained hypothesis (for practical purposes this would usually involve starting with $y_t \sim I(2)$), and then to reduce the order of differencing each time the null hypothesis is rejected until the first time the null is not rejected.

Thus, when $d = 2$ it is necessary to reformulate (3.5) as:

$$\Delta^2 y_t = \psi^* \Delta y_{t-1} + \sum_{i=1}^{p-2} \psi_i^* \Delta^2 y_{t-i} + \mu + u_t \qquad u_t \sim IID(0, \sigma^2) \tag{3.2.1}$$

To test the null hypothesis, we begin by calculating the ADF *t*-statistic ($\hat{\psi}^*/se(\hat{\psi}^*)$) which can be compared against the critical values in Table 3.1 (for τ_μ). If $\psi^* = 0$, against the alternative $\psi^* < 0$, is accepted then Δy_t is non-stationary and y_t contains two unit roots. If the null hypothesis is rejected then proceed to test the null of one unit root versus the stationary alternative using (3.5).

In practice, it seems intuitive to assume that there would be little difference whichever testing procedure is used since if $y_t \sim I(2)$ applying the ADF test using (3.5) should see an acceptance of the null 95 per cent of the time (using the 5 per cent critical values from the DF distribution) as long as there is at least one unit root. However, Dickey and Pantula (1987) found that on the basis of a Monte Carlo study this was not the case; the ability to reject the null of non-stationarity when more than one unit root was present (i.e., the series needs $d > 1$ differencing to induce stationarity) decreased when applying an equation such as (3.5) when compared to (3.2.1), *but not by very much*. Moreover, the empirical example they considered resulted in a rejection of non-stationarity whichever approach was applied (i.e., testing from lower (higher) to higher (lower) orders of integration), even though the series was judged to be $I(2)$.

Applying (3.2.1), both with and without a constant to the UK money-demand data analysed in Table 3.3, the results given in Table 3.2.1 were obtained.[18,19] Based on the ADF results, these suggest that prices are $I(2)$, while the nominal and real money supply, total domestic expenditure and the interest rate are $I(1)$ since we are able to reject the null of non-stationarity when the series are first differenced. It is usually assumed that if nominal money and/or prices are $I(2)$, and cointegrate, then $(m - p) \sim I(1)$, which is confirmed. However, several of the tests only weakly reject the

→

null hypothesis of non-stationarity. When the lag-length was set at 12 (see the earlier discussion) the null was never rejected using the ADF test, suggesting that this test has particularly low power. When Phillips–Perron-type tests (see Box 3.1) were used, the null hypothesis was rejected on every occasion except for prices. This suggests that, as stated earlier, there may be some concerns about the size of the PP test. Despite the problems with unit root testing, it seems reasonable to treat the real money supply, expenditure and the interest rate as *I*(1) and prices as *I*(2). The nominal money supply might be either, given its path over time (Figure 3.1).

Table 3.2.1 Augmented Dickey–Fuller tests of unit roots: UK money-demand data (1963:1–1989:2); seasonally unadjusted (dependent variable $=\Delta^2 y_t$)

Variable and lag-length		Test statistic (see Table 3.2)			
	Lag-length[a]	τ_μ	Φ_1	t	τ
ADF test					
log Real *M*1	8	−2.37	2.83	−2.37**	−2.24**
log Nominal *M*1	8	−2.01	2.14	−2.01**	−0.46
log *TDE*	8	−2.66*	3.56	−2.66**	−1.36
log *P*	1	−2.26	2.60	−2.26**	−0.99
R	10	−3.24**	5.24**	−3.24**	−3.26**
Phillips–Perron test					
log Real *M*1	8	− 9.31**	43.52**	−9.31**	−9.19**
log Nominal *M*1	8	−10.65**	56.92**	−10.65**	− 7.20**
log *TDE*	8	−18.16**	163.97**	−18.16**	−13.60**
log *P*	1	− 2.99*	4.42*	−2.99**	−1.44
R	10	−8.31**	34.34**	−8.31**	−8.36

Rejects the null hypothesis at the ** 5 per cent and * 10 per cent levels respectively.
[a] The lag-length was set by max $\bar{R}^2$ on every occasion (see text for details).

Note, the τ-statistic based on (3.1) is not calculated by *SHAZAM* unless the overall mean of the series is zero (cf. Figure 3.1). On the basis of the simple DF test the variable representing real output (log *TDE*) is found to be a trend-stationary series since, using the regression model (3.3), we can reject both the null of a unit root and the joint hypothesis that $\gamma_c = 0$ and $\rho_c = 1$. Other tests based on the DF statistic suggest that all the other series are non-stationary.

The results based on the DF test are questionable for all but the rate of interest, *R*, since significant lagged values of the dependent variable are found to be important when (3.5) is used to test for a unit root. The ADF tests where $\bar{R}^2$ is maximised suggest that all the series are non-stationary (similar results were obtained when the lag-length was set by the l_{12} formula). Note in particular that taking account of autocorrelation has significantly lowered τ_τ for log *TDE* and Φ_3 for the money supply variables. Given the above arguments about the reliability of the exact form of the test, it would seem reasonable to proceed on the basis that all the series are non-stationary.[20] As to whether each series is $I(1)$ or $I(2)$, this requires testing for more than one unit root (see Box 3.2).

Power and level of unit root tests

Choosing the correct form of the ADF model is problematic and using different lag-lengths often results in different outcomes with respect to rejecting the null hypothesis of non-stationarity. These problems are compounded by the fact that there are several issues related to the size and power of unit root tests, especially concerning the small sample properties of these tests.

Blough (1992) has recently extended what is known about the trade-off that exists between the size and power properties of unit root tests.[21] The usual requirements for a hypothesis test based on standard statistical inferences is that the size of the test should be close to its nominal value (see above), and it should have high power (through consistently rejecting the null when it is false) against at least some alternatives. However, in finite samples it can be shown that '... any trend-stationary process can be approximated arbitrarily well by a unit root process (in the sense that the autocovariance structures will be arbitrarily close)' (Campbell and Perron, 1991, p. 157). Similarly, any unit root process can be approximated by a trend-stationary process, especially when the sample size is small. That is, some unit root processes display finite sample behaviour closer to (stationary) 'white noise' than to a (non-stationary) random walk (while some trend-stationary processes behave more like random walks in finite samples). This implies that a unit root test '... with high power against *any* stationary alternative *necessarily* will have correspondingly high probability of false rejection of the unit root null when applied to near stationary processes' (Blough, 1992, p. 298). This follows from the closeness of the finite sample distribution of any statistic under a particular trend-stationary process and the finite sample distribution of the statistic under a difference-stationary process that approximates the trend-stationary process. Thus, Blough (op. cit., p. 299) states that there is a trade-off between size and power in that unit root tests must have either high probability of falsely rejecting the null of non-stationarity when the true d.g.p. is a nearly stationary process (poor size properties) or low power against any stationary alternative.[22]

The above problem concerning unit root tests, when there is near equivalence of non-stationary and stationary processes in *finite* samples, is in part due to using critical values based on the DF *asymptotic* distribution. The use of asymptotic critical values based on the strong assumptions of the simple DF model was also seen to be a limitation when considering the distribution of the augmented Dickey–Fuller test statistic. Thus, in Harris (1992b) it was suggested that bootstrap methods may be more applicable when using the ADF test of the unit root. Essentially, this amounts to replicating the underlying d.g.p. of the variable itself by sampling from the residuals of the ADF model and obtaining a sampling distribution (and critical values) for the

ADF statistic that is applicable to the underlying d.g.p. (instead of assuming that the underlying d.g.p. can be approximated asymptotically by equation (3.1)).

The problem of the size and power properties of unit root tests not only means that any results obtained must be treated with some caution but it raises the issue of whether current procedures are sufficiently robust to provide any substantial method of discriminating between non-stationary and trend-stationary processes. Blough (op. cit.) believes that unit root tests do have a role to play, stating: '... a unit root test which falsely rejects the null of a unit root for a given process may be properly indicating that that process should be treated as stationary for purposes of finite sample inference' (p. 304).

Structural breaks and unit root tests

Perron (1989) showed that if a series is stationary around a deterministic time trend which has undergone a permanent shift sometime during the period under consideration, failure to take account of this change in the slope will be mistaken by the usual ADF unit root test as a persistent innovation to a stochastic (non-stationary) trend. That is, a unit root test which does not take account of the break in the series will have (very) low power. There is a similar loss of power if there has been a shift in the intercept (possibly in conjunction with a shift in the slope of the deterministic trend).

If the break(s) in the series are known then it is relatively simple to adjust the ADF test by including (composite) dummy variables[23] to ensure there are as many deterministic regressors as there are deterministic components in the d.g.p. The relevant critical values for unit root tests involving shifts in the trend and/or intercept are found in Perron (1989, 1990). However, it is unlikely that the date of the break will be known *a priori*, as was assumed by Perron (op. cit). In such situations it is necessary to test for the possibility of a break using a recursive, rolling, or sequential approach (Banerjee, Lumsdaine and Stock, 1992). Several test statistics are available, including the usual ADF τ_τ-statistic (see Table 3.2) and also minimum ADF τ-statistics computed over various subsamples of the data. Banerjee, Lumsdaine and Stock (op. cit.) show that the standard ADF τ_τ-statistic is unreliable (which is to be expected, given the above discussion), but the new test statistics have reasonable size and power properties on the basis of some Monte Carlo experiments.

The recursive minimum ADF τ-statistic is computed using subsamples $t = 1, \ldots, k$, for $k = k_0, \ldots, T$, where k_0 is a start-up value and T is the size of the full sample.[24] The model given in (3.5) is estimated for each subsample and then the minimum value of $\tau_\tau(k/T)$ across all the subsamples is chosen and compared to the critical values provided in Table 1 of Banerjee, Lumsdaine and Stock, (op. cit.) to test the null of a unit root.[25] Rolling statistics are computed in a similar way, this time using

Table 3.4 Recursive, rolling and sequential augmented Dickey–Fuller tests of unit roots: UK money-demand data (1963:1–1989:2), seasonally unadjusted

Variable	Recursive:		Rolling:	Mean-shift statistics		Trend-shift statistics	
	τ_τ	min τ_τ	min τ_τ	min τ_τ	max *F*	min τ_τ	max *F*
log Real *M*1	−1.40	−3.60	−3.36	−3.11	7.31	−3.28	7.90
log Nominal *M*1	−2.20	−2.20	−3.30	−2.69	5.23	−2.67	4.83
log *TDE*	−1.85	−2.11	−3.85	−2.17	6.83	−1.93	7.62
log *P*	−2.38	−2.38	−3.41	−2.82	16.69†	−2.79	9.39
R	−2.00	−2.71	−3.22	−3.82	10.50	−3.76	10.01

†Rejects the null at 10% significance level. Critical values are obtained from Tables 1 and 2 in Banerjee, Lumsdaine and Stock (1992). See also the Statistical Appendix.

subsamples that are a constant fraction δ_0 of the full sample, rolling through the sample.[26] The sequential minimum ADF τ-statistic is likewise computed using the full sample and the following adaptation of (3.5):

$$\Delta y_t = \psi^* y_{t-1} + \sum_{i=1}^{p-1} \psi_i^* \Delta y_{t-i} + \mu_0 + \mu_1 t + \mu_2 D + u_t \qquad u_t \sim IID(0, \sigma^2) \tag{3.6}$$

where in the shift[27] in trend model:

$$D = t \quad \text{for } (t > k)$$
$$D = 0 \quad \text{for } (t \leqslant k)$$

while for the shift in mean model:

$$D = 1 \quad \text{for } (t > k)$$
$$D = 0 \quad \text{for } (t \leqslant k)$$

Allowing k (the unknown date of the hypothetical break or shift) to be increased sequentially, minimum values of $\tau_\tau(k/T)$ for the trend-shift and mean-shift models are compared to the critical values in Table 2 of Banerjee, Lumsdaine and Stock, (op. cit.). A further two test statistics with apparently reasonable size and power properties are F-statistics used to test the null H_0: $\mu_2 = \psi^* = 0$ in the trend-shift and mean-shift models. The largest values of these sequentially calculated F-statistics are compared to the critical values in Table 2 of Banerjee, Lumsdaine and Stock (op. cit.).

As an example of the approach, the various test statistics that have just been discussed were computed using the money-demand data considered earlier.[28] Results are reported in Table 3.4, and these show that there is little evidence for rejecting the unit root null even after allowing for the possibility of a break in the series. Only the price series shows any (weak) evidence of a break, and by examining the sequence of F-test statistics obtained it appears that if there was a break then it occurred in the third quarter of 1973 (see Figure 3.1(b)).

Seasonal unit roots

Time series data often comes in a seasonally *un*adjusted form and it has been argued that where possible such data are to be preferred to their seasonally adjusted counterpart, since the filters used to adjust for seasonal patterns often distort the underlying properties of the data (see section 19.6 in Davidson and MacKinnon, 1993, for some evidence). In particular, there is a tendency for the OLS estimate of ρ_b in the Dickey–Fuller test (3.2) to be biased towards 1 when y_t is a seasonally adjusted series, thus rejecting the null hypothesis of non-stationarity substantially less often than it should, according to the critical values in Table 3.1.

Certain variables (e.g., consumption spending) exhibit strong seasonal patterns which account for a major part of the total variation in the data and which are therefore important when model building. Such patterns may first of all result from stationary seasonal processes, which are conventionally modelled using seasonal dummies that allow some variation but no persistent change in the seasonal pattern over time. Alternatively, seasonal processes may be non-stationary if there is a varying and changing seasonal pattern over time. Such processes cannot be captured using deterministic seasonal dummies since the seasonal component drifts substantially over time; instead such a series needs to be seasonally differenced to achieve stationarity. This is more complicated than considering the possibility of a unit root (non-stationarity) at the zero frequency since *four* different unit roots are possible in a seasonal process. To see this, consider seasonally differencing quarterly data using the seasonal difference operator $\Delta_4 y_t = (1 - L^4)y_t = y_t - y_{t-4}$. Note, $(1 - L^4)$ can be factorised as:

$$\begin{aligned}(1 - L^4) &= (1 - L)(1 + L + L^2 + L^3)\\ &= (1 - L)(1 + L)(1 + L^2) = (1 - L)(1 + L)(1 - iL)(1 + iL)\end{aligned} \tag{3.7}$$

with each unit root corresponding to a different cycle in the time domain. The first $(1 - L)$ is the standard unit root considered so far, at the zero frequency. The remaining unit roots are obtained from the moving-average seasonal filter $S(L) = (1 + L + L^2 + L^3)$, and these correspond to the two-quarter (half-yearly) frequency $(1 + L)$ and a pair of complex conjugate roots at the four-quarter (annual) frequency, $(1 \pm iL)$. To simplify the interpretation of the seasonal unit roots Banerjee, *et al.* (1993, p. 122) show that a simple deterministic process $(1 + L)y_t = 0$ can be rewritten as $y_{t+2} = y_t$ (the process returns to its original value on a cycle with a period of 2); while $(1 - iL)y_t = 0$ can be rewritten as $y_{t+4} = y_t$(the process returns to its original value on a cycle with a period of 4).

Before considering testing for seasonal unit roots, it is useful to note that Osborn (1990) found that only five out of thirty UK macroeconomic series required seasonal differencing to induce stationarity; that is, seasonal unit roots are not encountered very often and macroeconomic time series can typically be described as $I(1)$ with a deterministic seasonal pattern superimposed (Osborn, 1993, p. 300). Second, if all three seasonal unit roots discussed above are actually present then no two quarters are cointegrated and '... the four quarter series for x go their separate ways in the long run ... the presence of seasonal unit roots begs the question of what sort of economic mechanism would give rise to this failure of cointegration' (Osborn, op. cit., p. 300). A third point to note before proceeding concerns the question of whether the usual ADF tests of the null hypothesis of a unit root at the zero frequency are valid, even when other unit roots at other seasonal frequencies are present. Put another way, does the presence of additional roots at other cycles invalidate the non-seasonal unit root test. Ghysels, Lee and Noh (1994) show that the usual ADF test is still valid, as long as a sufficient number of lagged terms are included in the test equation to take account of the seasonal terms in the data. However, they also show (on the basis of Monte Carlo experiments) that the test involves serious size distortions (worse than in the standard ADF case, as discussed earlier).[29]

To incorporate seasonal integration into the definition of integration at the zero frequency (see Box 2.4), it is useful to note as above that seasonal differencing involves using $(1-L)$ to difference at the zero frequency, d, in order to remove the zero frequency unit roots, and using the seasonal filter $S(L)$ to difference at the seasonal frequency, D, in order to remove the seasonal unit roots. Thus, it is said that the stochastic process y_t is integrated of orders d and D (denoted $I(d, D)$) if the series is stationary after first period differencing d times and seasonal differencing D times. To test the null hypothesis of $I(1, 1)$ against the alternatives $I(1, 0)$ and $I(0, 1)$, Osborn (1990, equation 1) proposed using:[30]

$$
\begin{aligned}
(1-L)(1-L^4)y_t &= \Delta\Delta_4 y_t = \alpha_1 D_{1t} + \alpha_2 D_{2t} + \alpha_3 D_{3t} + \alpha_4 D_{4t} + \beta_1 \Delta_4 y_{t-1} \\
&+ \beta_2 \Delta y_{t-4} + \sum_{i=1}^{p-1} \psi_i^* \Delta\Delta_4 y_{t-i} + u_t \qquad u_t \sim IID(0, \sigma^2)
\end{aligned}
\tag{3.8}
$$

where D_{qt} is the zero/one dummy corresponding to quarter q. If $\beta_1 < 0$ and $\beta_2 = 0$, then this implies accepting the alternative hypothesis $I(0, 1)$; while if $\beta_2 < 0$ and $\beta_1 = 0$, then accept $I(1, 0)$. Osborn (op. cit.) also reports an overall F-test of $\alpha_i = \beta_j = 0$ $(i = 1, 2, 3, 4; j = 1, 2)$.

Osborn (op. cit.) also proposes a different test involving the null hypothesis $I(1, 1)$ against the alternatives $I(2, 0)$ and $I(0, 1)$:

$$
\begin{aligned}
\Delta_4\Delta y_t &= \alpha_0 + \alpha_1(D_{1t} - D_{4t}) + \alpha_2(D_{2t} - D_{4t}) + \alpha_3(D_{3t} - D_{4t}) + \pi_1 Z_1 \Delta y_{t-1} \\
&\quad + \pi_2 Z_2 \Delta y_{t-1} + \pi_3 Z_3 \Delta y_{t-2} + \pi_4 Z_3 \Delta y_{t-1} + \sum_{i=1}^{p-1} \psi_i^* \Delta_4 \Delta y_{t-i} + u_t \\
&\qquad u_t \sim IID(0, \sigma^2)
\end{aligned}
\tag{3.9}
$$

where:

$$Z_1 = (1 + L + L^2 + L^3),$$

$$Z_2 = -(1 - L + L^2 - L^3),$$

$$Z_3 = -(1 - L^2).$$

If $\pi_1 < 0$ and $\pi_2 = \pi_3 = \pi_4 = 0$, then this implies accepting the alternative hypothesis $I(0, 1)$; while if $\alpha_0 = \pi_1 = 0$, $\pi_2 \neq 0$ and π_3 or $\pi_4 \neq 0$, then accept $I(2, 0)$.

To test the null of $I(1, 1)$ Osborn (op. cit.) advocates using both (3.8) and (3.9) because of potentially different power properties (the second equation uses up more degrees of freedom which may result in loss of power) and because (3.9) allows for the different alternative $I(2, 0)$. It can also be used to test for all possible unit roots in a seasonal process since Z_1 removes the seasonal unit roots and leaves in the zero frequency unit root; Z_2 leaves in the seasonal root at the two-quarter (half-yearly) frequency; and Z_3 leaves in the seasonal roots at the four-quarter (annual) frequency. Thus testing $\pi_i = 0$, $i = 2, 3, 4$, will determine if there are any seasonal unit roots and at what frequency.[31]

Another important point to note is that for both equations, if the null is true no intercept is expected because seasonal differencing has the particular property of removing conventional deterministic seasonality (i.e., it results in a zero mean). Consequently, it is unnecessary to include a trend in these equations to encompass the null and alternative hypotheses (as with the standard ADF test), but it is necessary to include four quarterly dummy variables when testing because even though there is no intercept under the null, tests of the unit root are not invariant to the starting values for the seasonal components of y_t (see the discussion of equations (3.1) and (3.2)). A second reason for not including a trend is that neither equation is a test against stationarity. If tests involving (3.8) and (3.9) point towards accepting the alternative $I(0, 1)$, then it is necessary to confirm this using the following to test the null hypothesis of $I(0, 1)$ against the alternatives of $I(1, 0)$ and $I(0, 0)$:

$$\Delta_4 y_t = \alpha_1 D_{1t} + \alpha_2 D_{2t} + \alpha_3 D_{3t} + \alpha_4 D_{4t} + \pi_1 Z_1 y_{t-1} + \pi_2 Z_2 y_{t-1} + \pi_3 Z_3 y_{t-2}$$

$$+\pi_4 Z_3 y_{t-1} + \sum_{i=1}^{p-1} \psi_i^* \Delta_4 y_{t-i} + \delta t + u_t \qquad u_t \sim IID(0, \sigma^2) \tag{3.10}$$

If $\pi_1 < 0$ and $\pi_i \neq 0$, for all $i = 2, 3, 4$, this implies the acceptance of the alternative hypothesis $I(0, 0)$; while if $\pi_1 = 0$, $\pi_2 \neq 0$ and π_3 or $\pi_4 \neq 0$, then accept $I(1, 0)$. As with (3.9), separately testing $\pi_i = 0$, $i = 2, 3, 4$, will determine if there are any seasonal unit roots and at what frequency.

Since (3.10) is a test against stationarity, both seasonal dummies and a trend are included. This ensures that the test procedure nests both the null hypothesis and alternative hypothesis and consequently the test is invariant to the drift parameter and starting values of y_0 when testing the $I(1)$ hypothesis with a non-constant drift term (but no deterministic trend).[32] This also means that it will be necessary to conduct a joint test of the hypothesis that $\pi_1 = \delta = 0$ since rejection of this suggests acceptance of trend-stationarity. Finally, if the tests involving (3.8) and (3.9) support the alternative $I(1, 0)$ and $I(2, 0)$, respectively, or if tests involving (3.10) support the alternative hypothesis $I(1, 0)$, then it is prudent to undertake a further test sequence using the conventional ADF model (equations (3.5) and (3.2.2)) and the testing procedure advocated by Perron (1988) as set out in Table 3.2.

Previous work using UK data has considered whether the consumption function comprises variables with seasonal unit roots (cf. Osborn, *et. al.*, 1988).[33] The variables considered are real non-durable consumers' expenditure (real C), real personal disposable income (real Y), the inflation rate (π), and end-of-period real liquid assets (real W). These series are plotted in Figure 3.2, and exhibit a clear seasonal pattern, especially real consumption and real liquid assets. Estimating (3.8)–(3.10) gave the results set out in Table 3.5. Real consumers' spending and real liquid assets would appear to be $I(1, 1)$ on the basis of (3.8), since neither $\beta_1 = 0$ and $\beta_2 = 0$ are rejected. The results from using (3.8) also support the alternative hypothesis that both real personal disposable income and the inflation rate are $I(1, 0)$ since $\beta_2 < 0$. In contrast, the results based on (3.9) present a less clear outcome: using the second set of results where the lag-length is set according to the formula reported in Schwert (1989, p.

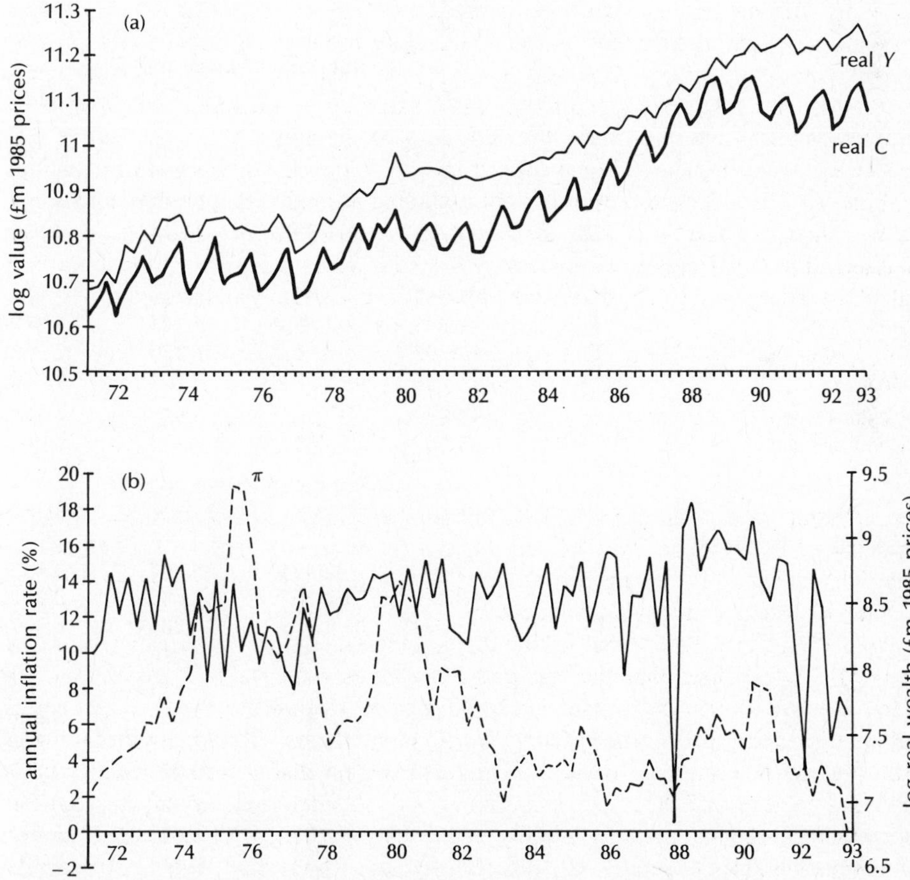

Figure 3.2 Quarterly UK consumption function data, seasonally unadjusted, 1971–93. (a) Log of real income and non-durable consumption. (b) Log of real wealth and annual retail inflation rate $\pi = \log(p_t - p_{t-4})$

Table 3.5 Seasonal unit roots tests: UK consumption function data (1971:2–1993:1)

Variable		(a) Test statistic based on (3.8)			
	Lag length	β_1	β_2	Overall *F*-test	
Lag length set by max $\bar{R}^2$					
real *C*	10	−1.062	−2.608	2.325	
real *Y*	10	−1.282	−4.522[b]	5.319[b]	
π	11	1.713	−5.440[b]	10.388[b]	
real *W*	7	−1.757	−1.966	1.994	
Lag length = int{12(*n*/100)$^{1/4}$}					
real *C*	11	−0.679	−2.781	12.273	
real *Y*	11	−1.240	−3.957[a]	4.668[a]	
π	11	1.713	−5.440[b]	10.388[b]	
real *W*	11	−1.456	−2.039	1.584	
5%critical value		−2.22	−3.75	3.79	
1% critical value		−2.82	−4.35	4.80	
		(b) Test statistic based on (3.9)			
		π_1	π_2	$\pi_3 \cap \pi_4$	$\alpha_0 \cap \pi_1$
Lag length set by max $\bar{R}^2$					
real *C*	0	−5.154[b]	−7.648[b]	2.866	2.866
real *Y*	6	−3.520[a]	−4.062[b]	4.772	3.302
π	11	−5.599[b]	−7.989[b]	21.170[b]	2.763
real *W*	10	−1.772	−1.797	1.314	3.090
Lag-length = int{12(*T*/100)$^{1/4}$}					
real *C*	11	−1.857	−2.491	2.129	2.866
real *Y*	11	−2.831	−2.983[a]	2.291	3.308
π	11	−5.599[b]	−7.989[b]	21.170[b]	2.763
real *W*	11	−1.846	−1.583	0.801	3.090
5% critical value		−2.94	−2.90	6.63	4.71
1% critical value		−3.56	−3.49	8.92	6.70
		(c) Test statistic based on (3.10)			
		π_1	π_2	$\pi_3 \cap \pi_4$	$\delta \cap \pi_1$
Lag-length set by max $\bar{R}^2$					
real *C*	10	−2.490	−2.371	1.892	3.415
real *Y*	11	−2.123	−2.265	2.663	3.308
π	5	−3.624[a]	−5.059[b]	18.285[b]	6.907
real *W*	7	−2.988	−2.895	2.015	4.614
Lag length = int{12(*T*/100)$^{1/4}$}					
real *C*	11	−2.340	−2.420	2.052	2.866
real *Y*	11	−2.123	−2.265	2.663	3.308
π	11	−2.342	−4.314[b]	10.021[b]	2.763
real *W*	11	−2.212	−2.443	1.045	3.090
5% critical value		−3.52	−2.93	6.62	6.33
1% critical value		− 4.15	−3.57	8.77	8.40

[a] reject null at 5 per cent significance level but not 1 per cent.

[b] reject null at 1 per cent significance level. Note all critical values are taken from Osborn (1990).

151 – see the discussion of the ADF test earlier), there is support for accepting that real C and real W contain unit roots at both the zero and seasonal frequencies. The picture for income is less obvious, given that there is evidence pointing to this variable possibly being $I(2, 0)$, while the outcome for inflation is not easily interpreted in terms of the null and alternative hypotheses (although the earlier result that π is $I(1, 0)$ may be deduced). Lastly, the results relating to (3.10) in Table 3.5 confirm that the inflation rate is $I(1, 0)$; moreover, since this test does not encompass the hypothesis $I(1, 1)$, the results based on (3.10) for real consumers' spending and real liquid assets can be ignored. However, based on using (3.10) there is evidence to support the contradictory notion that real Y is $I(0, 1)$.

It is reasonable to conclude that both real consumer spending and real liquid assets are $I(1, 1)$ while inflation is $I(1, 0)$, suggesting that the price level itself is $I(2, 0)$. The results for real personal disposable income are not clear-cut. As a check, standard ADF tests were undertaken based on (3.5) and (3.3.2) and setting $p = 11$. These confirm that each series contains a unit root at the zero frequency, providing support for the results obtained using (3.8). Osborn *et al.* (1988) (using similar unadjusted quarterly data for 1955–1985) report that real W, π, and real Y are $I(1, 0)$ while real C was tentatively classified as $I(1, 1)$.

Conclusion on unit root tests

This chapter has shown that while in principle it is necessary to test for the presence of unit roots in order to avoid the problem of spurious regression, this is by no means a simple exercise. An appropriate testing strategy is based on the augmented Dickey–Fuller test with a generous lag structure which allows for both constant and trend terms, and then follows the sequential testing strategy suggested by Perron (1988). This procedure needs to be amended if there is any evidence of structural breaks in the series under examination, and the testing procedure outlined in Banerjee, Lumsdaine and Stock (1992) should then be followed. Similarly, when using seasonally unadjusted data exhibiting strong seasonal patterns which may be changing over time, it is necessary to amend the ADF-type test to allow for possible seasonal unit roots. However, Osborn (1990) suggests that seasonal unit roots are not encountered very often and macroeconomic time series can typically be described as $I(1)$ with a deterministic seasonal pattern superimposed.

Clearly, the most important problem faced when applying unit root tests is their probable poor size and power properties (i.e., the tendency to over-reject the null when it is true and under-reject the null when it is false, respectively). This problem occurs because of the near equivalence of non-stationary and stationary processes in *finite* samples which makes it difficult to distinguish between trend-stationary and difference-stationary processes. It is not really possible to make such definitive statements as 'real GNP is non-stationary'; rather, unit root tests are more useful for indicating whether the finite sample data used exhibits stationary or non-stationary attributes.[34]

Appendix 1: Programming in SHAZAM: testing for structural breaks in unit root tests

```
*Note data are contained in the Statistical Appendix
file 11 uk_ms.dat
time 1963 4
smpl 1963.1 1989.2
read(11) y m p r
genr rm=m-p

* RESULTS FOR r
?ols m
genl t=$n
smpl 1 t
genr dr=r-lag(r)
genr lr=lag(r)
dim tstat 106 tsta 106 q 106 t1 106 t2 106 f1 106 f2 106
set nodoecho
genl n=int(.25*t)
smpl 5 t
?ols dr lr dr(1.4) trend/coef=b stderr=se
genl df=b/se
* PRINT ADF T-VALUE
print df
do %=n,t
sampl 5 %
?ols dr lr dr(1.4) trend/coef=beta stderr=e
genl tstat:%=(beta:1/e:1)*(%/t)
endo
smpl n t
* THE MINIMUM VALUE FOR TSTAT IS THE RECURSIVE MIN T-VALUE
stat tstat
smpl 1 t
genl n=int(.33*t)
do %=n,t
genl k=1+%-n
smpl k %
?ols dr lr dr(1.4) trend / coef=bet stderr=ee
genl tsta:%=(bet:1/ee:1)*(%/t)
endo
smpl n t
* THE MINIMUM VALUE FOR TSTA IS THE ROLLING MIN T-VALUE
stat tsta
smpl 1 t
```

```
genl n=int(.15*t)
genl k=t-n
genr dum=0
do %=n,k
smpl % t
genr dum=1
genr dumt=dum*trend
smpl 5 t
?ols dr lr dr(1.4) trend dum/coef=bl stderr=el
?test
?test lr=0
?test dum=0
?end
?genl fl:%=$f
genl tl:%=(bl/el)*(%/t)
?ols dr lr dr(1.4) trend dumt/coef=b2 stderr=e2
?test
?test lr=0
?test dumt=0
?end
?genl f2:%=$f
genl t2:%=(b2/e2)*(%/t)
genr dum=0
genr dumt=0
endo
smpl n k
print tl fl t2 f2
* THE MINIMUM VALUE FOR Tl IS THE MEAN-SHIFT MIN T-VALUE
* THE MINIMUM VALUE FOR T2 IS THE TREND-SHIFT MIN T-VALUE
* THE MAXIMUM VALUE FOR Fl IS THE MEAN-SHIFT MAX F-VALUE
* THE MAXIMUM VALUE FOR F2 IS THE TREND-SHIFT MAX F-VALUE
stat Tl T2 Fl F2
stop
```

Notes

1. Of course, it would be useful to test using both alternatives of the null, to ensure that each corroborates the other. In fact, when the Johansen model is discussed a unit root test procedure that takes the null of stationarity will be considered.
2. Note, we are not assuming that the residuals u_t are drawn from a normal distribution; rather they are drawn from the Dickey–Fuller distribution.
3. Note, if we reject $\rho^* = 0$ in favour $\rho^* < 0$ then we can safely reject $\rho^* > 0$.
4. Note, the d.g.p. underlying the DF distribution is that given in (3.1), containing no constant or trend. Critical values are then obtained for three models used to test the null

of a unit root: (i) a no constant/no trend regression (i.e., (3.1) in the text and the first block of values in Table 3.1); (ii) only a constant in the model ((3.2) and block 2 in Table 3.1); and (iii) both a constant and a trend ((3.3) and block 3 in Table 3.1). If the d.g.p. is altered to include a non-zero constant, the critical values obtained from (iii) are not affected; the DF distribution is invariant to the value of the constant in the d.g.p. and thus it is sufficient to use (3.1) as the underlying d.g.p. for calculating critical values (Fuller, 1976). This property of the DF distribution is known as similarity, and leads to similar tests (i.e., tests for which the distribution of the test statistic under the null hypothesis is independent of nuisance parameters in the d.g.p.).

5. Nankervis and Savin (1985) have shown that using (3.1) with $y_0 \neq 0$ can lead to problems of over-rejection of the null when it is true (i.e., there are problems with the size of the test).
6. *See also* footnote 4 for more details.
7. Thus, if the null hypothesis H_0: $(\rho_c - 1) = 0$ is true, we should expect the trend not to be significant in (3.3), otherwise we would need the extra block of DF critical values. Note, if the deterministic trend is significant under a joint test and dominates the stochastic trend then asymptotic normality of the *t*-statistic follows, as we now go on to discuss.
8. Note, Φ_3 is invariant with respect to y_0 and μ_c.
9. Note, Φ_1 is invariant with respect to y_0.
10. That is, a similar test having a DF distribution requires that the regression model used for testing contains more parameters than the d.g.p. (see Kiviet and Phillips, 1992).
11. Note, this will also be a problem when we consider adding lagged values of the Δy_{t-i} as additional regressors when using the augmented Dickey–Fuller test (see below).
12. This needs, however, to be counterbalanced by the fact that (in finite samples) as we add deterministic regressors to the regression model, there is a downward bias away from zero in the estimate of ρ and this bias increases as the number of deterministic regressors increases. However, even though this suggests that the asymptotic low power of the test and finite bias may help to cancel each other out, Monte Carlo simulation does tend to confirm that there still remains a problem in finite samples (e.g. Schwert, 1989).
13. In some packages (such as *PcGive*) the critical values used are those obtained by MacKinnon (1991), who calculated response surfaces to allow appropriate critical values to be obtained for various sample sizes (and not just those listed in the Dickey and Fuller tables).
14. Specifically, an additional term $1\text{-}j(\ell + 1)^{-1}$ follows the second summation sign in the formula for $S^2_{T\ell}$.
15. E.g., $u_t = \varepsilon_t - \theta\varepsilon_{t-1}$ where $\varepsilon_t \sim IID(0, \sigma^2)$.
16. This is an approximation to the Said–Dickey approach, since the latter do not include a model incorporating a deterministic trend, while the model with drift ($\mu \neq 0$) should necessitate that the first regressor in (3.5) become $(y_{t-1} - \bar{y})$, where $\bar{y}$ is the mean of y over the sample.
17. The COINT procedure in *SHAZAM* (developed by Ken White, at the University of British Columbia) provides the various forms of the test statistics as used here; it also calculates for the user the value p that maximises $\bar{R}^2$. Other packages typically report the ADF τ-statistic for various user specified lag-lengths (e.g., *PcGive* 7.7).
18. Note, we started testing with $d = 3$ and the null of non-stationarity was rejected in every case. The results presented therefore refer to the test of $I(2)$ against $I(1)$. Also, we

calculate the ADF τ-statistic since differenced series often have a mean of zero and no deterministic trend.

19. Usually a time trend is not included in (3.2.2) since this would imply that the variable has a quadratic trend, which is unlikely.
20. Note, using the Phillips–Perron test (see Box 3.1) produces similar results to the ADF test when $\bar{R}^2$ is maximised (including similar truncation lag-lengths); the major difference is that the PP test supports the notion that real output is a trend-stationary variable. This may result from the presence of negative MA terms in the d.g.p., which has been shown to affect the size of the PP test.
21. See also the results in DeJong, Nankervis and Savin (1992).
22. Put more technically, the unit root test must have power equal to its size against a near-stationary process.
23. I.e., dummy variables that take on a value of (0, 1) to allow for shifts in the intercept and dummies multiplied by a time trend to take into account any change in the slope of the deterministic trend.
24. Thus, the ADF statistic is computed for subsamples that increase by one observation until eventually the full sample is covered, with the first subsample running from 1 to k_0 with $k_0 = 0.25T$. Setting k_0 equal to one-quarter of the sample size is essentially arbitrary but this value was used by Banerjee *et al.* (op. cit.).
25. Note, each ADF τ-statistic is multiplied by (k/T), so, based on the full sample when $k = T$, the usual ADF τ-statistic must lie in the range of statistics computed.
26. Thus the first sub-sample covers 1 to k, with $k = 0.3T$, the second subsample is 2 to $0.3T + 1$, the third is 3 to $0.3T + 2$, and so on. Again choosing k equal to one-third of the sample size is essentially arbitrary but this value was used by Banerjee *et al.* (op. cit.).
27. The shift occurs at unknown k, and k is searched out between $0.15T$ and $T - 0.15T$. The use of the value 0.15 is again due to Banerjee *et al.* (op. cit.).
28. The need to set up looping procedures requires the use of a flexible program such as *SHAZAM* in order to compute the test statistics easily. Appendix 1 provides a copy of the program used.
29. This leads Ghysels *et al.* (1994) to point out: '... this faces the practical researcher with a difficult choice. Namely, either using unadjusted data resulting in tests with the wrong size, or using adjusted data, with adjustment procedures having adverse effects on power'.
30. Note, this test presumes that the underlying d.g.p. has seasonal deterministic components, captured by the seasonal dummies. If this is not true, the irrelevant inclusion of such terms should reduce the power of the test (see the earlier discussion on this for the standard ADF test). However, Ghysels *et al.* (1994) show in their experiments that omitting seasonal dummies when they should be included leads to a large bias in the size of the test or too low power. Hence, they believe the safe strategy is to include the (possibly irrelevant) seasonal dummies in the model.
31. Note, $\pi_3 = \pi_4 = 0$ must hold if there are seasonal roots at the four-quarter (annual) frequency.
32. See the discussion surrounding (3.1)–(3.3).
33. The data are available from the CSO databank, and are described in the appendix to the Osborn *et al.* (1988) paper. Note, total non-durable consumption is used here without excluding any components.
34. Note also, if anything, the problems of the size and power of the test are even worse in seasonal unit root models (Ghysels *et al.*, 1994).

4

Cointegration in single equations

Important terms and concepts

Engle–Granger approach 'Superconsistency' Finite sample bias Residual-based ADF test for cointegration Common factors Fully modified estimators Dynamic single-equation models Cointegration vector Speed of adjustment to equilibrium Diagnostic checking Seasonal cointegration

The Engle–Granger (EG) approach

In discussing cointegration in Chapter 2, it was shown that if two time series y_t and x_t are both $I(d)$, then in general any linear combination of the two series will also be $I(d)$; that is, the residuals obtained from regressing y_t on x_t are $I(d)$. If, however, there exists a vector β, such that the disturbance term from the regression ($\hat{\varepsilon}_t = y_t - \hat{\beta} x_t$) is of a lower order of integration, $I(d-b)$, where $b > 0$, then Engle and Granger (1987) define y_t and x_t as cointegrated of order (d, b). Thus, if y_t and x_t were both $I(1)$, and $\varepsilon_t \sim I(0)$, the two series would be cointegrated of order $CI(1, 1)$. This implies that if we wish to estimate the long-run relationship between y_t and x_t it is only necessary to estimate the static model:[1]

$$y_t = \beta x_t + \varepsilon_t \tag{4.1}$$

Estimating (4.1) using OLS achieves a consistent[2] estimate of the long-run steady-state relationship between the variables in the model, and all dynamics and endogeneity issues can be ignored asymptotically. This arises because of what is termed the 'superconsistency' property of the OLS estimator when the series are cointegrated. Before discussing this, recall the following simple dynamic model of short-run adjustment (cf. (2.11)):

$$y_t = \gamma_0 x_t + \gamma_1 x_{t-1} + \alpha y_{t-1} + u_t \tag{4.2}$$

This can be rewritten as:

$$y_t = \beta x_t + \lambda_1 \Delta x_t + \lambda_2 \Delta y_t + \nu_t \tag{4.3}$$

where $\beta = (\gamma_0 + \gamma_1/1 - \alpha)$; $\lambda_1 = -(\gamma_1/1 - \alpha)$; $\lambda_2 = -(\alpha/1 - \alpha)$; and $\nu_t = (u_t/1 - \alpha)$. Thus, estimating the static model (4.1) to obtain an estimate of the long-run parameter β is equivalent to estimating the dynamic model (4.3) without the short-run terms, Δx_t, Δy_t. According to the 'superconsistency' property, if y_t and x_t are both non-stationary $I(1)$ variables, and $\varepsilon_t \sim I(0)$, then as sample size, T, becomes larger the OLS estimator of β converges to its true value at a much faster rate than the usual OLS estimator with stationary $I(0)$ variables (Stock, 1987). That is, the $I(1)$ variables asymptotically dominate the $I(0)$ variables, Δx_t, Δy_t and ε_t. Of course, the omitted dynamic terms (and any bias due to endogeneity) are captured in the residual, ε_t, which will consequently be serially correlated.[3] But this is not a problem due to 'superconsistency'.

Nevertheless, in finite samples, it has been shown that bias *is* a problem, and this will be discussed later. Moreover, Phillips and Durlauf (1986) have derived the asymptotic distribution of the OLS estimator of β, and its associated t-statistic, showing these to be highly complicated and non-normal and thus invalidating standard tests of hypothesis. Thus, so far we have noted that there are problems of finite sample bias and an inability to draw inferences about the significance of the parameters of the static long-run model. A separate issue is whether tests of cointegration based directly on the residuals from (4.1) have good power properties (i.e., they do not under-reject the null when it is false).

To test the null hypothesis that y_t and x_t are not cointegrated amounts, in the Engle–Granger framework, to directly testing whether $\varepsilon_t \sim I(1)$ against the alternative that $\varepsilon_t \sim I(0)$. There are several tests that can be used, including the Dickey–Fuller and augmented Dickey–Fuller tests discussed at length in the last chapter (comparable Z-tests by Phillips, and Phillips and Perron, are also commonly used but Monte Carlo work suggests these have poorer size properties and thus they will not be explored here – see Box 3.1). Essentially, Engle and Granger (1987) advocated ADF tests of the following kind:

$$\Delta\hat{\varepsilon}_t = \psi^* \hat{\varepsilon}_{t-1} + \sum_{i=1}^{p-1} \psi_i^* \Delta\hat{\varepsilon}_{t-i} + \mu + \delta t + \omega_t \qquad \omega_t \sim IID(0, \sigma^2) \tag{4.4}$$

where the $\hat{\varepsilon}_t$ are obtained from estimating (4.1). The question of the inclusion of trend and/or constant terms in the test regression equation depends on whether a constant or trend term appears in (4.1). That is, deterministic components can be added to *either* (4.1) *or* (4.4), *but not to both*. As with the testing procedure for unit roots generally (cf. Chapter 3), it is important to include a constant if the alternative hypothesis of cointegration allows a non-zero mean for $\hat{\varepsilon}_t$ $(= y_t - \hat{\beta} x_t)$, while in theory a trend should be included if the alternative hypothesis allows a non-zero deterministic trend for $\hat{\varepsilon}_t$. However, Hansen (1992) has shown, on the basis of Monte Carlo experimentation, that irrespective of whether ε_t contains a deterministic trend or not, including a time trend in (4.4) results in a loss of power (i.e., leads to under-rejecting the null of no cointegration when it is false).[4] Since, it is generally unlikely that the $\hat{\varepsilon}_t$ obtained from estimating (4.1) will have a zero mean, and given Hansen's results, this form of testing for cointegration should be based on (4.1) and (4.4) with δ set equal to zero.

As with univariate unit root tests, the null hypothesis of a unit root and thus no cointegration (H_0: $\psi^* = 0$) is based on a *t*-test with a non-normal distribution. However, unless β is already known (and not estimated using equation (4.1)) it is not possible to use the standard Dickey–Fuller tables of critical values. There are two major reasons for this; first, because of the way it is constructed the OLS estimator 'chooses' the residuals in (4.1) to have the smallest sample variance,[5] even if the variables are not cointegrated, making the ε_t appear as stationary as possible. Thus, the standard DF distribution (cf. Table 3.1) would tend to over-reject the null. Second, the distribution of the test statistic under the null is affected by the number of regressors (n) included in (4.1). Thus, different critical values are needed as n changes. Since the critical values also change depending on whether a constant and/or trend are included in (4.4), and with the sample size, there are a large number of permutations, each requiring a different set of critical values with which to test the null hypothesis.

Fortunately, MacKinnon (1991) has linked the critical values for particular tests to a set of parameters of an equation of the response surfaces. That is, with this table of response surfaces (see Table 4.1 for an extract), and the following relation:

$$C(p) = \phi_\infty + \phi_1 T^{-1} + \phi_2 T^{-2} \tag{4.5}$$

Table 4.1 Response surfaces for critical values of cointegration tests

n	Model	% point	ϕ_∞	ϕ_1	ϕ_2
1	no constant,	1	−2.5658	−1.960	−10.04
	no trend	5	−1.9393	−0.398	0.0
		10	−1.6156	−0.181	0.0
1	constant,	1	−3.4336	−5.999	−29.25
	no trend	5	−2.8621	−2.738	−8.36
		10	−2.5671	−1.438	−4.48
1	constant +	1	−3.9638	−8.353	−47.44
	trend	5	−3.4126	−4.039	−17.83
		10	−3.1279	−2.418	−7.58
3	constant,	1	−4.2981	−13.790	−46.37
	no trend	5	−3.7429	−8.352	−13.41
		10	−3.4518	−6.241	−2.79

Source: MacKinnon (1991).

where $C(p)$ is the p per cent critical value, it is possible to obtain the appropriate critical value for any test involving the residuals from an OLS equation where the number of regressors (excluding the constant and trend) lies between: $1 \leqslant n \leqslant 6$. For instance, the estimated 5 per cent critical value for 105 observations when $n = 3$ in (4.1), and with a constant but no trend included in (4.4), is given by $(-3.7429 - 8.352/105 - 13.41/105^2) \approx -3.82$. Thus reject the null of no cointegration at the 5 per cent significance level if the t-value associated with ψ^* is more negative than -3.82. Note also, the critical values calculated with $n = 1$ will be the same as those given in Table 3.1 for the univariate DF test.

The residual-based ADF test for cointegration that has just been discussed assumes that the variables in the OLS equation are all $I(1)$, such that the test for cointegration is whether $\varepsilon_t \sim I(1)$ against the alternative that $\varepsilon_t \sim I(0)$. If some of the variables are in fact $I(2)$ then cointegration is still possible if the $I(2)$ series cointegrates down to an $I(1)$ variable in order to cointegrate potentially with the other $I(1)$ variables (see Box 2.4). However, Haldrup (1994) shows that the critical values for the ADF test will now depend (particularly in small samples) on the *number* of $I(1)$ and $I(2)$ *regressors* in the equation. Consequently, when testing for cointegration when there is a mix of $I(1)$ and $I(2)$ variables, the critical values provided in Haldrup (op. cit., Table 1) must be used.[6]

A potential problem with using the ADF test can now be considered (although for simplicity of exposition the DF test which involves no lagged values of the dependent variable is presented). Kremers, Ericsson and Dolado (1992) examine the common factor 'problem' of the DF statistic (a problem which applies to any single equation unit-root-type cointegration test, such as the Phillips Z-test). Suppose the underlying d.g.p. is given by (4.2), with the residuals from (4.1) used to test the null of no cointegration. The DF test comprises:

$$\Delta\hat{\varepsilon}_t = \psi\hat{\varepsilon}_{t-1} + \omega_t \tag{4.6}$$

which can be rewritten to obtain the equivalent error-correction model (evaluated at $\hat{\beta} = \beta$):

$$\Delta(y_t - \beta x_t) = \psi(y_{t-1} - \beta x_{t-1}) + \omega_t \quad \text{OR}$$

$$\Delta y_t = \beta\Delta x_t + \psi(y_{t-1} - \beta x_{t-1}) + \omega_t \tag{4.7}$$

But this is *not* the unrestricted ECM underlying (4.2); this can be shown to be given by (cf. equation (2.13)):

$$\Delta y_t = \gamma_0\Delta x_t - (1 - \alpha)[y_{t-1} - \beta x_{t-1}] + u_t \tag{4.8}$$

For (4.8) to be the same as (4.7), it is necessary to impose $(\gamma_1 = -\gamma_0\alpha)$ since then (4.2) can be rewritten as:

$$(1 - \alpha L)y_t = (\gamma_0 + \gamma_1 L)x_t + u_t \quad \text{OR}$$

$$(1 - \alpha L)y_t = \gamma_0(1 - \alpha L)x_t + u_t \tag{4.9}$$

and both sides of this equation contain the common factor $(1 - \alpha L)$. What the DF

Box 4.1 Engle–Granger–Yoo three-step approach

Engle and Yoo (1991) propose a 'third step' to the standard Engle–Granger procedure which seeks to overcome some of the problems inherent in using the static first-step model (4.1) to obtain an estimate of the long-run parameter β. In particular, the latter is generally biased in finite samples and its distribution is generally non-normal, which means that standard t-statistics cannot be used to test hypotheses concerning β. Assuming that there is both a unique cointegration vector *and* weak exogeneity of the right-hand-side variables in the short-run ECM, then the third step provides a correction to the first-stage estimate of β and ensures that it has a normal distribution.

After estimating the static model (cf. (4.1)), a first-stage estimate is obtained of $\hat{\beta}$, which we can label $\hat{\beta}^1$. The residuals from the static model provide estimates of the disequilibrium ($\hat{\varepsilon}_{t-1} = y_{t-1} - \hat{\beta}x_{t-1}$) which then enter the second-stage short-run ECM (cf. (4.10)). The latter itself provides an estimate of the speed-of-adjustment parameter $-(1-\hat{\alpha})$ and a set of residuals, $\hat{u}_t$, which are then used in a third-stage regression:

$$\hat{u}_t = \delta[(1-\hat{\alpha})x_{t-1}] + \nu_t \tag{4.1.1}$$

The estimate of δ obtained (together with its standard deviation, which provides the correct standard deviation for β^3 below) is used to correct the first-stage estimates:

$$\hat{\beta}^3 = \hat{\beta}^1 + \hat{\delta} \tag{4.1.2}$$

As an indication of the type of results obtained, the residuals from the first-stage static demand for real money (4.11b) are entered (lagged one period) into a short-run ECM with $\Delta(m-p)_t$ as the dependent variable and an estimate of the speed of adjustment is obtained of -0.05. Thus, each of the (lagged) right-hand-side variables in (4.11b) are multiplied by 0.05, and the new variables form the regressors in the third-stage model with the residuals from the short-run ECM as the dependent variable (cf. (4.1.1)). Using the resultant parameter estimates of δ (and associated standard errors which are used to calculate t-ratios), the corrected long-run relationship comes out as:

$$m - p = \underset{(1.90)}{5.082}\Delta p + \underset{(5.28)}{0.813}y - \underset{(3.38)}{5.563}R + \underset{(1.11)}{2.011} + \hat{\varepsilon} \tag{4.13}$$

Comparing these results with (4.13), it can be seen that the EG three-stage approach improves the estimates of y, R and the constant but the estimate for Δp is still wrongly signed.

test imposes through the common factor restriction in (4.9) is that the short-run reaction of y_t to a change in x_t (i.e., γ_0) now becomes the same as the long-run effect (i.e., β) that would occur if the model were in equilibrium.[7] Kremers, Ericsson and Dolado (op. cit.) point out that if invalid (as is often likely), this restriction imposes a loss of information (and so a loss of power) relative to a test, say, based on the unrestricted ECM.[8]

So why is the Engle–Granger procedure so popular, given that (i) this test for cointegration is likely to have lower power against alternative tests; (ii) its finite sample estimates of long-run relationships are potentially biased; and (iii) inferences cannot be drawn using standard t-statistics about the significance of the parameters of the static long-run model? First, it is of course easy to estimate the static model by OLS and then perform unit root tests on the residuals from this equation. Second, estimating (4.1) is only the first stage of the EG procedure, with stage two comprising estimating the short-run ECM itself using the estimates of disequilibrium ($\hat{\varepsilon}_{t-1}$) to obtain information on the speed of adjustment to equilibrium. That is, having obtained ($\hat{\varepsilon}_{t-1} = y_{t-1} - \hat{\beta}x_{t-1}$) from (4.1), it is possible to estimate:

$$\Delta y_t = \gamma_0 \Delta x_t - (1-\alpha)\hat{\varepsilon}_{t-1} + u_t \quad \text{OR}$$

$$A(L)\Delta y_t = B(L)\Delta x_t - (1-\pi)\hat{\varepsilon}_{t-1} + u_t \tag{4.10}$$

where the second form allows for a general dynamic structure to be determined by the data (see the discussion of (2.14)). Note also that if y_t and x_t are $I(1)$, and cointegration between them exists (thus $\varepsilon_t \sim I(0)$), then all the terms in (4.10) are $I(0)$, and statistical inferences using standard t- and F-tests are applicable.

To illustrate the approach, estimating static demand for money equations using seasonally unadjusted data for 1963:1 – 1989:2 produced the following results:[9]

$$m = 0.774p + 1.212y - 3.448R - 2.976 + \hat{\varepsilon}_1 \qquad R^2 = 0.99 \quad DW = 0.33 \tag{4.11a}$$

$$m - p = 0.769\Delta p + 0.409y - 3.981R + 6.682 + \hat{\varepsilon}_2 \quad R^2 = 0.69 \quad DW = 0.24 \tag{4.11b}$$

Using (4.4), with $\mu = \delta = 0$ imposed, the residuals, $\hat{\varepsilon}_1$ and $\hat{\varepsilon}_2$, were tested for a unit root under the null hypothesis of no cointegration. The value of p was set by both the maximum $\bar{R}^2$ approach and by the formula suggested in Schwert (1989): both produced a similarly long lag-length for the ADF test and consequently similar results. The τ-value associated with testing the null hypothesis that H_0: $\psi^* = 0$ based on the $\hat{\varepsilon}_1$ is -1.56, while the corresponding test statistic for $\hat{\varepsilon}_2$ is -2.62. The critical value for rejecting the null is obtained from Table 4.1 and in both instances is -3.09 (at the 10 per cent significance level).[10] These results indicate that there is no long-run stable relationship for money demand. As will be seen, this is in contradiction to some of the results from other tests of cointegration.

Alternative approaches

There are a number of alternative tests for cointegration. The simplest is the cointegration regression Durbin–Watson (CRDW) test proposed by Sargan and Bhargava (1983). This is based on the standard DW statistic obtained from a regression involving (4.1), and it is known to be the uniformly most powerful invariant test[11] of the null hypothesis that ε_t is a simple non-stationary random walk (i.e., $\varepsilon_t = \varepsilon_{t-1} + z_t$; where $z_t \sim IN(0, \sigma^2)$) against the alternative that ε_t is a stationary first-order autoregressive process (i.e., $\varepsilon_t = \rho\varepsilon_{t-1} + z_t$; where $|\rho| < 1$ and $z_t \sim IN(0, \sigma^2)$). In

Box 4.2 Dynamic analysis and the long-run model: estimates from *PcGive* (ver. 7.7)

AR Model estimated:

$$A(L)(m-p)_t = B_1(L)y_t + B_2(L)R_t + B_3(L)\Delta p_t + u_t$$

$R^2 = 0.996349$ $F(26, 73) = 766.19$ [0.0000] $\sigma = 0.0138893$ DW = 2.08

RSS = 0.01408263468 for 27 variables and 100 observations

Information criteria:

SC = -7.62459; HQ = -8.04331; FPE = 0.000244999

Diagnostic tests of the u_t

AR 1- 5 F(5, 68) = 1.8769 [0.1098]

ARCH 4 F(4, 65) = 0.67035 [0.6149]

Normality $\chi^2(2) = 4.204$ [0.1222]

X_i^2 F(49, 23) = 0.53713 [0.9658]

RESET F(1, 72) = 0.2299 [0.6331]

Solved static long run equation

$$m-p = -0.3931 + 1.052\ y - 6.871\ R - 7.332\ \Delta p + 0.2379\ \text{Seasonal}$$
$$(SE)\quad (1.376)\ (0.1218)\ (0.5737)\ (1.693)\quad (0.1869)$$

WALD test $\chi^2(4) = 155.92$ [0.0000] **

Analysis of lag structure

Lag=	0	1	2	3	4	5	Σ
m -p	-1	0.58	0.127	-0.185	0.442	-0.102	-0.138
SE	0	0.123	0.131	0.122	0.123	0.108	0.0311
Constant	-0.0544	0	0	0	0	0	-0.0544
SE	0.185	0	0	0	0	0	0.185
y	-0.00243	0.25	0.0487	-0.385	0.138	0.0969	0.146
SE	0.102	0.112	0.114	0.113	0.119	0.11	0.0281
R	-0.413	-0.355	-0.274	0.0774	0.172	-0.159	-0.952
SE	0.129	0.198	0.2	0.198	0.198	0.147	0.198
Δp	-0.649	0.045	0.103	-0.25	-0.315	0.0502	-1.02
SE	0.24	0.286	0.28	0.276	0.257	0.22	0.241
Seasonal	-0.0119	0.0197	0.0251	0	0	0	0.0329
SE	0.0101	0.0106	0.00916	0	0	0	0.0242

→

<u>Tests of the significance of each variable</u>

variable	F(num, denom)	Value	Probability	Unit Root t-test
m-p	F(5, 73) =	279.92	[0.0000] **	-4.4577*
Constant	F(1, 73) =	0.086917	[0.7690]	-0.29482
y	F(6, 73) =	7.2548	[0.0000] **	5.1892
R	F(6, 73) =	11.655	[0.0000] **	-4.795
Δp	F(6, 73) =	4.438	[0.0007] **	-4.2184
Seasonal	F(3, 73) =	5.0883	[0.0030] **	1.3642

<u>Tests on the significance of each lag</u>

Lag	F(num, denom)	Value	Probability
1	F(4, 73) =	12.288	[0.0000] **
2	F(4, 73) =	0.84412	[0.5018]
3	F(4, 73) =	3.3472	[0.0143] *
4	F(4, 73) =	5.7871	[0.0004] **
5	F(4, 73) =	0.60177	[0.6626]

<u>Tests on the significance of all lags up to 5</u>

Lag	F(num, denom)	Value	Probability
1- 5	F(20, 73) =	305.38	[0.0000] **
2- 5	F(16, 73) =	4.0287	[0.0000] **
3- 5	F(12, 73) =	4.6031	[0.0000] **
4- 5	F(8, 73) =	3.6411	[0.0013] **
5- 5	F(4, 73) =	0.60177	[0.6626]

<u>COMFAC WALD test statistic table</u>

Order	χ^2df	Value	p-value	Incr. χ^2df	Value	p-value
5	3	0.55972	[0.9056]	3	0.55972	[0.9056]
4	6	0.80294	[0.9920]	3	0.24322	[0.9703]
3	9	2.414	[0.9831]	3	1.6111	[0.6569]
2	12	13.293	[0.3481]	3	10.879	[0.0124] *
1	15	34.894	[0.0025] **	3	21.601	[0.0001] **

terms of the money-demand model, the critical value for rejecting the null of no cointegration is 0.48 (see Sargan and Bhargava (1983)), which is not exceeded in (4.11). However, this critical value is only relevant when ε_t follows a first-order process, that is, there is no higher-order residual autocorrelation (as is usually present, e.g., in the example considered here). Thus, the CRDW test is generally not a suitable test statistic.[12]

An alternative that has been suggested by Kremers, Ericsson and Dolado (1992) is to directly test the null hypothesis that $\alpha = 1$ in (4.10), which is the error-correction formulation of the model.[13] If this null holds, then there is no cointegration. Under the null hypothesis, such a t-type test has a non-normal distribution, and Kremers *et al.* (op. cit.) suggest using the MacKinnon critical values associated with the comparable ADF test of the null. Banerjee *et al.* (1993), however, show that the distribution of the t-statistic associated with testing $\alpha = 1$ is closer to the normal distribution than it is to the ADF distribution (also, under the alternative hypothesis of cointegration, the t-value is known to be asymptotically normally distributed). However, despite this problem of what set of critical values to use, both Kremers *et al.* (op. cit.) and Banerjee *et al.* (op. cit.) show that this approach produces a more powerful test in comparison to the ADF test (presumably because no common factor restrictions are imposed). To make the test operational, it is necessary to assume that x_t is weakly exogenous (see below for a discussion of this property) and an estimate of ε_{t-1} is needed. The latter can either be obtained, for example, from imposing $\beta = 1$ (on theoretical grounds), and thus $\varepsilon_{t-1} = y_{t-1} - x_{t-1}$, or an estimate of the long-run relationship must be obtained in advance (i.e., we require an unbiased estimate of β). Another approach equivalent to that suggested by Kremers *et al.* (op. cit.), is to estimate the unrestricted dynamic model in distributed-lag form rather than as an ECM, and then to solve for the long-run model (i.e., to estimate equation (4.2), or a more general form directly, and then to solve for equation (4.1)). This procedure is standard in certain econometric packages, in particular *PcGive* (v7.7), and the output from applying this approach to the money-demand model is given in Box 4.2 (see the next section for a discussion of the approach). In line with the results from using the ECM formulation, the test of the null hypothesis of no cointegration is more powerful in comparison to using the ADF test, and Inder (1993) shows that there are other desirable properties, namely that the unrestricted dynamic model gives '... precise estimates (of long-run parameters) and valid t-statistics, even in the presence of endogenous explanatory variables' (Inder, op. cit., p. 68).

Dynamic models

When the simple dynamic model, as represented by (4.2), is a sufficient representation of the underlying economic relationship, the EG approach of estimating the (static) (4.1) is equivalent to omitting the short-run elements of the dynamic model. As more complicated dynamic models become necessary to capture the relationship between x and y, then estimating the static model to obtain an estimate of the long-run parameter β will push more complicated dynamic terms into the residual, ε_t, with the result that the latter can exhibit severe autocorrelation. As has been stated, 'superconsistency' ensures that it is asymptotically valid to omit the stationary $I(0)$ terms in equations such as (4.3), but in finite samples the estimates of the long-run relationship will be biased (and, as shown by Phillips, 1986, this is linked to the degree of serial correlation).[14] The Monte Carlo work of Banerjee *et al.* (1993) and Inder (1993), shows that this bias is often substantial. Thus, it seems reasonable to consider estimating the full model which includes the dynamics, that is, (4.2) or its equivalent, since this leads to greater precision in estimating β in finite samples.

One of the results to emerge from the Monte Carlo work is that it is preferable to over-parameterise the dynamic model (i.e., a generous lag-length should be chosen) since this reduces any bias when compared to an under-parameterised model, even when the 'true' model involves a simple d.g.p. with few dynamic terms. Thus, the following model should be estimated:

$$A(L)y_t = B(L)x_t + u_t \tag{4.12}$$

where $A(L)$ is the polynomial lag operator $1 - \alpha_1 L - \alpha_2 L^2 - \ldots - \alpha_p L^p$; $B(L)$ is the polynomial lag operator $\gamma_0 + \gamma_1 L + \gamma_2 L^2 + \ldots + \gamma_q L^q$; and $L^r x_t = x_{t-r}$.[15] The long-run parameter(s)[16] can be obtained by solving the estimated version of (4.12) for $\hat{\beta}$, which in the simple model (equation (4.2)) amounts to $\hat{\beta} = (\hat{\gamma}_0 + \hat{\gamma}_1 / 1 - \hat{\alpha}_1)$.[17] Standard errors of $\hat{\beta}$ can be obtained using a (non-linear) algorithm (the procedure used in *PcGive* v7.7 involves numerical differentiation), and thus not only are long-run estimates obtained but t-tests concerning the statistical significance of $\hat{\beta}$ can also be undertaken. Inder (1993) shows that t-tests of this kind, using critical values from the standard normal distribution, have good size and power properties (even when x_t is endogenous) and therefore valid inferences can be made concerning $\hat{\beta}$.[18]

In addition to providing generally unbiased estimates of the long-run model and valid t-statistics, it is possible to carry out a unit root test of the null hypothesis of no cointegration since the sum of the $\hat{\alpha}_i$ $(i = 1, \ldots, p)$ in (4.12) must be less than one for the dynamic model to converge to a long-run solution. Thus, dividing $(1 - \Sigma\hat{\alpha}_i)$ by the sum of their associated standard errors provides a t-type test statistic which can be compared against the critical values given in Banerjee, Dolado, and Mestre (1992), in order to test the null hypothesis.[19]

As an example of the approach, recall that when applying unit root tests to the residuals from the static demand for money equation there is no evidence to reject the null hypothesis of no cointegration. Setting $p = q = 5$, and then testing to ensure that this parameterisation of (4.12) is general enough to pass various diagnostic tests[20] relating to the properties of the residuals, $\hat{u}_t$, the following (cf. Box 4.2) long-run relationship is found (with t-values in parentheses):

$$m - p = \underset{(4.33)}{-7.332\Delta p} + \underset{(8.64)}{1.052y} - \underset{(11.98)}{6.871R} - \underset{(0.29)}{0.393} + \underset{(1.27)}{0.238SEAS} + \hat{\varepsilon} \tag{4.13}$$

A Wald test decisively rejects the null that all of the long-run coefficients (except the constant term) are zero. The unit root test of the null hypothesis of no cointegration results in a test statistic of −4.46 which rejects the null at the 5 per cent significance level.[21] Thus, this approach suggests that contrary to the results obtained from the static (4.4), there is a long-run stable relationship for money demand. Furthermore, tests of common factors in the lag polynomials reject the hypothesis of four common factors, which helps to explain the results from applying the different tests for cointegration. Lastly, it can be seen that the estimates of long-run parameters are also different (cf. equations (4.11b) and (4.13)), with the estimate for Δp wrongly signed, and the estimate for real income unexpectedly small, in the static model.[22]

Fully modified estimators

Using a dynamic modelling procedure results in a more powerful test for cointegration, as well as giving generally unbiased estimates of the long-run relationship and standard t-statistics for conducting statistical hypothesis testing. In large part the better performance of the dynamic model is the result of not pushing the short-run dynamics into the residual term of the estimated OLS regression. As with the tests for unit roots discussed in the last chapter (Box 3.1), the alternative to modelling the dynamic processes is to apply a non-parametric correction to take account of the impact on the residual term of autocorrelation (and possible endogeneity if the right-hand-side variables in the cointegration equation are not weakly exogenous). Such an approach is often termed Modified OLS (see especially Phillips and Hansen, 1990), and amounts to applying adjustments to the OLS estimates of both the long-run parameter(s) β and its associated t-value(s) to take account of any bias, due to autocorrelation and/or endogeneity problems, which show up in the OLS residuals.[23] Thus, tests involving the Modified OLS t-statistics are asymptotically normal.

Inder (1993) found that the Modified OLS estimates of the long-run relationship yielded little or no improvement on the precision of the standard OLS estimator. Thus, bias remained a problem in many of his Monte Carlo experiments, leading him to conclude that '... it seems that the semiparametric correction is insufficient to remove the autocorrelation in the error when the data-generating process includes a lagged dependent variable' (p. 61). Furthermore '... Modified OLS gives t-statistics whose sizes are generally no better than the OLS results. ... The poor performance of (such) t-statistics suggests that in this case a very large sample is required for the asymptotics to take effect' (p. 66). This is perhaps fortunate since implementation of the Phillips-type non-parametric corrections is somewhat complicated, and Inder's results suggest that there is little to be gained over the static EG approach.

Problems with the single equation approach

It was stated in Box 2.4 that if there are $n > 2$ variables in the model, there can be more than one cointegration vector. That is, the variables in a model (e.g., (2.1) which depicts the money-demand function) may feature as part of several equilibrium relationships governing the joint evolution of the variables. It is possible for up to $n - 1$ linearly independent cointegration vectors to exist and only when $n = 2$ is it possible to show that the cointegration vector is unique.

Assuming that there is only one cointegration vector, when in fact there are more, leads to inefficiency in the sense that we can only obtain a linear combination of these vectors when estimating a single equation model. However, the drawbacks of this approach extend beyond its inability to validly estimate the long-run relationships between the variables; even if there is only one cointegration relationship, estimating a single equation is potentially inefficient (i.e., it does not lead to the smallest variance against alternative approaches). As will be seen, information is lost unless each endogenous variable appears on the left-hand side of the estimated equations in the multivariate model, except in the case where all the right-hand-side variables in the cointegration vector are weakly exogenous.

It is useful to extend the single equation ECM to a multivariate framework by defining a vector $\mathbf{z}_t = [y_{1t}, y_{2t}, x_t]'$ and allowing all three variables in $\mathbf{z}_t$ to be potentially endogenous, namely:

$$\mathbf{z}_t = \mathbf{A}_1\mathbf{z}_{t-1} + \ldots \mathbf{A}_k\mathbf{z}_{t-k} + \mathbf{u}_t \qquad \mathbf{u}_t \sim IN(0, \Sigma) \tag{4.14}$$

This is comparable to the single equation dynamic model (4.12) and in a similar way can be reformulated into a *vector* error-correction (*V*ECM) form:

$$\Delta\mathbf{z}_t = \mathbf{\Gamma}_1\Delta\mathbf{z}_{t-1} + \ldots + \mathbf{\Gamma}_{k-1}\Delta\mathbf{z}_{t-k+1} + \mathbf{\Pi}\mathbf{z}_{t-1} + \mathbf{u}_t \tag{4.15}$$

where $\mathbf{\Gamma}_i = -(\mathbf{I} - \mathbf{A}_1 - \ldots - \mathbf{A}_i)$, $(i = 1, \ldots, k-1)$, *and* $\mathbf{\Pi} = -(\mathbf{I} - \mathbf{A}_1 - \ldots - \mathbf{A}_k)$. The (3×3) $\mathbf{\Pi}$ matrix contains information on the long-run relationships; in fact, $\mathbf{\Pi} = \boldsymbol{\alpha}\boldsymbol{\beta}'$, where $\boldsymbol{\alpha}$ represents the speed of adjustment to disequilibrium[24] while $\boldsymbol{\beta}$ is a matrix of long-run coefficients. Thus, the term $\boldsymbol{\beta}'\mathbf{z}_{t-1}$ embedded in (4.15) is equivalent to the error-correction term $(y_{t-1} - \beta x_{t-1})$ in (4.8), except that $\boldsymbol{\beta}'\mathbf{z}_{t-1}$ contains up to $(n-1)$ vectors in a multivariate model.[25]

Setting the lag-length in (4.15) to $k = 2$, and writing out the model in full gives:

$$\begin{bmatrix} \Delta y_{1t} \\ \Delta y_{2t} \\ \Delta x_t \end{bmatrix} = \Gamma_1 \begin{bmatrix} \Delta y_{1t-1} \\ \Delta y_{2t-1} \\ \Delta x_{t-1} \end{bmatrix} + \begin{bmatrix} \alpha_{11} & \alpha_{12} \\ \alpha_{21} & \alpha_{22} \\ \alpha_{31} & \alpha_{32} \end{bmatrix} \begin{bmatrix} \beta_{11} & \beta_{21} & \beta_{31} \\ \beta_{12} & \beta_{22} & \beta_{32} \end{bmatrix} \begin{bmatrix} y_{1t-1} \\ y_{2t-1} \\ x_{t-1} \end{bmatrix} \tag{4.16}$$

It is now possible to illustrate more fully the problems incurred when estimating only a single equation model. Using (4.16) and writing out just the error-correction part of, say, the first equation (i.e., the equation with Δy_{1t} on the left-hand side) gives:[26,27]

$$\Pi_1\mathbf{z}_{t-1} = [(\alpha_{11}\beta_{11} + \alpha_{12}\beta_{12}) \quad (\alpha_{11}\beta_{21} + \alpha_{12}\beta_{22}) \quad (\alpha_{11}\beta_{31} + \alpha_{12}\beta_{32})] \begin{bmatrix} y_{1t-1} \\ y_{2t-1} \\ x_{t-1} \end{bmatrix} \tag{4.17}$$

where $\mathbf{\Pi}_1$ is the first row of $\mathbf{\Pi}$. That is, if only a single equation with Δy_{1t} as the left-hand side variable is estimated then it is not possible to obtain an estimate of either of the cointegration vectors since all that can be obtained is an estimate of $\mathbf{\Pi}_1$ which is a linear combination of the two long-run relationships (and this applies equally to the static or dynamic form of the single equation model – cf. equations (4.1) and (4.12)). This result applies whichever element of $\mathbf{z}_t$ is used as the left-hand side in the single equation model, since only estimates of $\mathbf{\Pi}_i$ can be obtained ($i = 1, 2, 3$).

Alternatively, when there is only one cointegration relationship ($\beta_{11}y_{1t-1} + \beta_{21}y_{2t-1} + \beta_{31}x_{t-1}$), rather than two, entering into all three ECMs with differing speeds of adjustment $[\alpha_{11}, \alpha_{21}, \alpha_{31}]'$, then using a single equation approach will obtain an estimate of the cointegration vector since writing out just the error-correction part of, say, the first equation gives:

$$\alpha_{11}(\beta_{11}y_{1t-1} + \beta_{21}y_{2t-1} + \beta_{31}x_{t-1}) \tag{4.18}$$

However, there is information to be gained from estimating the other equations in the system since α_{21} and α_{31} are not zero. That is, more efficient estimates of $\boldsymbol{\beta}$ can be obtained by using all the information the model has to offer. Indeed, Johansen (1992a) shows that in situations where $\mathbf{z}_t$ is endogenous and there is one cointegration vector, then the variance of the estimator of $\boldsymbol{\beta}_{\text{part}} > \boldsymbol{\beta}_{\text{full}}$, where 'part' refers to a partial estimator (e.g., a single equation OLS estimator) and 'full' refers to a modelling approach that estimates the full system (equation 4.16).

Only when, say, $\alpha_{21} = \alpha_{31} = 0$ will a single equation estimator of the unique cointegration vector be efficient. Then the cointegration relationship does not enter the other two equations, that is, Δy_{2t} and Δx_t do not depend on the disequilibrium changes represented by $(\beta_{11}y_{1t-1} + \beta_{21}y_{2t-1} + \beta_{31}x_{t-1})$. As will be shown in the next chapter, this means that when estimating the parameters of the model (i.e., $\mathbf{\Gamma}_1, \mathbf{\Pi}, \boldsymbol{\alpha}, \boldsymbol{\beta}$) there is no loss of information from *not* modelling the determinants of Δy_{2t} and Δx_t; so, these variables can enter on the right-hand side of a single equation ECM.[28] For now, it is sufficient to state that $\alpha_{21} = \alpha_{31} = 0$ amounts to y_{2t} and x_t being weakly exogenous. When all the right-hand-side variables in a single equation model are weakly exogenous, this approach is sufficient to obtain an efficient estimator of $\boldsymbol{\beta}$ such that (4.12) should provide the same results as a multivariate (or system) estimator (e.g., the Johansen approach, as set out in the next chapter).[29]

As has just been explained, it is only really applicable to use the single equation approach when there is a single unique cointegration vector and when all the right-hand-side variables are weakly exogenous. Inder (1993), on the basis of his Monte Carlo experiments, has suggested that the problem of endogeneity may be relatively unimportant in many situations, but there is still a question as to whether it is possible to perform tests of weak exogeneity in a single equation framework. Urbain (1992) suggests that the usual approach based on a Wu–Hausman-type orthogonality test is unlikely to provide clear results. This approach amounts to regressing the right-hand-side variable of interest (e.g., Δy_{2t}) on all the lagged first-differenced variables in the model (e.g., $\Sigma_i^{k-1}\Delta\mathbf{z}_{t-i}$)[30] and then testing whether the residuals from this equation are significant in the short-run ECM (cf. equation (4.10)). That is, if Δy_{2t} is weakly exogenous then the residuals from the equation determining it will be orthogonal to (i.e., non-correlated with) the short-run ECM determining Δy_{1t}. However, Urbain (op. cit.) points out that orthogonality will be present anyway (on the basis of the multivariate normal distribution), and suggests that it would be more appropriate to test whether the error-correction term embedded in the short-run ECM (i.e., $\hat{\boldsymbol{\varepsilon}}_{t-1} = \hat{\boldsymbol{\beta}}_1' \mathbf{z}_{t-1}$) is significant in the equation determining Δy_{2t}. As mentioned previously, if Δy_{2t} is weakly exogenous then it does not depend on the disequilibrium changes represented by the $\hat{\boldsymbol{\varepsilon}}_{t-1}$. However, even though it is possible in principle to test for weak exogeneity, there is still the more important issue of how many possible $(n-1)$ cointegration relations exist in a model which includes n variables. Since this must be established, it is better to undertake testing for weak exogeneity as part of a multivariate procedure. As will be seen, this can be done easily using the Johansen approach.

As an example of the single equation approach when there is more than one cointegration relationship, consider the UK purchasing-power parity (PPP) and uncovered interest rate parity (UIP) model estimated by Johansen and Juselius (1992). This model is examined in detail in the next chapter, where multivariate testing suggests that there are at least two cointegration relationships between the five variables p_1 (the UK wholesale price index), p_2 (trade weighted foreign wholesale price index), e (UK effective exchange rate), i_1 (three-month UK treasury bill rate), and i_2 (three-month Eurodollar interest rate). Theory suggests that if PPP holds in the goods market (i.e., internationally produced goods are perfect substitutes for domestic goods) we should expect to find *in the long-run* that price differentials between two countries are equal to differences in the nominal exchange rate ($p_1 - p_2 = e$), while UIP in the capital market relates the interest rates of the two countries to expected changes in exchange rates ($i_1 - i_2 = e^e - e$). If markets are efficient, expected changes in exchange rates will be increasingly influenced by deviations from long-run PPP (especially as the forecast horizon grows – see Juselius, 1994) and thus $e^e = (p_1 - p_2)$, providing a link between the capital and the goods market. If parity holds in the long-run we should expect $(i_2 - i_2) = (p_1 - p_2 - e)$, and estimated parameter values of $(\pm)1$ for all the variables in the model.

Estimating the static model using seasonally unadjusted data for 1972:1–1987:2 produced the following result:

$$p_1 = 1.442p_2 + 0.468e - 0.937i_1 + 1.114i_2 + \hat{\varepsilon} \qquad R^2 = 0.99 \quad DW = 19 \tag{4.19}$$

and using (4.4), with $\delta = 0$ imposed, the residuals, ε, were tested for a unit root under the null hypothesis of no cointegration. The τ-value associated with testing the null hypothesis that H_0: $\psi^* = 0$ based on the ε was −2.40, while the critical value for rejecting the null was −4.64 (at the 5% significance level obtained from Table 4.1 with $n = 5$ and $T = 62$). Thus, these results indicate that there is no long-run stable relationship.[31]

Setting $p = q = 5$, and then testing to ensure that this parameterisation of (4.12) is general enough to pass various diagnostic tests relating to the properties of the residuals, u_t, the following long-run relationship is found using the dynamic modelling approach (with t-values in parentheses):

$$p_1 = \underset{(29.92)}{1.331}\, p_2 + \underset{(8.51)}{0.402}e + \underset{(3.48)}{3.765}\, i_1 - \underset{(0.88)}{0.606}\, i_2 + \hat{\varepsilon} \tag{4.20}$$

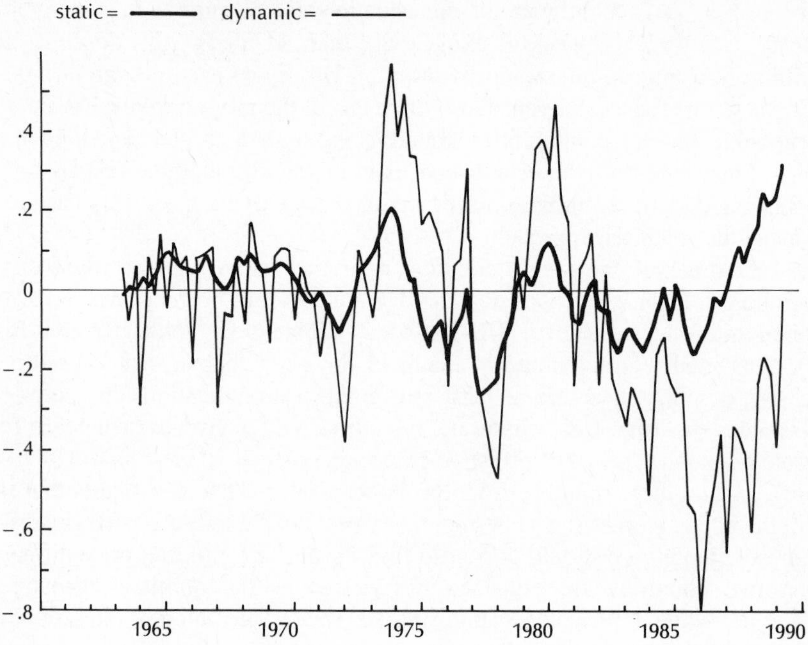

Figure 4.1 Cointegration relations for UK money supply based on equations (4.11b) and (4.13)

A Wald test decisively rejects the null that all of the long run coefficients are zero. However, the unit root test of the null hypothesis of no cointegration results in a test statistic of −2.97, which does not reject the null at the 10 per cent significance level (based on a critical value of −3.65 obtained from Table 4 in Banerjee, Dolado and Mestre (1992)). Thus, using the single equation approach, cointegration is not established and the estimates of long-run parameters seem remote from their expected values.

Estimating the short-run dynamic model

Having obtained an estimate of the long-run relationship, the second stage of the EG procedure comprises estimating the short-run ECM itself (e.g., equation (4.10)) using the estimates of disequilibrium ($\hat{\varepsilon}_{t-1}$) to obtain information on the speed of adjustment to equilibrium. The $\hat{\varepsilon}_{t-1}$ associated with the cointegration relations obtained from the static and dynamic models (equations (4.11b) and (4.13)) are plotted in Figure 4.1. These show that real M1 was considerably off its equilibrium value (which occurs when $\hat{\varepsilon}_{t-1} = 0$), especially (according to the dynamic approach)

Table 4.2 *F*-statistics for the sequential reduction from the fifth-order AR model in Box 4.2

Model reduction	Degrees-of-freedom	Test statistic [significance level]
Model 1 → 2:	$F(3, 73)$	0.01906 [0.9964]
Model 1 → 3:	$F(7,73)$	0.46212 [0.8587]
Model 2 → 3:	$F(4, 76)$	0.82641 [0.5124]
Model 1 → 4:	$F(11, 73)$	0.64029 [0.7885]
Model 2 → 4:	$F(8, 76)$	0.90842 [0.5142]
Model 3 → 4:	$F(4, 80)$	0.99911 [0.4131]
Model 1 → 5:	$F(15, 73)$	0.72135 [0.7553]
Model 2 → 5:	$F(12, 76)$	0.93305 [0.5192]
Model 3 → 5:	$F(8, 80)$	0.99501 [0.4465]
Model 4 → 5:	$F(4, 84)$	0.99096 [0.4171]
Model 1 → 6:	$F(17, 73)$	0.75495 [0.7364]
Model 2 → 6:	$F(14, 76)$	0.94940 [0.5118]
Model 3 → 6:	$F(10, 80)$	1.00730 [0.4447]
Model 4 → 6:	$F(6, 84)$	1.01290 [0.4226]
Model 5 → 6:	$F(2, 88)$	1.05720 [0.3518]

after 1982. Thus, it will be interesting to see whether the money supply adjusts quickly or slowly to such disequilibrium.

The initial model (denoted Model 1) is the autoregressive distributed-lag model with $p = q = 5$ used to obtain $\hat{\varepsilon}_{t-1} = (m-p)_{t-1} + 7.332\Delta p_{t-1} - 1.052y_{t-1} + 6.871R_{t-1} + 0.393 - 0.238SEAS$ (see Box 4.2). Model 2 is the equivalent short-run ECM obtained by setting $p = q = 4$ in (4.10). Next the Hendry-type 'general-to-specific' procedure is used to reduce this short-run ECM to its parsimonious form (see Ericsson, Hendry and Tran (1992) for full details relating to this data-set). This resulted in Models 3–6, and involved dropping insignificant variables and reparameterising the estimated equation as follows:

- *Model 3*: since $\Delta R_{t-1} = \Delta R_{t-2} = \Delta R_{t-3} = \Delta R_{t-4} = 0$, these variables are dropped;
- *Model 4*: since $\Delta p_t = -\Delta p_{t-1}$, these variables are dropped and $\Delta^2 p_t$ is introduced instead; since $\Delta p_{t-2} = \Delta p_{t-3} = \Delta p_{t-4} = 0$ these variables are also dropped;
- *Model 5*: since $\Delta y_{t-2} = -\Delta y_{t-3}$, these variables are dropped and $\Delta^2 y_{t-2}$ is introduced instead; also as $\Delta y_t = \Delta y_{t-1} = \Delta y_{t-4} = 0$ these variables are dropped;
- *Model 6*: $\Delta(m-p)_{t-1} = \Delta(m-p)_{t-2} = \Delta(m-p)_{t-3}$, and these variables are replaced by $[(m-p)_t - (m-p)_{t-3}]/3$ instead.

The *F*-statistics (and associated probabilities of rejecting the null in square brackets) for testing each Model in the sequential reduction process are given in Table 4.2. The complete reduction from Model 1 to Model 6 is not rejected with $F_{17,73} = 0.75$ [0.74], and none of the reductions between model pairs reject at the 5 per cent significant level. The final model obtained was:

$$\Delta(m-p)_t = \underset{(1.36)}{0.005} - \underset{(4.717)}{0.880}\,\Delta^2 p_t + \underset{(3.203)}{0.149}\,\Delta^2 y_{t-2} - \underset{(5.025)}{0.646}\,\Delta_3(m-p)_t/3 +$$
$$\underset{(3.395)}{0.188}\,\Delta(m-p)_{t-4} - \underset{(3.517)}{0.387}\,\Delta R_t - \underset{(10.802)}{0.116}\,\hat{\varepsilon}_{t-1} - \underset{(2.312)}{0.012}\,SEAS_{1t} -$$
$$\underset{(4.476)}{0.022}\,SEAS_{2t} + \underset{(1.710)}{0.012}\,SEAS_{3t} \qquad (4.21)$$

Diagnostics

$\bar{R}^2 = 0.833$; $F(9, 90) = 50.044$ [0.0000]; $\sigma = 0.0135641$; $DW = 2.15$;
AR 1 – 5 F(5, 85) = 1.0355 [0.4021]; ARCH 4 $F(4, 82) = 0.70884$ [0.5882];
X_i^2 $F(15, 74) = 0.78657$ [0.6881]; $X_i^* X_j$ $F(48, 41) = 0.70269$ [0.8804];
RESET $F(1, 89) = 0.26072$ [0.6109]; Normality $\chi^2(2)$; = 3.4735 [0.1761].

None of the diagnostic tests reported are significant at the 95 per cent critical value (except the F-test that all the slope coefficients are zero), and therefore there is nothing to suggest that the model is misspecified. These tests cover, respectively, the goodness-of-fit of the model (i.e., what percentage of the total variation in the dependent variable is explained by the independent variables); an F-test that all the right-hand-side explanatory variables except the constant have zero parameter coefficients; the standard deviation of the regression; the Durbin–Watson test for first-order autocorrelation (which is strictly not valid in a model with lagged dependent variables); a Breusch–Godfrey LM test for serial autocorrelation up to the fifth lag, obtained by regressing the residuals from the original model on all the regressors of that model and the lagged residuals; an ARCH test for autoregressive conditional heteroscedasticity, obtained by regressing the squared residuals from the model on their lags (here up to the fourth lag) and a constant; White's test for heteroscedasticity, involving the auxiliary regression of the squared residuals on the original regressors and all their squares; White's heteroscedasticity/functional for misspecification test, based on the auxiliary regression of the squared residuals on all squares and cross-products of the original regressors; Ramsey's RESET general test of misspecification, obtained by adding powers of the fitted values from the model (e.g., $\hat{y}_t^2$, $\hat{y}_t^3$, etc.,) to the original regression equation; and the Doornik and Hansen (1993) univariate test for normality. Significance levels for rejecting the null hypothesis are given in [ ] brackets. Full references for each test are available in most standard econometric texts, such as Johnston (1984). Econometric software packages, which usually contain similar batteries of tests, also provide good references and explanations.

Another important aspect of diagnostic checking is testing for structural breaks in the model which would be evidence that the parameter estimates are non-constant. Sequential one-step ahead Chow-tests[32] and one-step ahead residuals($\tilde{u}_t = y_t - x_t'\hat{\beta}_t$) can be obtained from applying recursive least squares to the model over successive time periods by increasing the sample period by one additional observation for each estimation. Plots of these Chow tests and residuals are given in Figure 4.2 for the estimated short-run ECM. The graph of one-step ahead residuals are shown bordered

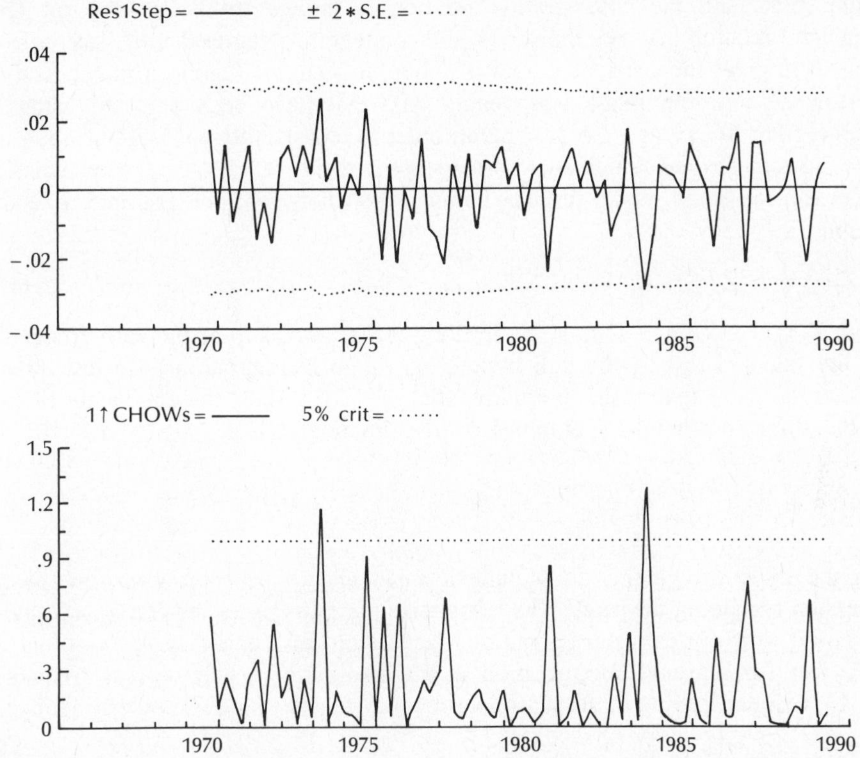

Figure 4.2 Diagnostic testing of the short-run ECM: one-step ahead residuals and Chow tests

by two standard deviations from the mean of zero (i.e., $0 \pm 2\hat{\sigma}_t$), and points outside this region are either outliers or are associated with coefficient changes. There is some evidence to suggest that there is a problem around the 1983:3 observation. The Chow tests also suggest that parameter instability is evident around the 1973:2 and 1983:3 time periods.

Returning to (4.21), the speed-of-adjustment coefficient indicates that the UK money supply adjusted relatively slowly to changes to the underlying equilibrium relationship since the parameter estimate on $\hat{\varepsilon}_{t-1}$ shows that economic agents removed only 11.6 per cent of the resulting disequilibrium each period. This helps to explain the considerable deviations from equilibrium depicted in Figure 4.1.

Seasonal cointegration[33]

If series exhibit strong seasonal patterns they may contain seasonal unit roots; consequently, any potential cointegration may occur at seasonal cycles as well as (or instead of) at the zero frequency domain. In cases where there are seasonal unit roots in the series and the cointegration relation is thought to be a long-run (zero frequency) relation between the series, the cointegration regression of, say, c_t on y_t using (4.1) gives inconsistent estimates. Thus, in such a situation it is necessary to test for the long-run relationship using data that have been adjusted using the seasonal filter $S(L) = (1 + L + L^2 + L^3)$ in order to remove the seasonal unit roots and leave the zero frequency unit root corresponding to $(1 - L)$. That is, when series are all $I(1, 1)$, the static model test for cointegration between, for example, c_t and y_t becomes

$$(Z_1 c_t) = \beta_1 (Z_1 y_t) + \varepsilon_t \tag{4.22}$$

where $Z_1 = (1 + L + L^2 + L^3)$, β_1 is the long-run relationship at the zero frequency, and the standard test of the null hypothesis of no cointegration is to test directly whether $\varepsilon_t \sim I(1)$ against the alternative that $\varepsilon_t \sim I(0)$. Thus, the equivalent of (4.4) can be estimated using the $\hat{\varepsilon}_t$ obtained from estimating (4.22):

$$\Delta\hat{\varepsilon}_t = \pi_1 \hat{\varepsilon}_{t-1} + \sum_{i=1}^{p-1} \psi_i^* \Delta\hat{\varepsilon}_{t-i} + \mu + \delta t + \omega_t \qquad \omega_t \sim IID(0, \sigma^2) \tag{4.23}$$

with the issue of whether to include a trend and/or constant terms in the test regression remaining the same. The test statistic is a t-type test of H_0: $\pi_1 = 0$ against H_1: $\pi_1 < 0$, with critical values given by MacKinnon (cf. Table 4.1).

To test for seasonal cointegration at the two-quarter (half-yearly) frequency, $(1 + L)$, requires leaving in the seasonal root at this cycle using Z_2 and estimating:

$$(Z_2 c_t) = \beta_2 (Z_2 y_t) + \nu_t \tag{4.24}$$

where $Z_2 = -(1 - L + L^2 - L^3)$, and β_2 is the long-run relationship at the two-quarter frequency. Testing the null hypothesis of no cointegration uses the residuals $\hat{\nu}_t$ from (4.24), and the following version of the ADF test:

$$(\hat{\nu}_t + \hat{\nu}_{t-1}) = \pi_2(\hat{\nu}_{t-1}) + \sum_{1=1}^{p-1} \psi_i^* (\hat{\nu}_{t-i} + \hat{\nu}_{t-i-1}) + \mu + \sum_{i=1}^{3} \delta_i D_{it} + \omega_t$$

$$\omega_t \sim IID(0, \sigma^2) \tag{4.25}$$

where D_{qt} is the zero/one dummy corresponding to quarter q. The test statistic is a t-type test of H_0: $\pi_2 = 0$ against H_1: $\pi_2 < 0$, with critical values given by MacKinnon (cf. Table 4.1).

Finally, testing for seasonal cointegration at the four-quarter (annual) frequency, $(1 \pm iL)$, requires leaving in the seasonal roots at this cycle using Z_3 and estimating:

$$(Z_3 c_t) = \beta_3 (Z_3 y_t) + \beta_4 (Z_3 y_{t-1}) + \zeta_t \tag{4.26}$$

where $Z_3 = -(1 - L^2)$, and β_3 and β_4 are the long-run relationships at the four-quarter frequency. Testing the null hypothesis of no cointegration uses the residuals $\hat{\zeta}_t$ from (4.26), and the following version of the ADF test:

$$(\hat{\zeta}_t + \hat{\zeta}_{t-2}) = \pi_3(-\hat{\zeta}_{t-2}) + \pi_4(-\hat{\zeta}_{t-1}) + \sum_{i=1}^{p-1} \psi_i^* (\hat{\zeta}_{t-i} + \hat{\zeta}_{t-i-1}) + \mu$$

$$+ \sum_{i=1}^{3} \delta_i D_{it} + \omega_t \qquad \omega_t \sim IID(0, \sigma^2) \tag{4.27}$$

where the test of the null hypothesis requires a joint F-test H_0: $\pi_3 = \pi_4 = 0$. Critical values for this test and individual t-tests of H_0: $\pi_3 = 0$, H_0: $\pi_4 = 0$, when there are two variables in the cointegration equation, are given in Engle, Granger, Hylleberg and Lee (1993, Table A.1).

Assuming that cointegration occurs at all frequencies, that is, $[\varepsilon_t, \nu_t, \zeta_t] \sim I(0)$ in (4.22), (4.24) and (4.26), the following short-run ECM for c_t and y_t (see Engle *et al.*, op. cit.) can be estimated:

$$(1 - L^4)c_t = \Delta_4 c_t = \sum_{j=0}^{q} a_j \, \Delta_4 y_{t-j} + \sum_{i=1}^{p} b_i \, \Delta_4 c_{t-i} + \gamma_1 \hat{\varepsilon}_{t-1} + \gamma_2 \hat{\upsilon}_{t-1}$$

$$+ (\gamma_3 + \gamma_4 L)\hat{\zeta}_{t-1} + u_t \tag{4.28}$$

where the γ_i are speed-of-adjustment parameters, and it is assumed that y_t is weakly exogenous.[34]

In the last chapter, tests for seasonal integration using UK data suggested that both real consumer spending and real liquid assets are $I(1, 1)$ while inflation is $I(1, 0)$. The results for real personal disposable income were not clear-cut. Tests for seasonal cointegration are reported in Table 4.3; these suggest that cointegration between c_t, y_t, w_t, and π_t (and sub-groups) can be rejected at the zero (or long-run)

Table 4.3 Test for cointegration at frequencies $0, \frac{1}{2}, \frac{1}{4}(\frac{3}{4})$: UK consumption function data (1971:2–1993:1) (based on equations (4.23), (4.25), and (4.27))

Variables	Deterministic components included[a]	t_{π_1}	t_{π_2}	t_{π_3}	t_{π_4}	$F_{\pi_3 \cap \pi_4}$
c_t, y_t	I + TR/SD	−2.36	−2.43	−3.46	−2.48[b]	10.24[b]
c_t, y_t	I	−2.33	−1.63	−1.91	−1.37	2.86
c_t, w_t	I + TR/SD	−1.20	−3.50	−3.58	−3.12[d]	13.16[c]
c_t, w_t	I	1.69	−2.76	−1.58	−0.91	1.70
c_t, y_t, w_t, π_t	I + TR/SD	−2.01	−3.12	−3.58	−2.20	9.79
c_t, y_t, w_t, π_t	I	−1.95	−2.77	−2.56	−1.06	3.93

[a] TR = trend, I = intercept, SD = seasonal dummies; [b] rejects null at 5 per cent significance level; [c] rejects null at 2.5 per cent significance level; [d] rejects null at 1 per cent significance level.

frequency, and at the two-quarter frequency.[35] However, there is evidence to suggest that variables are cointegrated at the four-quarter (or annual) frequency, given the values of the F-statistics obtained.[36] Similar results were obtained using Japanese data for c_t and y_t, by Engle *et al.*, op. cit., and they argued: '... if a slightly impatient borrowing-constrained consumer has the habit of using his bonus payments to replace worn out clothes, furniture, etc., when the payment occurs, one may expect cointegration at the annual frequency' (p. 292). Given that such bonus payments are not typical in the British labour market, some other (although similar) rationale has to be sought. Lastly, these results confirm those in Hylleberg, Engle, Granger and Yoo (1990), who also found some evidence of seasonal cointegration between c_t and y_t at the half-yearly frequency using UK data.

Conclusions

Testing for cointegration using a single equation is problematic. If there are $n > 2$ variables in the model, and if $n - 1$ of these are not weakly exogenous, the single equation approach can be misleading, particularly if more than one cointegration relationship is present. If single equation methods are to be used, it would seem that the unrestricted dynamic modelling approach is most likely to produce unbiased estimates of the long-run relationship, with appropriate t- and F-statistics. The test of cointegration associated with this approach is also more powerful against alternatives, such as the usual Engle–Granger static model. However, given that the number of cointegration vectors is unknown, and given the need to allow all variables to be potentially endogenous (and then testing for exogeneity), there seems little advantage in *starting* from the single equation model. Rather, the multivariate VAR approach developed by Johansen (1988) is the more obvious place to begin testing for cointegration.

Notes

1. The issue of whether the model should include an intercept or an intercept and time trend will be discussed later when considering the testing strategy for determining whether $\varepsilon_t \sim I(0)$.
2. That is, as $T \to \infty$, the estimate of $\hat{\beta}$ converges to the true β (denoted plim $\hat{\beta} = \beta$). Any bias (and its variance) in finite samples should tend to zero as the sample size T tends to infinity.
3. If there is a simultaneity problem, then $E(x_t\ u_t) \neq 0$ is also true.
4. Including or excluding the time trend in the model appears to have little effect on the size of the test (i.e., over-rejecting the null when it is true).
5. The OLS estimator minimises the (sum of the squared) deviations of the $\hat{\varepsilon}_t$ from the OLS regression line obtained from $\hat{y}_t = \hat{\beta}x_t$; that is, OLS obtains $\hat{\beta}$ that will minimise $\hat{\sigma}^2$.
6. For instance, he gives the example (which is also used later on – see equation (4.11)) of testing for cointegration in the UK money-demand function, where m_t and p_t are

potentially $I(2)$. In a test in which homogeneity is not imposed (i.e., m_t and p_t are not combined into $(m_t - p_t)$), so that the OLS regression comprises $m = \beta_0 + \beta_1 p + \beta_2 y - \beta_3 R + \varepsilon$, there is one $I(2)$ regressor, and therefore Haldrup's Table 1 must be used with $m_1 = 2$ and $m_2 = 1$.

7. Note, in (4.9) the long-run elasticity between Y and X is $\beta = (\gamma_0(1 - \alpha L)/1 - \alpha L) = \gamma_0$, assuming that $\alpha < 1$ (which is necessary for the short-run model to converge to a long-run solution).
8. They also point out that using the ADF version of the test, it may be necessary to have a lag-length longer than that required in the ECM in order to generate white noise errors, which may lead to poorer size properties (i.e., the likelihood of over-rejecting the null when it is true) for the ADF test when compared to the a test (outlined below) based on the unrestricted ECM.
9. The data are the same as those used previously (e.g., see Figure 3.1) and are based on Hendry and Ericsson (1991). The statistical sources are discussed by Hendry and Ericsson, although they concentrate on using seasonally adjusted data. The data are reproduced in the Statistical Appendix.
10. The critical value from Haldrup (1994, Table 1) for the case where homogeneity is not imposed (4.11a) and m_t and p_t are both potentially $I(2)$ is -3.93 (at the 10 per cent level).
11. The use of the term 'invariant' means that the test is not affected by a trend entering (4.1).
12. Note, the CRDW test also suffers from the 'problem' that it imposes a common factor restriction – see the discussion relating to the ADF test on this matter.
13. In the more general formulation of the ECM, the test amounts to whether the parameter coefficient on the error correction term, $\hat{\varepsilon}_{t-1}$, equals zero.
14. Banerjee *et al.* (1986) show that bias is inversely related to the value of R^2 in the static OLS regression model, but they point out that it does not necessarily follow that high values of R^2 imply low biases, since R^2 can always be increased by the addition of more (*ad hoc*) regressors.
15. For instance, choosing $p = q = 4$ results in the following dynamic model: $y_t = \gamma_0 x_t + \gamma_1 x_{t-1} + \gamma_2 x_{t-2} + \gamma_3 x_{t-3} + \gamma_4 x_{t-4} + \alpha_1 y_{t-1} + \alpha_2 y_{t-2} + \alpha_3 y_{t-3} + \alpha_4 y_{t-4} + u_t$.
16. If x_t is a single variable then there is a single long-run parameter β (which may include the long-run estimate of the constant as well as slope – see equation (2.12) – and therefore $\boldsymbol{\beta} = [\beta_0, \beta_1]'$); however, if $\mathbf{x}_t$ is a vector of variables, then a vector of long-run parameters is obtained.
17. In more complicated models, the long-run parameters are the sum of the parameters associated with the variable being considered, that is, $\Sigma\hat{\gamma}_i$ $(i = 0, \ldots, q)$ in (4.12), divided by one minus the sum of the parameters associated with the dependent variable, that is, $1 - \Sigma\hat{\alpha}_i$ $(i = 1, \ldots, p)$.
18. He states that the test statistics based on the simple OLS static model are '... hopelessly unreliable' (p. 67).
19. Note, dividing the sum of the parameter estimates associated with x (i.e., $\Sigma\gamma_i$) by the sum of their associated standard errors provides a t-type test of the null hypothesis that there is no significant long-run effect of x on y. This test is *not* equivalent to a test involving the t-values obtained from the solution to the long-run equation and in small samples it is possible that there will be conflicting outcomes from these alternative approaches.
20. These tests (reported in Box 4.2), and how to interpret them, will be discussed below in the section on estimating the short-run model. For now it is sufficient to note that the significance levels for rejecting the null of no serial correlation (AR test), autoregressive conditional heteroscedasticity (ARCH test), etc., are given in [ ] brackets after each test

statistic, and are such as to suggest we should have little confidence in rejecting the various null hypotheses.

21. Note, $(1-\Sigma\alpha_i) = -0.138$, with a standard error of 0.0311.
22. Applying the dynamic modelling approach to the nominal money balances model give the following long-run equation:

$$m = \underset{(11.22)}{0.967p} + \underset{(3.82)}{1.153y} - \underset{(7.76)}{6.573R} - \underset{(0.45)}{1.627} + \underset{(1.23)}{0.221SEAS}$$

while the unit root test for cointegration yields a test statistic of −4.526 (significant at the 5 per cent level). Note, since results discussed in Box 3.2 suggest that m and p are probably $I(2)$, it is assumed that a $I(1)$ cointegration relation between these variables exists which in turn cointegrates with the other $I(1)$ variables in the model (see Box 2.4) to result in an $I(0)$ error term. In (4.13) if $(m-p) \sim I(1)$, as suggested in Table 3.2.1, then it is easier to justify the existence of a cointegration relationship for real money demand, given that the other variables are also $I(1)$, including Δp since $p \sim I(2)$.

23. The non-parametric correction for bias due to autocorrelation is akin to the Phillips–Perron correction (Box 3.1); a second correction uses a non-parametric estimate of the long-run covariance between x and y to deal with any endogeneity. It is also possible to correct the unrestricted dynamic model (equation (4.12)) for possible endogeneity using a similar non-parametric correction to that proposed for the modified OLS (see Inder, 1993).
24. See the discussion surrounding $(1-\alpha_1)$ in (2.13) for an analogous interpretation in the single equation model.
25. In fact, the matrix $\boldsymbol{\beta}'\mathbf{z}_{t-1}$ contains n column vectors in a multivariate model but only $(n-1)$ of these can possibly represent long-run relationships, and often the number of steady-state vectors is less than $(n-1)$. The whole issue of testing for stationary cointegration vectors in $\boldsymbol{\beta}$ is considered in the next chapter when we test for the reduced rank of $\boldsymbol{\beta}$.
26. Note, since there are two cointegration relationships, both enter each of the equations in the system. Also, neither of the two equations has been normalised in (4.16), and so all the β_{ij} are included. Normalisation, say to obtain a coefficient of 1 on y_{1t-1}, would entail multiplying each long-run relationship by its respective estimate of $1/\beta_{1j}$ $(j=1,2)$.
27. Equation (4.17) can also be written as:

$$\alpha_{11}(\beta_{11}y_{1t-1} + \beta_{21}y_{2t-1} + \beta_{31}x_{t-1}) + \alpha_{12}(\beta_{11}y_{1t-1} + \beta_{21}y_{2t-1} + \beta_{31}x_{t-1})$$

which shows clearly the two cointegration vectors with associated speed-of-adjustment terms in the equation for Δy_{1t}.

28. More technically, this is referred to as conditioning on these variables.
29. Note, estimating the long-run relationship using a static model (equation (4.1)) will not produce the same result because of small sample bias; that is, both (4.12) and (4.15) incorporate short-run adjustments. In fact, with weak exogeneity assumed, (4.12) and (4.15) are equivalent.
30. Other variables known to determine Δy_{2t} but not already included in the model since they are assumed exogenous to it, may also enter.
31. Note, the CRDW test also fails to reject the null.
32. These are calculated as the *change* in the sum of the squared residuals (Σu_t^2) from the model as it is estimated over successive time periods (adjusted for degrees of freedom), and an F-test that β changes is obtained.

33. The reader is advised to review the discussion of seasonal unit roots in Chapter 3 before tackling this section.
34. Otherwise, the term $\Delta_4 y_t$ on the right-hand side of the ECM would not be allowed and we could write a second ECM with $\Delta_4 y_t$ as the dependent variable. The latter would have the same cointegration relations but the speed-of-adjustment parameters, γ_i, would potentially be of a different magnitude.
35. Note, lag-lengths set to maximise $\bar{R}^2$ and in accordance with the arguments in Schwert (1989) are used. Results reported in Table 4.3 are based on max-$\bar{R}^2$.
36. Note, because critical values for cointegration equations involving more than two variables are not available at the four-quarter frequency, it is not possible to draw any definite conclusions surrounding the tests of the full consumption function model.

5

Cointegration in multivariate systems

Important terms and concept

Johansen technique Reduced rank regression Cointegration relationship Vector autoregressive (VAR) model Vector error-correction (VECM) model Testing for cointegration rank Conditioning on weakly exogenous variables *I*(2) models Pantula principle Testing for weak exogeneity Cointegration space Unique cointegration vectors Identification of the long-run model

The Johansen technique is fast becoming an essential tool for applied economists wishing to estimate time series models. The implication that non-stationary variables can lead to spurious regressions unless at least one cointegration vector is present means that some form of testing for cointegration is almost mandatory. Earlier use of the Engle–Granger (EG) procedure (Chapter 4) is giving way to the determination of cointegration rank, given the consequences for the EG approach if more than one cointegration relationship exists. The major problem facing those wishing to use Johansen's (1988) technique is that it is only just becoming available in a user-friendly fashion, following the release of *PcFiml* (version 8) and *Cats* (in Rats version 4).[1]

The problems facing the user who wishes to implement the technique include, *inter alia*:

- testing the order of integration of each variable that enters the multivariate model;
- setting the appropriate lag-length of the VAR model (in order to ensure Gaussian error terms in the VECM) and determining whether the system should be

conditioned on any predetermined $I(0)$ variables (including dummies to take account of possible policy interventions);

- testing for reduced rank, including the issue of testing whether the system should be treated as an $I(2)$ rather than an $I(1)$ system;
- identifying whether there are trends in the data and therefore whether deterministic variables (a constant and trend) should enter the cointegration space or not;
- testing for weak exogeneity (which leads to the modelling of a partial system with exogenous variables);
- testing for linear hypotheses on cointegration relations;
- testing for unique cointegration vectors;
- joint tests involving restrictions on $\boldsymbol{\alpha}$ and $\boldsymbol{\beta}$.

Each of these will be considered in turn and examples provided (in particular based on the PPP and UIP model estimated by Johansen and Juselius (1992) as discussed in the last chapter). However, it is necessary first to briefly outline the Johansen model and the method of reduced rank regression used to estimate it.

The Johansen approach

The multivariate autoregressive model was discussed briefly in the last chapter when considering the deficiencies of the single equation cointegration approach. Defining a vector $\mathbf{z}_t$ of n potentially endogenous variables, it is possible to specify the following d.g.p. and model $\mathbf{z}_t$ as an unrestricted vector autoregression (VAR) involving up to k-lags of $\mathbf{z}_t$:

$$\mathbf{z}_t = \mathbf{A}_1\mathbf{z}_{t-1} + \ldots + \mathbf{A}_k\mathbf{z}_{t-k} + \mathbf{u}_t \qquad \mathbf{u}_t \sim IN(0, \Sigma) \tag{5.1}$$

where $\mathbf{z}_t$ is $(n \times 1)$ and each of the $\mathbf{A}_i$ is an $(n \times n)$ matrix of parameters. This type of VAR-model has been advocated most notably by Sims (1980) as a way to estimate dynamic relationships among jointly endogenous variables without imposing strong *a priori* restrictions (such as particular structural relationships and/or the exogeneity of some of the variables). The system is in reduced form with each variable in $\mathbf{z}_t$ regressed on only lagged values of both itself and all the other variables in the system. Thus, OLS is an efficient way to estimate each equation comprising (5.1) since the right-hand side of each equation in the system comprises a common set of (lagged and thus predetermined) regressors.

Equation (5.1) can be reformulated into a *vector* error-correction (*V*ECM) form:

$$\Delta\mathbf{z}_t = \boldsymbol{\Gamma}_1\Delta\mathbf{z}_{t-1} + \ldots + \boldsymbol{\Gamma}_{k-1}\Delta\mathbf{z}_{t-k+1} + \boldsymbol{\Pi}\mathbf{z}_{t-k} + \mathbf{u}_t \tag{5.2}$$

where $\boldsymbol{\Gamma}_i = -(\mathbf{I} - \mathbf{A}_1 - \ldots - \mathbf{A}_i)$, $(i = 1, \ldots, k-1)$, and $\boldsymbol{\Pi} = -(\mathbf{I} - \mathbf{A}_1 - \ldots - \mathbf{A}_k)$. This way of specifying the system contains information on both the short- and long-run adjustment to changes in $\mathbf{z}_t$, via the estimates of $\hat{\boldsymbol{\Gamma}}_i$ and $\hat{\boldsymbol{\Pi}}$ respectively. As will be seen, $\boldsymbol{\Pi} = \boldsymbol{\alpha\beta}'$, where $\boldsymbol{\alpha}$ represents the speed of adjustment to disequilibrium, while

Box 5.1 The Johansen method of reduced rank regression

Rewriting (5.2) as:

$$\Delta \mathbf{z}_t + \boldsymbol{\alpha\beta}'\mathbf{z}_{t-k} = \boldsymbol{\Gamma}_1 \Delta \mathbf{z}_{t-1} + \ldots + \boldsymbol{\Gamma}_{k-1} \Delta \mathbf{z}_{t-k+1} + \mathbf{u}_t \tag{5.1.1}$$

it is possible to correct for short-run dynamics (i.e., take out their effect) by regressing $\Delta \mathbf{z}_t$ and $\mathbf{z}_{t-k}$ separately on the right-hand side of (5.1.1). That is, the vectors $\mathbf{R}_{0t}$ and $\mathbf{R}_{kt}$ are obtained from:

$$\Delta \mathbf{z}_t = \mathbf{P}_1 \Delta \mathbf{z}_{t-1} + \ldots + \mathbf{P}_{k-1} \Delta \mathbf{z}_{t-k+1} + \mathbf{R}_{0t} \tag{5.1.2}$$

$$\mathbf{z}_{t-k} = \mathbf{T}_1 \Delta \mathbf{z}_{t-1} + \ldots + \mathbf{T}_{k-1} \Delta \mathbf{z}_{t-k+1} + \mathbf{R}_{kt} \tag{5.1.3}$$

which can then be used to form residual (product moment) matrices:

$$\mathbf{S}_{ij} = T^{1} \sum_{i=1}^{T} \mathbf{R}_{it} \mathbf{R}'_{jt} \qquad i,j = 0, k \tag{5.1.4}$$

The maximum likelihood estimate of $\boldsymbol{\beta}$ is obtained as the eigenvectors corresponding to the r largest eigenvalues from solving the equation

$$|\, \lambda \mathbf{S}_{kk} - \mathbf{S}_{k0} \mathbf{S}_{00}^{-1} \mathbf{S}_{0k} \,| = 0 \tag{5.1.5}$$

which gives the n eigenvalues $\hat{\lambda}_1 > \hat{\lambda}_2 > \ldots > \hat{\lambda}_n$ and the corresponding eigenvectors $\hat{\mathbf{V}} = (\hat{v}_1, \ldots, \hat{v}_n)$.[62] Those r elements in $\hat{\mathbf{V}}$ which determine the linear combinations of stationary relationships can be denoted $\hat{\boldsymbol{\beta}} = (\hat{v}_1 \ldots, \hat{v}_r)$, that is, these are the cointegration vectors. This is because the eigenvalues are the *largest* squared canonical correlations between the 'levels' residuals $\mathbf{R}_{kt}$ and the 'difference' residuals $\mathbf{R}_{0t}$, that is, we obtain estimates of all the distinct $\hat{\mathbf{v}}_i'\mathbf{z}_t$ $(i = 1, \ldots, r)$ combinations of the $I(1)$ levels of $\mathbf{z}_t$ which produce high correlations with the stationary $\Delta \mathbf{z}_t \sim I(0)$ elements in (5.2), such combinations being the cointegration vectors by virtue of the fact that they must themselves be $I(0)$ to achieve a high correlation. Thus the magnitude of $\hat{\lambda}_i$ is a measure of how strongly the cointegration relations $\hat{\mathbf{v}}_i'\mathbf{z}_t$ (which we can now denote as $\hat{\boldsymbol{\beta}}_i'\mathbf{z}_t$) are correlated with the stationary part of the model. The last $(n - r)$ combinations obtained from solving (5.1.5), that is, $\hat{\mathbf{v}}_i'\mathbf{z}_t$ $(i = r + 1, \ldots, n)$, indicate the non-stationary combinations, and theoretically these are uncorrelated with the stationary elements in (5.2). Consequently, for the eigenvectors corresponding to the non-stationary part of the model, $\hat{\lambda}_i = 0$ for $i = r + 1, \ldots, n$. So, for example, Johansen (1992b) points out that the test that $r = 1$ is really a test that $\hat{\lambda}_2 = \hat{\lambda}_3 = \ldots = \hat{\lambda}_n = 0$, whereas $\hat{\lambda}_1 > 0$. Since he also shows that $\hat{\lambda}_i = \hat{\boldsymbol{\alpha}}_i' \mathbf{S}_{00}^{-1} \boldsymbol{\alpha}_i$ a test involving these eigenvalues (which we shall see is the standard way to test for cointegration) is equivalent to testing that the $\boldsymbol{\alpha}_i$ are insignificantly small for $i = r + 1, \ldots, n$. Finally, note that estimates of $\hat{\boldsymbol{\alpha}} = \mathbf{S}_{0k}\hat{\boldsymbol{\beta}}$.

$\boldsymbol{\beta}$ is a matrix of long-run coefficients such that the term $\boldsymbol{\beta}'\mathbf{z}_{t-k}$ embedded in (5.2) represents up to $(n-1)$ cointegration relationships in the multivariate model which ensure that the $\mathbf{z}_t$ converge to their long-run steady-state solutions. Assuming $\mathbf{z}_t$ is a vector of non-stationary $I(1)$ variables, then all the terms in (5.2) which involve $\Delta\mathbf{z}_{t-i}$ are $I(0)$ while $\boldsymbol{\Pi}\mathbf{z}_{t-k}$ must also be stationary for $\mathbf{u}_t \sim I(0)$ to be 'white noise'. There are three instances when this requirement that $\boldsymbol{\Pi}\mathbf{z}_{t-k} \sim I(0)$ is met; first, when all the variables in $\mathbf{z}_t$ are in fact stationary, which is an uninteresting case in the present context since it implies that there is no problem of spurious regression and the appropriate modelling strategy is to estimate the standard Sims-type VAR in levels (i.e., equation (5.1)). The second instance is when there is no cointegration at all, implying that there are no linear combinations of the $\mathbf{z}_t$ that are $I(0)$, and consequently $\boldsymbol{\Pi}$ is an $(n \times n)$ matrix of zeros. In this case, the appropriate model is a VAR in first differences involving no long-run elements. The third way for $\boldsymbol{\Pi}\mathbf{z}_{t-k}$ to be $I(0)$ is when there exists up to $(n-1)$ cointegration relationships: $\boldsymbol{\beta}'\mathbf{z}_{t-k} \sim I(0)$. In this instance $r \leqslant (n-1)$ cointegration vectors exist in $\boldsymbol{\beta}$ (i.e., r columns of $\boldsymbol{\beta}$ form r linearly independent combinations of the variables in $\mathbf{z}_t$, each of which is stationary), together with $(n-r)$ non-stationary vectors (i.e., $n-r$ columns of $\boldsymbol{\beta}$ form $I(1)$ common trends). Only the cointegration vectors in $\boldsymbol{\beta}$ enter (5.2), otherwise $\boldsymbol{\Pi}\mathbf{z}_{t-k}$ would not be $I(0)$, which implies that the last $(n-r)$ columns of $\boldsymbol{\alpha}$ are insignificantly small (i.e., effectively zero).[3] Thus the typical problem faced, of determining how many $r \leqslant (n-1)$ cointegration vectors exist in $\boldsymbol{\beta}$, amounts to equivalently testing which columns of $\boldsymbol{\alpha}$ are zero. Consequently, testing for cointegration amounts to a consideration of the rank of $\boldsymbol{\Pi}$, that is, finding the number of r linearly independent columns in $\boldsymbol{\Pi}$.

To recap, if $\boldsymbol{\Pi}$ has full rank (i.e., there are $r = n$ linearly independent columns) then the variables in $\mathbf{z}_t$ are $I(0)$, while if the rank of $\boldsymbol{\Pi}$ is zero then there are no cointegration relationships. Neither of these two cases is particularly interesting. More usually, $\boldsymbol{\Pi}$ has reduced rank; that is, there are $r \leqslant (n-1)$ cointegration vectors present. Later on we shall consider actual tests for the (reduced) rank of $\boldsymbol{\Pi}$, which, as noted earlier, are equivalent to testing which columns of $\boldsymbol{\alpha}$ are zero. However, this presupposes that it is possible to factorise $\boldsymbol{\Pi}$ into $\boldsymbol{\Pi} = \boldsymbol{\alpha}\boldsymbol{\beta}'$, where $\boldsymbol{\alpha}$ and $\boldsymbol{\beta}$ can both be reduced in dimension to $(n \times r)$.[4] It is generally not possible to apply ordinary regression techniques to the individual equations comprising the system in (5.2) since what is obtained is an $(n \times n)$ estimate of $\boldsymbol{\Pi}$.[5,6] Rather, Johansen (1988) obtains estimates of $\boldsymbol{\alpha}$ and $\boldsymbol{\beta}$ using the procedure known as reduced rank regression. Since this is quite complicated the details are confined to Box 5.1.

Testing the order of integration of the variables

When using time series data, it is often assumed that the data are non-stationary, and thus that a stationary cointegration relationship(s) needs to be found in order to avoid the problem of spurious regression. However, it is clear from the discussion in Chapter 3 that unit root tests often suffer from poor size and power properties (i.e., the tendency to over-reject the null hypothesis of non-stationarity when it is true and under-reject the null when it is false, respectively). This has meant that in practical applications, it is quite common for there to be tests for cointegration even when the preceding unit root analysis suggests that the properties of the variables in the equation(s) are unbalanced (i.e., they cannot cointegrate down to a common lower order of integration — see Box 2.4).[7] This might be justified on the grounds that the unit root tests are not reliable, and consequently the variables may indeed all be, say, $I(1)$. However, it is not necessary for all the variables in the model to have the same order of integration (unless $n=2$) but it is important to understand and take account of the implications when all the variables are not $I(1)$.

Indeed, it is possible that cointegration is present when there is a mix of $I(0)$, $I(1)$ and $I(2)$ variables in the model. Stationary $I(0)$ variables might play a key role in establishing a sensible long-run relationship between non-stationary variables, especially if theory *a priori* suggests that such variables should be included.[8] However, in the multivariate model, for every stationary variable included, the number of cointegration equations will increase correspondingly. To see this, recall from the above discussion of the Johansen procedure that testing for cointegration amounts to a consideration of the rank of $\mathbf{\Pi}$, that is, finding the number of r linearly independent columns in $\mathbf{\Pi}$. Since each $I(0)$ variable is stationary by itself, it forms a 'cointegration relation' by itself, and consequently forms a linearly independent column in $\mathbf{\Pi}$. To take the argument one step further, suppose we have two $I(0)$ variables in the model; by definition any linear combination (i.e., a single $\boldsymbol{\beta}_i$) cointegrates. This does not imply that these two $I(0)$ variables form only one cointegration relationship since we could combine the two columns of $\boldsymbol{\beta}$ linearly, each containing just the one $I(0)$ variable, to obtain the cointegration relationship being sought.[9] Thus the practical implication of including $I(0)$ variables is that cointegration rank will increase and a number of the cointegration vectors in $\boldsymbol{\beta}$ should contain only one variable. Knowledge of this (or at least the expectation) may help in interpreting the initial (unrestricted) results obtained from using the Johansen approach.

If the model contains $I(2)$ variables, the situation becomes far more complicated. Some (or all) of the $I(2)$ variables may cointegrate down to $I(1)$ space and then further cointegrate with other $I(1)$ variables to obtain a cointegration vector(s). Thus, the presence of variables that require to be differenced *twice* to induce stationarity does not preclude the possibility of stationary relationships in the model.[10] However, applying the standard Johansen approach, which is designed to handle $I(1)$ and $I(0)$ variables, will not provide the necessary stationary vectors. When there are $I(2)$ variables in the model, we must either replace these with an $I(1)$ alternative through some form of differencing (e.g., if money supply and prices are $I(2)$, we could reformulate the model to consider real money, $m_t - p_t$), or it will be necessary to use the approach developed by Johansen (1994) for $I(2)$ models. Again, knowing that there are $I(2)$ variables in the model can help in formulating the right approach to estimating cointegration relationships in such situations.

Finally, it will become apparent that the Johansen approach provides an alternative means of testing for unit roots in each variable, where the null hypothesis is that of stationarity rather than non-stationarity. The procedure will be discussed once we have considered how to test for restrictions on each vector in $\boldsymbol{\beta}$, although it is not currently known whether the Johansen approach to testing for unit roots (which is equivalent to a multivariate augmented-Dickey–Fuller-type test) has better size and power than the standard tests considered in Chapter 3.

Formulation of the dynamic model

So far the VECM to be estimated (equation (5.2)) contains no deterministic components (such as an intercept and trend, or seasonal dummies). There is also the issue of setting the appropriate lag-length of the $\Delta\mathbf{z}_{t-k+1}$ to ensure that the residuals are Gaussian (i.e., they do not suffer from autocorrelation, non-normality, etc.). Setting the value of k is also bound up with the issue of whether there are variables that only affect the short-run behaviour of the model and which, if they are omitted, will become part of the error term, $\mathbf{u}_t$. Residual misspecification can arise as a consequence of omitting these important conditioning variables, and increasing the lag-length k is often not the solution (as it usually is when, for example, autocorrelation is present).[11,12] The question of whether there are trends in the data and therefore whether deterministic variables (a constant and trend) should enter the cointegration space or not will be taken up after considering how to test for the number of cointegration vectors in the model, since testing for the inclusion of these deterministic components is undertaken *jointly* with testing for cointegration rank. In this section, we consider the other issues surrounding the appropriate value for k.

For notational simplicity assume that $k=2$ and that there exist other variables that are both weakly exogenous and insignificant in the long-run cointegration space such that we can condition on the set of such $I(0)$ variables, $\mathbf{D}_t$. The latter will only affect the short-run model, and it is possible to rewrite (5.2) as:

$$\Delta\mathbf{z}_t = \boldsymbol{\Gamma}_1\Delta\mathbf{z}_{t-1} + \boldsymbol{\Pi}\mathbf{z}_{t-2} + \boldsymbol{\Psi}\mathbf{D}_t + \mathbf{u}_t \tag{5.3}$$

The variables in $\mathbf{D}_t$ are often included to take account of short-run 'shocks' to the system, such as policy interventions and the impact of the two oil-price shocks in the 1970s which had an important effect on macroeconomic conditions. Such variables often enter as dummy variables, including seasonal dummies when the data are observed more frequently than annually. Seasonal dummies are centred to ensure that they sum to zero over time[13] and thus they do not affect the underlying asymptotic distributions upon which tests (including tests for cointegration rank) depend. However, it is worth noting at the outset that including any other dummy or dummy-type variable *will* affect the underlying distribution of test statistics, such that the critical values for these tests are different depending on the number of dummies included. This will mean that the published critical values provided by Johansen and others (e.g., Osterwald-Lenum, 1992) are only indicative in such situations.[14]

As an example, consider the PPP and UIP model estimated using UK data by

Johansen and Juselius (1992). This was set out briefly in the last chapter, and comprises the five variables p_1 (the UK wholesale price index), p_2 (trade weighted foreign wholesale price index), e (UK effective exchange rate), i_1 (three-month UK treasury bill rate), and i_2 (three-month Eurodollar interest rate). Using OLS to estimate the system denoted by (5.3), and restricting $\mathbf{D}_t$ to include only seasonal dummies and an intercept produces the output in Table 5.1 (*PcFiml* was used,[15] leaving the cointegration rank unrestricted as $r = n$). The diagnostic tests[16] involve F-tests for the hypothesis that the i-period lag ($F_{k=i}$) is zero; that there is no serial correlation (F_{ar}, against fourth-order autoregression); that there is no autoregressive conditional heteroscedasticity (F_{arch}, against fourth order); that there is no heteroscedasticity (F_{het}); and lastly a χ^2-test for normality (χ^2_{nd}: see Doornik and Hansen, 1993). Analogous system (vector) tests are also reported (see the *PcFiml* manual), with the last test F_{ur} representing the test against the significance of the regressors in $\mathbf{D}_t$.

The results based on $k = 2$ indicate that the second-period lag is significant in at least one of the equations in the model (and cointegration analysis requires the model to have a common lag-length). Non-normal residuals are a problem in the equations determining p_2 and i_2. The impact of the outlier observations is seen more clearly in Figure 5.1. Increasing the lag-length to $k = 3$ (or higher) has little impact and the additional lags are generally not significant.

Johansen and Juselius (1992) argued that by looking at residual plots the above

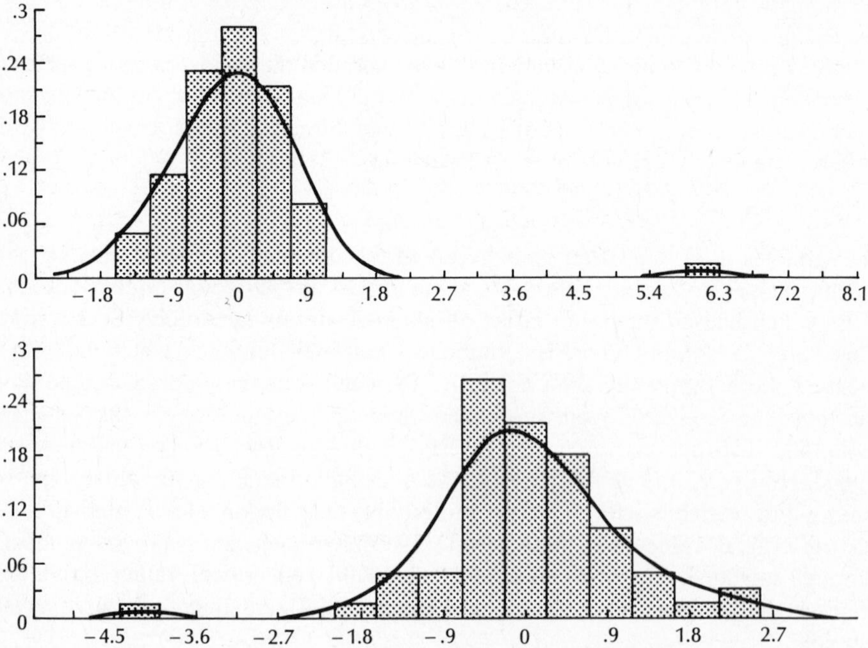

Figure 5.1 Residual densities for p_2 and i_2: excluding Δpo_t, Δpo_{t-1} and D_{usa} in the model

Table 5.1 Model evaluation diagnostics: PPP and UIP model using UK data (only an intercept and seasonal dummies in $\mathbf{D}_t$)

Statistic	p_1	p_2	e	i_1	i_2
Lag-length=2					
$F_{k=1}$ (5, 42)	20.49**	11.91**	14.11**	20.94**	6.51**
$F_{k=2}$ (5, 42)	2.03	1.59	1.04	3.89**	0.88
$\hat{\sigma}$	0.85%	1.23%	3.32%	1.23%	1.45%
F_{ar} (4, 42)	1.10	0.34	1.76	0.85	2.36
F_{arch} (4, 38)	2.53	0.03	0.59	0.41	1.59
F_{het} (20, 25)	1.09	2.08*	0.33	0.92	1.57
χ^2_{nd} (2)	7.71*	68.87**	1.63	2.59	23.56**
Multivariate tests: F_{ar}(100, 111)=1.28; F_{het}(300, 176)=0.86; χ^2_{nd}(10)=97.68**; F_{ur}(50,194)=120.12**					
Lag-length = 3					
$F_{k=1}$(5, 36)	22.47**	12.11**	12.59**	13.98**	6.72**
$F_{k=2}$ (5, 36)	3.23*	0.70	1.75	2.99*	3.15*
$F_{k=3}$ (5, 36)	1.37	1.86	1.64	2.09	3.42*
$\hat{\sigma}$	0.78%	1.20%	3.35%	1.23%	1.30%
F_{ar} (4, 36)	1.52	1.56	1.50	0.99	1.18
F_{arch}(4, 32)	1.90	0.02	0.31	1.51	2.07
F_{het}(30, 9)	0.41	0.78	0.24	0.53	0.92
χ^2_{nd}(2)	4.15	72.30**	8.32*	2.58	19.43**
Multivariate tests: F_{ar}(100, 82)=1.02; χ^2_{het}(450)=494.53; χ^2_{nd}(10)=96.44**; F_{ur}(75, 176)=74.38**					

**Rejects null hypothesis at 1 per cent significance level; *rejects null hypothesis at 5 per cent significance level.

problems of excess kurtosis were found to coincide with significant changes in the oil price, and thus they conditioned their model on Δpo_t and Δpo_{t-1}, where po measures the world price of crude oil. These $I(0)$ variables are presumed to be exogenous and to have only a short-run effect and thus they are presumed to enter $\mathbf{D}_t$ only. The residual diagnostics which now result are shown in the top half of Table 5.2, and Figure 5.2. There is a significant reduction in the kurtosis associated with the foreign wholesale price index,[17] but little change in the residuals of the Eurodollar interest rate equation. Johansen and Juselius (op. cit.) stopped at this point in terms of the specification of $\mathbf{D}_t$, arguing that if these two variables prove to be weakly exogenous (as was the case for p_2) then non-normality is less of a problem since we can condition on the weakly exogenous variables (although they remain in the long-run model) and therefore improve the stochastic properties of the model. In practice, as will be seen later when we consider testing for weak exogeneity, this means that the exogenous variables only enter the right-hand side of (5.2) and do not therefore have to be modelled themselves, which is an advantage, especially '... if there have been many interventions during the period and the weakly exogenous variable exhibits all the "problematic" data features' (Hansen and Juselius, 1994).

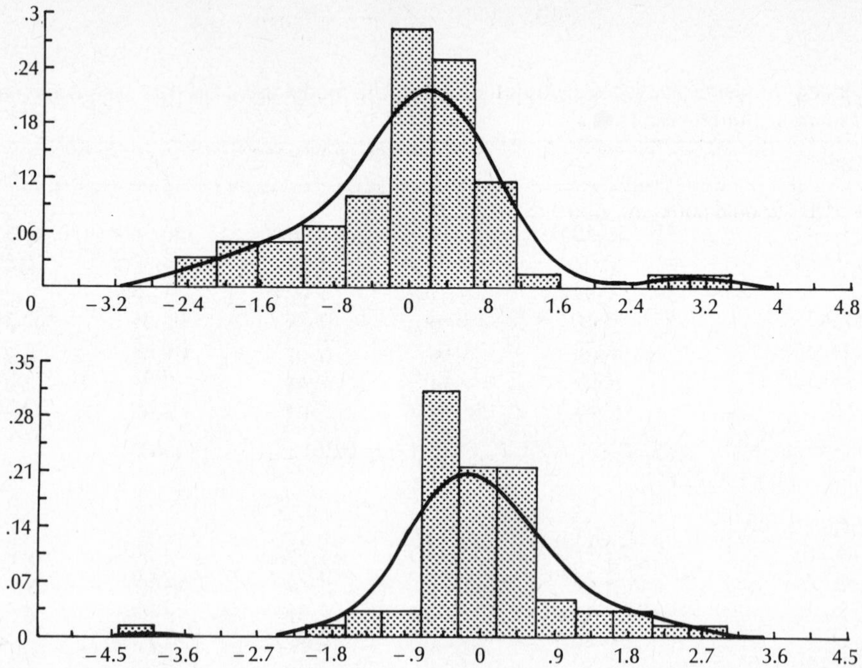

Figure 5.2 Residual densities for p_2 and i_2: including Δpo_t, Δpo_{t-1} but excluding D_{usa} in the model

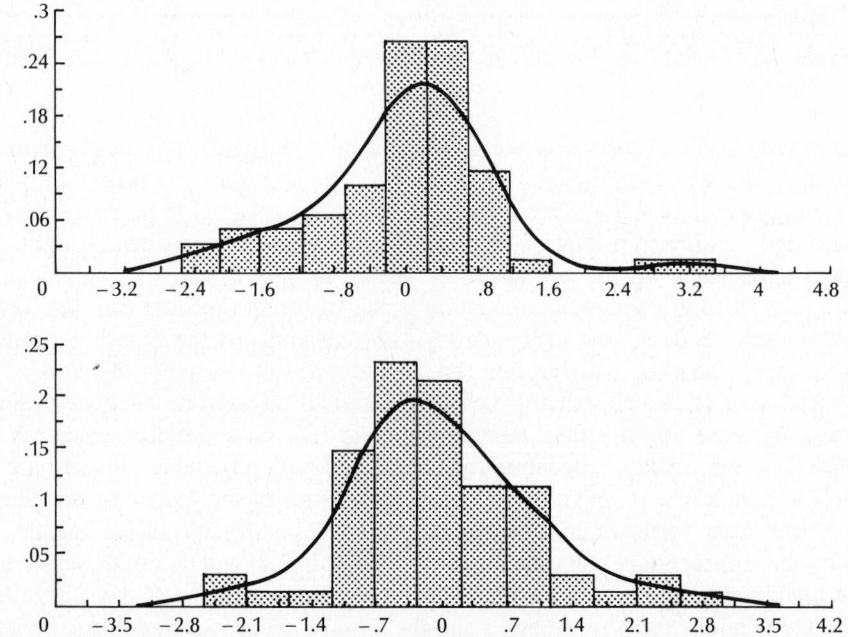

Figure 5.3 Residual densities for p_2 and i_2: including Δpo_t, Δpo_{t-1} and D_{usa} in the model

Table 5.2 Model evaluation diagnostics: PPP and UIP model using UK data (1972:1–1987:2) (lag-length $k = 2$)

Statistic	p_1	p_2	e	i_1	i_2
Intercept, seasonal dummies, Δpo_t, Δpo_{t-1} in $\boldsymbol{D}_t$					
$F_{k=1}(5, 40)$	16.65**	13.07**	11.95**	19.53**	6.15**
$F_{k=2}(5, 40)$	1.42	1.14	0.72	3.59**	0.68
$\hat{\sigma}$	0.80%	0.83%	3.35%	1.24%	1.47%
$F_{ar}(4, 40)$	1.16	1.59	1.53	0.56	2.94
$F_{arch}(4, 36)$	1.48	0.49	0.46	0.37	1.70
$F_{het}(20, 23)$	0.60	1.34	0.30	0.79	1.34
$\chi^2_{nd}(2)$	5.75	12.19**	1.17	3.74	23.29**
Multivariate tests: $F_{ar}(100, 102)=1.13$; $F_{het}(300, 152)=0.64$; $\chi^2_{nd}(10)=46.23$**; $F_{ur}(50, 185)=130.90$**					
Intercept, seasonal dummies, Δpo_t, Δpo_{t-1} and D_{usa} in $\boldsymbol{D}_t$					
$F_{k=1}(5, 39)$	16.62**	12.77**	11.32**	17.88**	9.35**
$F_{k=2}(5, 39)$	1.48	1.21	0.74	2.96*	0.83
$\hat{\sigma}$	0.81%	0.83%	3.34%	1.25%	1.33%
$F_{ar}(4, 39)$	1.16	1.54	1.94	0.51	2.03
$F_{arch}(4, 35)$	1.39	0.47	0.22	1.32	0.82
$F_{het}(20, 22)$	0.59	1.27	0.28	0.68	0.68
$\chi^2_{nd}(2)$	5.30	12.31**	2.03*	4.37	4.24
Multivariate tests: $F_{ar}(100, 97)=1.24$; $F_{het}(300, 140)=0.54$; $\chi^2_{nd}(10)=26.24$**; $F_{ur}(50, 181)=132.74$**					

**Rejects null hypothesis at 1 per cent significance level; *rejects null hypothesis at 5 per cent significance level.

The residual plot for i_2 indicates that the outlier problem is associated with the first quarter of 1979 and especially the second quarter of 1980. Thus, a second dummy was included, taking on the value of 1 for both these periods and labelled D_{usa} (since it coincided in the later period with depository institutions deregulation and the Monetary Control Act in the USA, which had a strong impact on interest rate determination outside the USA). The new set of residual diagnostics is reported in the lower half of Table 5.2, and Figure 5.3, showing yet a further improvement in the stochastic properties of the model.

A different example of the problems associated with specifying the value of k and the elements in $\mathbf{D}_t$, involves OLS estimation of the demand for money model. Setting $k=2$, and restricting $\mathbf{D}_t$ to include only seasonal dummies and an intercept, the results as set out in Table 5.3 are obtained. The null hypothesis of no serial correlation is rejected in the univariate case for the real money supply and real output (cf. the F_{ar} statistics against fifth-order autoregression), and for the system as a whole. There is also some evidence that the residuals from the real output and inflation equations are non-normally distributed. Increasing the lag-length to $k=4$ produces the results in the second half of Table 5.3; the extra lags on $(m-p)_t$ and y_t

Table 5.3 Model evaluation diagnostics: UK demand for money (1963:1–1989:2) (only an intercept and seasonal dummies in $\mathbf{D}_t$)

Statistic	$m-p$	y	Δp	R
Lag-length = 2				
$F_{k=1}(4, 88)$	12.22**	10.36**	5.80**	12.22**
$F_{k=2}(4, 88)$	5.10**	6.00**	5.33**	5.10**
$\hat{\sigma}$	2.00%	1.71%	0.77%	1.31%
$F_{ar}(5, 86)$	4.19**	2.77*	0.51	0.34
$F_{arch}(4, 83)$	0.78	0.87	1.14	2.42
$F_{het}(16, 74)$	0.94	1.00	0.78	1.79*
$\chi^2_{nd}(2)$	3.39	7.88*	6.26*	3.04
Multivariate tests: $F_{ar}(80, 270)=2.02$**; $F_{het}(160, 574)=1.09$; $\chi^2_{nd}(8)=19.54$*; $F_{ur}(32, 326)=248.47$**				
Lag-length = 4				
$F_{k=1}(4, 78)$	9.25**	9.79**	5.95**	23.60**
$F_{k=2}(4, 78)$	2.56*	1.41	3.33*	1.39
$F_{k=3}(4, 78)$	1.59	4.52**	0.37	0.18
$F_{k=4}(4, 78)$	4.79**	5.18**	1.71	0.72
$\hat{\sigma}$	1.62%	1.58%	0.73%	1.36%
$F_{ar}(5, 76)$	1.92	1.66	0.93	1.04
$F_{arch}(4, 73)$	1.02	1.09	0.64	3.31*
$F_{het}(32, 48)$	0.52	0.73	0.76	0.89
$\chi^2_{nd}(2)$	2.50	5.28	5.44	2.82
Multivariate tests: $F_{ar}(80, 231)=0.96$; $F_{het}(320, 400)=0.59$; $\chi^2_{nd}(8)=18.76$*; $F_{ur}(64, 307)=124.42$**				

**Rejects null hypothesis at 1 per cent significance level; *rejects null hypothesis at 5 per cent significance level.

are significant[18] and serial correlation is no longer a problem, although the test for ARCH is significant for the interest rate equation. Checking the plot of the residuals for the latter indicates outliers associated with the first two quarters of 1977, and adding a dummy to cover this period removes the ARCH process.[19] Alternatively, on the assumption that the interest rate is weakly exogenous, it may be appropriate to condition on R instead of adding the extra dummy variable, especially if no economic rationale is available to justify its inclusion.[20]

Testing for reduced rank

It was stated earlier that if a model contains $\mathbf{z}_t$, a vector of non-stationary $I(1)$ variables, then $\mathbf{\Pi z}_{t-k}$ in (5.2) contains the stationary long-run error-correction relations and must be stationary for $\mathbf{u}_t \sim I(0)$ to be 'white noise'. This occurs when $\mathbf{\Pi}$ $(=\boldsymbol{\alpha\beta}')$ has reduced rank; that is, there are $r \leqslant (n-1)$ cointegration vectors present in $\boldsymbol{\beta}$ so that testing for cointegration amounts to finding the number of r linearly independent columns in $\boldsymbol{\Pi}$, which is equivalent to testing that the last $(n-r)$ columns of $\boldsymbol{\alpha}$ are insignificantly small (i.e., effectively zero). In Box 5.1, it is shown that Johansen's maximum likelihood approach to solving this problem amounts to a reduced rank regression which provides n eigenvalues $\hat{\lambda}_1 > \hat{\lambda}_2 > \ldots > \hat{\lambda}_n$ and *their corresponding* eigenvectors $\hat{\mathbf{V}} = (\hat{\mathbf{v}}_1, \ldots, \hat{\mathbf{v}}_n)$. Those r elements in $\hat{\mathbf{V}}$ which determine the linear combinations of stationary relationships can be denoted $\hat{\boldsymbol{\beta}} = (\hat{\mathbf{v}}_1, \ldots, \hat{\mathbf{v}}_r)$; that is, the distinct $\hat{\mathbf{v}}_i'\mathbf{z}_t$ $(i = 1, \ldots, r)$ combinations of the $I(1)$ levels of $\mathbf{z}_t$ which produce high correlations with the stationary $\Delta\mathbf{z}_t \sim I(0)$ elements in (5.2) are the cointegration vectors by virtue of the fact that they must themselves be $I(0)$ to achieve a high correlation. Since each eigenvector $\hat{\mathbf{v}}_i$ has a corresponding eigenvalue, then the magnitude of $\hat{\lambda}_i$ is a measure of how strongly the cointegration relations $\hat{\mathbf{v}}_i'\mathbf{z}_t$ (which we can now denote as $\hat{\boldsymbol{\beta}}_i'\mathbf{z}_t$) are correlated with the stationary part of the model. The last $(n-r)$ combinations obtained from the Johansen approach, that is, $\hat{\mathbf{v}}_i'\mathbf{z}_t$ $(i = r+1, \ldots, n)$, indicate the non-stationary combinations, and theoretically these are uncorrelated with the stationary elements in (5.2). Consequently, for the eigenvectors corresponding to the non-stationary part of the model, $\hat{\lambda}_i = 0$ for $i = r+1, \ldots, n$.

Thus to test the null hypothesis that there are at most r cointegration vectors (and thus $(n-r)$ unit roots) amounts to:

$$H_0\colon \lambda_i = 0 \qquad i = r+1, \ldots, n$$

where only the first r eigenvalues are non-zero. This restriction can be imposed for different values of r and then the log of the maximised likelihood function for the restricted model is compared to the log of the maximised likelihood function of the unrestricted model and a standard likelihood ratio test computed (although with a non-standard distribution). That is, it is possible to test the null hypothesis using what has become known as the *trace* statistic:

$$\lambda_{\text{trace}} = -2\log(Q) = -T\sum_{i=r+1}^{n} \log(1-\hat{\lambda}_i) \qquad r = 0, 1, 2, \ldots, n-2, n-1. \tag{5.4}$$

Table 5.4 Tests of the cointegration rank for the PPP and UIP model using UK data (1972:1–1987:2)[a]

$H_0{:}r$	$n-r$	$\hat{\lambda}_i$	$-T\log(1-\hat{\lambda}_{r+1})$	$\lambda_{\max}$ (0.95)	$-T\Sigma\log(1-\hat{\lambda}_i)$	λ_{trace} (0.95)
0	5	0.407	31.33	33.5	80.75**	68.5
1	4	0.285	20.16	27.1	49.42*	47.2
2	3	0.254	17.59	21.0	29.26	29.7
3	2	0.102	6.46	14.1	11.67	15.4
4	1	0.083	5.19*	3.8	5.19*	3.8

[a]See Johansen and Juselius (1992, Table 2).

**Denotes rejection at the 1 per cent significance level; *denotes rejection at the 5 per cent. significance level.

where Q = (restricted maximised likelihood ÷ unrestricted maximised likelihood). Asymptotic critical values are provided in Osterwald-Lenum (1992), although if dummy variables enter the deterministic part of the multivariate model (i.e., $\mathbf{D}_t$ above), then these critical values are only indicative. Similarly, if the practitioner only has a small sample of observations on $\mathbf{z}_t$ then there are likely to be problems with the power and size properties of the above test when using asymptotic critical values. The implications of this, and other similar problems with the trace statistic, are considered later.

Another test of the significance of the largest λ_r is the so-called maximal-eigenvalue or λ-*max* statistic:

$$\lambda_{\max} = -T \log(1 - \hat{\lambda}_{r+1}) \qquad r = 0, 1, 2, \ldots, n-2, n-1 \tag{5.5}$$

This tests that there are r cointegration vectors against the alternative that $r+1$ exist. An example of testing for the reduced rank of $\mathbf{\Pi}$ is now presented to make clear the use of the tests outlined above.

The results obtained from applying the Johansen reduced rank regression approach (see Box 5.1) to the PPP and UIP model discussed above (with intercept, seasonal dummies and Δpo_t, Δpo_{t-1} in $\mathbf{D}_t$ and $k=2$) are given in Table 5.4. The various hypotheses to be tested, from no cointegration (i.e., $r=0$ or alternatively $n-r=5$) to increasing numbers of cointegration vectors, are presented in the first column. The eigenvalues associated with the combinations of the $I(1)$ levels of $\mathbf{z}_t$ are in the second column, ordered from highest to lowest. Next come the $\lambda_{\max}$ statistics which test whether $r=0$ against $r=1$, or $r=1$ against $r=2$, etc. That is, a test of the significance of the largest λ_r is performed, and the present results suggest that the hypothesis of no cointegration ($r=0$) cannot be rejected at the 5 per cent level (with the 5 per cent critical values given in the fourth column). The λ_{trace} statistics test the null that $r=q$ ($q=1, 2, \ldots, n-1$) against the unrestricted alternative that $r=n$. On the basis of this test it is possible to accept that there are two cointegration vectors since the trace statistic associated with the null hypothesis that $r=1$ is rejected but the null hypothesis that $r=2$ is not rejected.[21] This apparent contradiction in the tests for cointegration rank is not uncommon. As has already been stated, the inclusion of dummy or dummy-type variables in $\mathbf{D}_t$ affects the underlying distribution of the test statistics, such that the critical values for these tests are different depending on the number of dummies included. The problem of small samples has also been mentioned, and Reimers (1992) suggests that in such a situation the Johansen procedure over-rejects when the null is true. Thus he suggests taking account of the number of parameters to be estimated in the model and making an adjustment for degrees of freedom by replacing T in (5.4) and (5.5) by $T-nk$, where T is the sample size, n is the number of variables in the model and k is the lag-length set when estimating (5.2).[22] Using both Reimers adjusted trace and $\lambda_{\max}$ statistics, we could not reject the null of no cointegration given that we would now be using a value of $T-nk=50$ rather than $T=60$ in calculating the test statistics. However, as pointed out by Doornik and Hendry (1994), it is unclear yet whether this is the preferred correction, although Cheung and Lai (1993) report that their results

'... support that the finite-sample bias of Johansen's tests is a positive function of $T/(T-nk)$ ... furthermore, the finite-sample bias toward over-rejection of the no cointegration hypothesis magnifies with increasing values of n and k'.

The Monte Carlo experiments reported in Cheung and Lai (op. cit.) also suggest that '... between Johansen's two LR tests for cointegration, the trace test shows more robustness to both skewness and excess kurtosis in (the residuals) than the maximal eigenvalue (λ_{max}) test'. Since the PPP and UIP model suffers from excess kurtosis, it may be preferable to place greater weight on the trace test. However, it is also important to use any additional information that can support the choice of r. Juselius (1994) suggests looking at the dynamics of the VAR model (equation (5.1)) and in particular whether it converges in the long-run. Thus the eigenvalues (i.e., roots) of what is termed the 'companion matrix' (**A**) are considered since these provide additional confirmation of how many $(n-r)$ roots are on the unit circle and thus the number of r cointegration relations. The matrix **A** is defined by:

$$\mathbf{A} = \begin{bmatrix} \mathbf{A}_1 & \mathbf{A}_2 & \cdots & \mathbf{A}_{k-1} & \mathbf{A}_k \\ \mathbf{I}_n & 0 & \cdots & 0 & 0 \\ 0 & \mathbf{I}_n & \cdots & 0 & 0 \\ & & & & \\ 0 & 0 & \cdots & \mathbf{I}_n & 0 \end{bmatrix}$$

5x2=10

with the $\mathbf{A}_i$ defined by (5.1) and $\mathbf{I}_n$ is the n-dimensional identity matrix. There are ten roots of the companion matrix in the present example, since $n \times k = 10$. The moduli[23] of the three largest roots are 0.979, 0.918 and 0.918, respectively, indicating that all roots are inside the unit circle, with the three largest close to unity. This suggests that $(n-r)=3$, and thus there are two cointegration relations. The fact that all roots are inside the unit circle is consistent with $\mathbf{z}_t$ comprising $I(1)$ processes, although it is certainly possible that the largest root is not significantly different from 1. If any of the roots are on or outside the unit circle, this would tend to indicate an $I(2)$ model, requiring second-order differencing to achieve stationarity.[24]

The estimates of $\hat{\boldsymbol{\alpha}}$ and $\hat{\boldsymbol{\beta}}$ obtained from applying the Johansen technique (using the *Cats* program) are presented in Box 5.2.[25] Note, the $\hat{\boldsymbol{\beta}}$-matrix is presented in normalised form, with the latter having one element of each row of $\boldsymbol{\beta}'$ set equal to 1. This is achieved by simply dividing each row by the chosen element.[26] Normalising the $\hat{\boldsymbol{\beta}}$-matrix leads to a normalised $\hat{\boldsymbol{\alpha}}$-matrix and different normalisations applied to $\hat{\boldsymbol{\beta}}$ lead to different values in the $\hat{\boldsymbol{\alpha}}$-matrix. Figure 5.4 plots the first four relations associated with the first four rows in $\hat{\boldsymbol{\beta}}'$ to see if any of the $\hat{\boldsymbol{\beta}}_i'\mathbf{z}_t$ are stationary. The first two vectors correspond to the most stationary relations in the model but there is some evidence that both relationships are upward trending. The other two vectors are clearly non-stationary. The plots in Figure 5.5 present a different version of the same relations as are given in Figure 5.4, since instead of multiplying the $\hat{\boldsymbol{\beta}}_i$ by $\mathbf{z}_t$, where $\mathbf{z}_t$ captures all the short-run dynamics (including seasonals) in the model, the $\hat{\boldsymbol{\beta}}_i$ are multiplied by a vector, $\mathbf{R}_{kt}$, which is equivalent to $\mathbf{z}_t$ but with all the short-run dynamic effects removed (i.e., $\mathbf{R}_{kt} = \mathbf{z}_{t-k} - (\hat{\boldsymbol{\Gamma}}_1 \Delta\mathbf{z}_{t-1} + \ldots + \hat{\boldsymbol{\Gamma}}_{k-1}\Delta\mathbf{z}_{t-k+1})$ — see

T–n·k =5⟩

Box 5.2   Output from *Cats* for PPP and UIP model

Eigenv.	λ-max	Trace	H$_0$: r=	n−r=	λ-max90	Trace90
0.4067	31.33	80.75	0	5	30.90	64.84
0.2854	20.16	49.42	1	4	24.73	43.95
0.2542	17.59	29.26	2	3	18.60	26.79
0.1023	6.48	11.67	3	2	12.07	13.33
0.0829	5.19	5.19	4	1	2.69	2.69

adjusted

Normalised

β′

r=1 → β$_1$
r=2 → β$_2$

	p$_1$	p$_2$	e	i$_1$	i$_2$
	1.000	−0.909	−0.932	−3.375	−1.891
	0.028	−0.032	−0.095	1.000	−0.934
	0.364	−0.463	0.405	1.000	−1.032
	1.000	−2.400	1.122	−0.409	2.986
	1.000	−1.453	−0.481	2.278	0.763

α   a$_1$↓   ↓α$_2$

−0.068	0.042	−0.008	0.001	−0.013
−0.018	0.004	−0.039	0.013	0.008
0.101	−0.005	−0.153	−0.035	−0.047
0.034	−0.147	−0.028	0.012	−0.024
0.058	0.292	0.013	0.027	−0.010

T-VALUES FOR **α**   α$_{11}$ α$_{12}$

α$_1$	−4.635	0.795	−0.671	0.156	−1.519
α$_2$	−1.167	0.080	−3.293	1.452	0.833
α$_3$	1.633	−0.023	−3.190	−0.962	−1.280
α$_4$	1.500	−1.801	−1.600	0.900	−1.752
α$_5$	2.138	3.043	0.632	1.676	−0.626

Π

p$_1$	p$_2$	e	i$_1$	i$_2$
−0.082	0.080	0.064	0.233	0.092
−0.011	−0.009	0.012	0.037	0.115
−0.038	0.133	−0.172	−0.590	−0.169
0.008	−0.008	−0.004	−0.351	0.120
0.088	−0.118	−0.041	0.077	−0.322

equations (5.1) and (5.1.3)). The first two graphs in Figure 5.5 now suggest that the first two vectors are stationary, confirming that $r = 2$. Note, however, the advice given by Hansen and Juselius (1994) that when '... $\boldsymbol{\beta}'\mathbf{z}_t$ and $\boldsymbol{\beta}'\mathbf{R}_{kt}$ look widely different, in particular if the former looks $\mathbf{I}(1)$ whereas the latter looks stationary, it is a good idea to check whether your data vector $\mathbf{z}_t$ is second-order instead of first-order non-stationary'.

As another check of the adequacy of the model, Figure 5.6 plots recursive estimates of the first four non-zero eigenvalues. This type of graph corresponds to a standard plot of parameter estimates in the usual regression model since non-constancy of $\hat{\boldsymbol{\alpha}}$ or $\hat{\boldsymbol{\beta}}$ should be reflected in non-constancy of the $\hat{\lambda}_i$. Generally, for the PPP and UIP model there is no evidence of parameter instability due to, for example, the failure to account for structural breaks.

As an example of a likely $I(2)$ system, consider the UK demand for money model again, but in terms of nominal money balances (cf. the unit root tests associated with Table 3.2.1). Applying the Johansen approach to seasonally *un*adjusted data for the 1963:1–1989:2 period[27] results in one cointegration vector being accepted after testing for reduced rank, with the largest eigenvalue of the companion matrix having a modulus of 1.006. Estimating the real money-demand model with the potentially $I(2)$ variables m_t and p_t replaced by $(m-p)_t$ also produces support for a single cointegration relationship, but this time with the largest eigenvalue of the companion matrix having a modulus of 0.991. Johansen (1994) has developed a more exact test for whether the model contains any $I(2)$ variables (see Box 5.3), but the procedure is

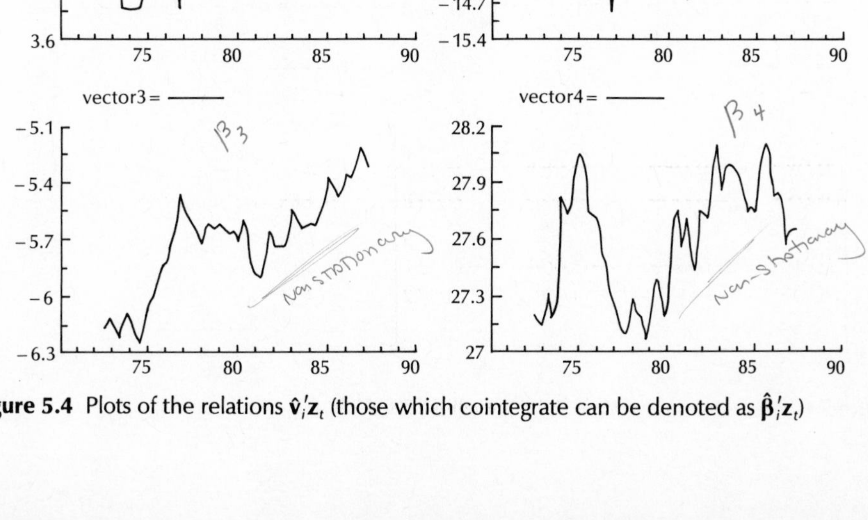

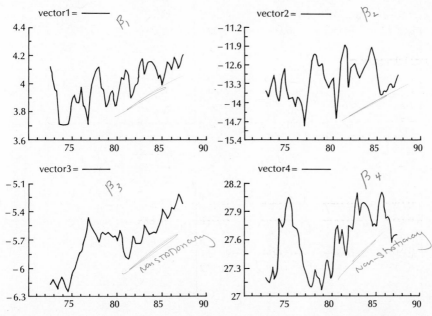

Figure 5.4 Plots of the relations $\hat{\mathbf{v}}_i'\mathbf{z}_t$ (those which cointegrate can be denoted as $\hat{\boldsymbol{\beta}}_i'\mathbf{z}_t$)

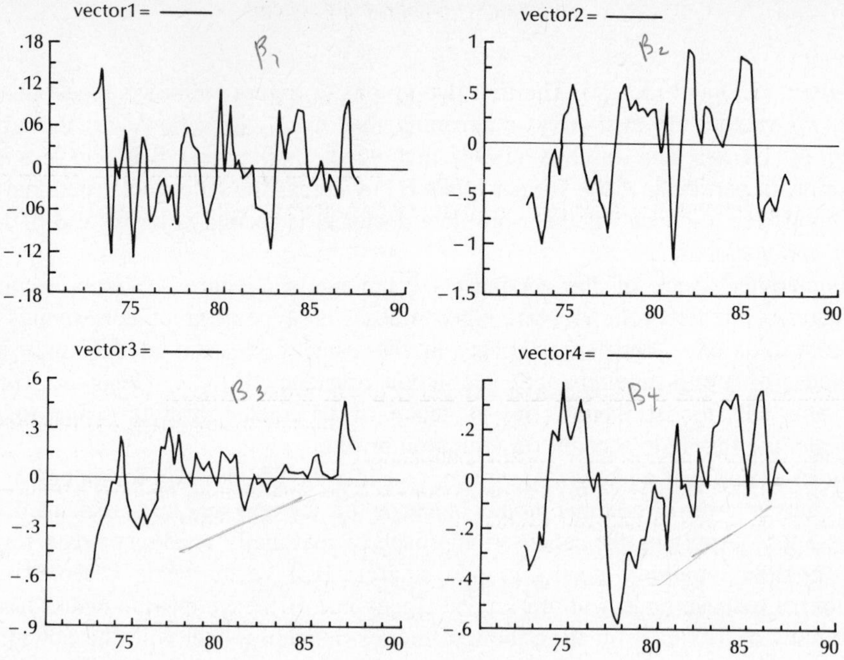

Figure 5.5 Plots of the relations $\hat{\mathbf{v}}_i'\hat{\mathbf{R}}_{kt}$ (those which cointegrate can be denoted as $\hat{\boldsymbol{\beta}}_i'\hat{\mathbf{R}}_{kt}$)

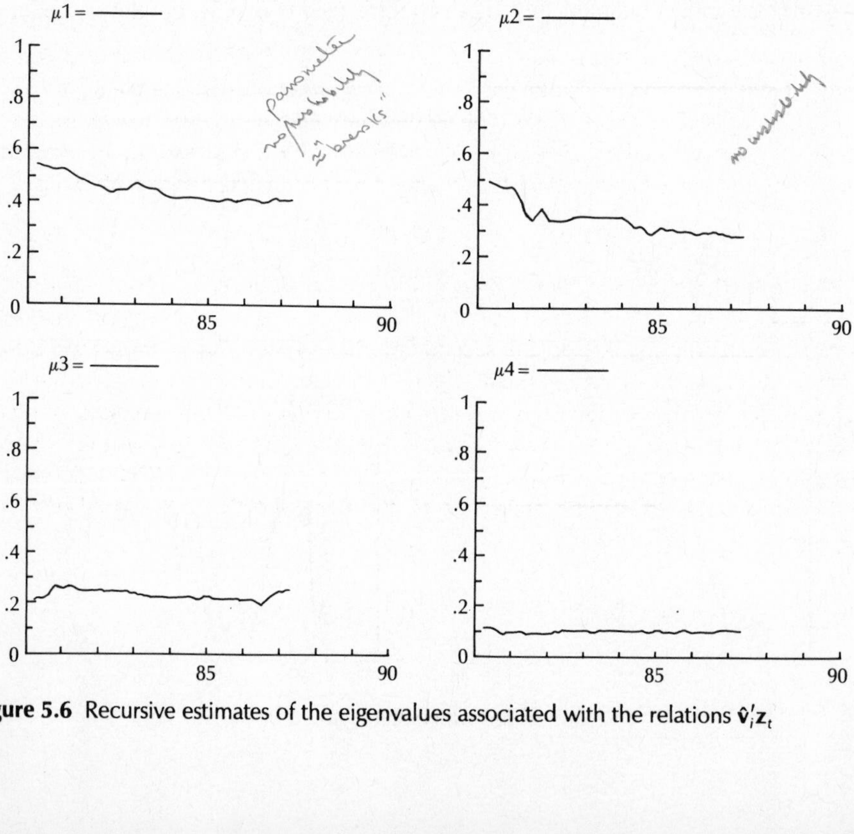

Figure 5.6 Recursive estimates of the eigenvalues associated with the relations $\hat{\mathbf{v}}_i'\mathbf{z}_t$

Box 5.3 Formal testing of the I(2) model using Johansen's two-step approach

There is an additional condition (associated with *just* the non-stationary $(n-r)$ part of the model) that (5.2) must satisfy for the model to contain only $I(1)$ variables:

$$\text{rank}\,(\boldsymbol{\alpha}_{\perp}'\boldsymbol{\Gamma}\boldsymbol{\beta}_{\perp}) = n-r \qquad \textit{when}\ \boldsymbol{\Gamma} = -\sum_{j=1}^{k} j\boldsymbol{\Gamma}_i \tag{5.3.1}$$

where $\boldsymbol{\Gamma}$ is the mean lag matrix of (5.2), while $\boldsymbol{\alpha}_{\perp}$ and $\boldsymbol{\beta}_{\perp}$ are $n \times (n-r)$ orthogonal matrices to $\boldsymbol{\alpha}$ and $\boldsymbol{\beta}$ such that $\boldsymbol{\alpha}_{\perp}'\boldsymbol{\alpha} = \mathbf{0}$ and $\boldsymbol{\beta}_{\perp}'\boldsymbol{\beta} = \mathbf{0}$. If this condition is met, then the non-stationary part of the model comprises $(n-r)$ linearly independent $I(1)$ relations, which can be added to the r linearly independent stationary relations contained in the reduced rank matrix $\boldsymbol{\Pi}$ $(= \boldsymbol{\alpha\beta}')$. If the condition is not met then $(\boldsymbol{\alpha}_{\perp}'\boldsymbol{\Gamma}\boldsymbol{\beta}_{\perp})$ has a reduced rank of $s_1 < (n-r)$ and the overall model will contain r cointegration relations, s_1 common $I(1)$ trends and $s_2 = (n-r-s_1)$ common $I(2)$ trends. The problem now becomes one of separating out the three dimensions of the model.

First, note that when $I(2)$ trends are present the appropriate VECM model is the second-differenced version akin to (5.2):

$$\Delta^2\mathbf{z}_t = \boldsymbol{\Gamma}\Delta\mathbf{z}_{t-1} + \boldsymbol{\Gamma}_1^*\Delta^2\mathbf{z}_{t-1} + \ldots + \boldsymbol{\Gamma}_{k-2}^*\Delta^2\mathbf{z}_{t-k+2} + \boldsymbol{\Pi}\mathbf{z}_{t-k} + \mathbf{u}_t \tag{5.3.2}$$

Johansen (1994) proposes a two-step procedure to determine the dimensions of r, s_1 and s_2. The first step is to proceed as in the case of the standard $I(1)$ model and obtain estimates of $\hat{r}$, $\hat{\boldsymbol{\alpha}}$ and $\hat{\boldsymbol{\beta}}$, that is, in terms of testing for cointegration rank, this step uses a reduced rank regression procedure based on (5.2) in order to determine the number of cointegration relations in the model. The second step amounts to determining the rank of $(\boldsymbol{\alpha}_{\perp}'\boldsymbol{\Gamma}\boldsymbol{\beta}_{\perp})$, which is conditional on having estimates of $\hat{\boldsymbol{\alpha}}$ and $\hat{\boldsymbol{\beta}}$, and uses a reduced rank regression procedure based on (5.3.2) after it has been multiplied through by $\boldsymbol{\alpha}_{\perp}'$:

$$\boldsymbol{\alpha}_{\perp}'\Delta^2\mathbf{z}_t = \boldsymbol{\alpha}_{\perp}'\boldsymbol{\Gamma}\Delta\mathbf{z}_{t-1} + \boldsymbol{\alpha}_{\perp}'\boldsymbol{\Gamma}_1^*\Delta^2\mathbf{z}_{t-1} + \ldots + \boldsymbol{\alpha}_{\perp}'\boldsymbol{\Gamma}_{k-2}^*\Delta^2\mathbf{z}_{t-k+2} + \boldsymbol{\alpha}_{\perp}'\mathbf{u}_t \tag{5.3.3}$$

Note that the term involving the stationary long-run relations $\boldsymbol{\Pi}\mathbf{z}_{t-k}$, has dropped out since $\boldsymbol{\alpha}_{\perp}'\boldsymbol{\Pi} = (\boldsymbol{\alpha}_{\perp}'\boldsymbol{\alpha})\boldsymbol{\beta}' = \mathbf{0}$, and (5.3.3) comprises an $(n-r) \times (n-r)$ dimensional system of equations in only first- and second-order differences. That is, the second step only operates on the non-stationary part of the model, and from it we can determine s_1, the rank of $(\boldsymbol{\alpha}_{\perp}'\boldsymbol{\Gamma}\boldsymbol{\beta}_{\perp})$. In fact, the reduced rank analysis of (5.3.3) provides $(n-r)$ eigenvalues $\hat{\mu}_1 > \hat{\mu}_2 > \ldots > \hat{\mu}_{n-r}$ which can be used to test the null hypothesis that there are at most s_1 common $I(1)$ trends (and thus $s_2 = (n-r-s_1)$ common $I(2)$ trends) using a likelihood ratio test statistic equivalent to the trace statistic in the standard $I(1)$ approach:

$$Q_{r,s_1} = -T\sum_{i=s+1}^{n-r} \log(1-\hat{\lambda}_i) \qquad s = 0, 1, 2, \ldots, n-r-1 \tag{5.3.4}$$

→

Table 5.3.1 The results of the $I(2)$ analysis of the UK money-demand data

r		Q_{r,s_1}			$Q_r = \lambda_{trace}$	λ_{trace} (0.95)	$p - r$
0	108.46	57.97	14.68	4.39	77.54	47.18	4
	$s_1=0$	$s_1=1$	$s_1=2$	$s_1=3$			
1		62.32	12.20	4.07	30.50	29.51	3
		$s_1=0$	$s_1=1$	$s_1=2$			
2			24.89	5.76	12.35	15.20	2
			$s_1=0$	$s_1=1$			
3				0.29	0.15	3.96	1
				$s_1=0$			
Q_r (0.95)	47.18	29.51	15.20	3.96			
$p - r - s_1$	4	3	2	1	0		

Source: Johansen (1992b).

Note, this tests for the rank s_1 conditional on the value of r, and thus tests are carried out after having determined the number of cointegration vectors in the model.[28] The critical values are the same as those given in Osterwald-Lenum (1992), since Johansen has shown that Q_{r,s_1} and λ_{trace} have the same asymptotic distributions.

As an example, of the $I(2)$ approach, Johansen (1992b) uses the two-step reduced rank regression procedure and seasonally adjusted UK money-demand data to obtain the results presented in Table 5.3.1. Each row of test statistics involving Q_{r,s_1} has been obtained after setting r (i.e., the rank of $\mathbf{\Pi}$), thus for $r = 0$, the options available for testing in the non-stationary part of the model are from 0 to 3 common $I(1)$ trends (or, reading along the last row of the table, from 4 to 0 common $I(2)$ trends). Thus, we start by determining r on the basis of the trace test statistics in the Q_r column. In fact, it is possible to reject the null that $r = 1$ (since $\lambda_{trace} = 30.5 > 29.51$), but only just, and Johansen preferred to accept this hypothesis on the basis of the power of the test and other evidence. Having chosen $r = 1$, allowing for at most three non-stationary columns in $\boldsymbol{\beta}$, we now wish to test for the rank of the non-stationary part of the model. Starting with the null that $s_1 = 0$, we compare the Q_{r,s_1} statistic of 62.32 with its critical value of 29.51 (in the penultimate row of the table), and reject this hypothesis. Next, we test the null that $s_1 = 1$, which we cannot reject at the 5 per cent significance level. This suggests that the model comprises a single common $I(1)$ trend and s_2 $(= p - r - s_1)$ common $I(2)$ trends. However, this is a borderline case, and can be compared with the next borderline case that we can reject the null that $s_1 = 2$, implying that all three non-stationary vectors are common $I(1)$ trends. The results are somewhat ambiguous, and Johansen argues that economic reasoning would suggest that a plausible outcome is at most one common $I(2)$ variable in the model.

not yet available in software packages such as *Cats* and *PcFiml* (although it is planned to extend the former to include the $I(2)$ model). So, presently, the issue of whether there are $I(2)$ variables in the system requires a certain degree of subjective judgement. If there are $I(2)$ variables and the rank test procedure outlined above for the $I(1)$ model indicates that there are cointegration relationships, then these are valid but they are not necessarily stationary (which has implications for the next stage of econometric modelling, e.g., estimating dynamic error-correction models which include these cointegration relationships). In such a situation, as noted above, it is necessary to replace the $I(2)$ variables with $I(1)$ alternatives through some form of differencing, or it is necessary to use the (as yet not easily implemented) approach for $I(2)$ variables developed by Johansen (1994).

Lastly, having determined how many cointegration vectors there are, it is now necessary to consider whether these are unique and consequently whether they tell us anything about the structural economic relationships underlying the long-run model. The PPP and UIP model (see Box 5.2) appears to have two cointegration vectors (i.e., the first two rows of $\hat{\boldsymbol{\beta}}'$, since these correspond to the largest eigenvalues and thus have the highest correlation with the stationary part of the model). As Johansen and Juselius (1992) point out, the first vector seems to contain the assumed PPP relation in the first three variables and the second to contain the interest rate differential in the last two variables. However, when interpreting the cointegration vectors obtained from the Johansen approach it needs to be stressed that what the reduced rank regression procedure provides is information on how many unique cointegration vectors *span* the cointegration space, while any linear combination of the stationary vectors is itself a stationary vector and thus the estimates produced for any particular column in $\boldsymbol{\beta}$ are not necessarily unique. This can easily be seen by noting that $\boldsymbol{\alpha\beta}' = \boldsymbol{\alpha\xi}^{-1}\boldsymbol{\xi\beta}' = \boldsymbol{\alpha}^{*}\boldsymbol{\beta}'^{*}$, where $\boldsymbol{\xi}$ is any $r \times r$ non-singular matrix. Thus, if we can find a $\boldsymbol{\xi}$-matrix that transforms $\boldsymbol{\beta}$ into $\boldsymbol{\beta}^{*}$, we still have the same unique number of cointegration vectors, but the vectors themselves are not unique. This is very important, and it would be a major limitation if we could not determine unique structural relationships for each cointegration vector (assuming such uniqueness exists). Fortunately, it is possible to test for unique vectors (see below) as well as to test more generally to see if particular relationships span the cointegration space (e.g., does the $(1, -1, -1, *, *)'$ vector exist anywhere within the space spanned by the two vectors comprising the PPP model).[29]

Deterministic components in the multivariate model

In discussing the formulation of the dynamic model, the question of whether an intercept and trend should enter the short- and/or long-run model was raised. For notational simplicity assuming that $k=2$, and omitting the other deterministic variables in $\mathbf{D}_t$, we can expand the VECM (equation (5.2)) to include the various options that need to be considered:

$$\Delta z_t = \Gamma_1 \Delta z_{t-1} + \alpha \begin{bmatrix} \beta \\ \mu_1 \\ \delta_1 \end{bmatrix} \tilde{z}_{t-k} + \alpha_\perp \mu_2 \, \delta + \alpha_\perp \delta_2 t + u_t \qquad (5.6)$$

Model #1

where $\tilde{z}'_{t-k} = (z'_{t-k}, 1, t)$. Although it is possible to specify a model where $\delta_1 = \delta_2 = \mu_1 = \mu_2 = 0$, that is, there are no deterministic components in the data or in the cointegration relations, this is unlikely to occur in practice, especially as the intercept is generally needed to account for the units of measurement of the variables in z_t.[30] Three models can realistically be considered:

Model #2
CIMEAN
*Table 1**

- If there are no linear trends in the levels of the data, such that the first-differenced series have a zero mean, then $\delta_1 = \delta_2 = \mu_2 = 0$. Thus, the intercept is restricted to the long-run model (i.e., the cointegration space) to account for the units of measurement of the variables in z_t. The critical values for this model are taken from Table (1*) in Osterwald-Lenum (1992). For consistency with the *Cats* program, we shall label this Model 2.[31] *"Cimean"*

Model #3
Drift
Table 1

- If there are linear trends in the levels of the data, then we specify a model that allows the non-stationary relationships in the model to drift, so $\delta_1 = \delta_2 = 0$. However, it is assumed that the intercept in the cointegration vectors is cancelled by the intercept in the short-run model, leaving only an intercept in the short-run model (i.e., in estimating (5.6), μ_1 combines with μ_2 to provide an overall intercept contained in the short-run model). The critical values for this Model (3) are in Table 1 in Osterwald-Lenum (1992). *"Drift"*

Model #4
CI Drift
*Table 2**

- If there are no quadratic trends in the levels of the data then there will be no time trend in the short-run model, but if there is some long-run linear growth which the model cannot account for, given the chosen data-set, then we allow for a linear trend in the cointegration vectors. Thus, the only restriction imposed is $\delta_2 = 0$ and the cointegration space includes time as a trend-stationary variable, to take account of unknown exogenous growth (e.g., technical progress).[32,33] For Model (4) the critical values are available in Table (2*) in Osterwald-Lenum (1992). *CI drift*

Another model (Model 5 in *Cats*) that could be considered is to extend Model 4 to allow for linear trends in the short-run model determining Δz_t, and thus quadratic trends in z_t. Thus δ_2 is also unrestricted, although this is economically difficult to justify (especially since if the variables are entered in logs, this would imply an implausible ever-increasing or decreasing rate of change).

The question of which model (2–4) should be used is not easily answered *a priori*; the vector z_t could be plotted in levels (and first differences) and examined for trends so that variables such as interest rates, which show no indication to drift upwards or downwards over time, might require the intercept to be restricted to lie in the cointegration space. However, plots of the data would provide little information on whether Model 4 should be used, since this choice arises when the available data

Table 5.5 Determining cointegration rank and the model for the deterministic components: UK real demand for money data (1963:1–1989:2)

H_0:	r	$n-r$	Model 2	Model 3	Model 4
λ_{max} *test:*					
	0	4	77.76 →	77.74	78.13
	1	3	35.10	13.41*	21.64
	2	2	7.58	7.23	7.83
	3	1	5.93	0.13	→ 6.10
Trace test:					
	0	4	126.37 →	98.51	113.70
	1	3	48.61	20.77*	35.57
	2	2	13.51	7.36	13.93
	3	1	5.93	0.13	→ 6.10

cannot account for other unmeasured factors that induce autonomous growth in (some or all of the variables) in $\mathbf{z}_t$. Thus, Johansen (1992c) suggests the need to test the joint hypothesis of both the rank order and the deterministic components, based on the so-called Pantula principle. That is, all three models are estimated and the results are presented from the most restrictive alternative (i.e., $r=0$ and Model 2) through to the least restrictive alternative (i.e., $r=n-1$ and Model 4).[34] The test procedure is then to move through from the most restrictive model and at each stage to compare the trace (or λ_{max}) test statistic to its critical value and only stop the first time the null hypothesis is not rejected.

As an example, consider the UK real money-demand model, with seasonally unadjusted data ($k=4$ and seasonal dummies are included in $\mathbf{D}_t$). The results from estimating Models 2–4 and then applying the Pantula principle are given in Table 5.5. Starting with the most restrictive model (and concentrating on the λ_{max} test statistic), the rank test statistic of 77.76 exceeds its 95 per cent critical value of 28.14. Then proceed to the next most restrictive model (keeping to the same value of r), as shown by the arrow in the table, which again exceeds its critical value in Osterwald-Lenum (op. cit., Table 1). Moving through the table row by row from left-to-right, the first time the null is not rejected is indicated by the $*$. Thus, we would accept that there is one cointegration vector and there are deterministic trends in the levels of the data (Model 3). Looking at Figure 3.1, this choice of Model 3 may not be obvious, given that real money supply, real total domestic expenditure and the inflation and interest rates are not strongly trending for most of the period covered.

Having now considered the full set of $I(0)$ variables to enter $\mathbf{D}_t$ (i.e., dummies as well as constant and trend components), we can proceed to testing restrictions on the $\boldsymbol{\alpha}$ and $\boldsymbol{\beta}$. First, we test for weak exogeneity, and then for linear hypotheses on the cointegration relations. This leads to tests for unique cointegration vectors, and finally joint tests involving restrictions on $\boldsymbol{\alpha}$ and $\boldsymbol{\beta}$.

Testing for weak exogeneity

α : speed of
Adj b
diseq.

In the VECM, (5.2), it has been shown that the Π-matrix contains information on the long-run relationships, where $\Pi = \alpha\beta'$, and α represents the speed of adjustment to disequilibrium and β is a matrix of long-run coefficients. Furthermore, it was explained that if there are $r \leqslant (n-1)$ cointegration vectors in β then this implies that the last $(n-r)$ columns of α are zero.[35] Thus the typical problem faced, of determining how many $r \leqslant (n-1)$ cointegration vectors exist in β, amounts to equivalently testing which columns of α are zero.

β : Lr coefficient

r : CI vectors

n-r : trend

Turning to the role of the non-zero columns of α, suppose that $r = 1$, and $z_t = [y_{1t}, y_{2t}, x_t]'$; then $\alpha = [\alpha_{11}, \alpha_{21}, \alpha_{31}]'$.[36] The first term in α represents the speed at which Δy_{1t}, the dependent variable in the first equation of the VECM, adjusts towards the single long-run cointegration relationship $(\beta_{11}y_{1t-1} + \beta_{21}y_{2t-1} + \beta_{31}x_{t-1})$, while α_{21} represents the speed at which Δy_{2t} adjusts, and α_{31} shows how fast Δx_t responds to the disequilibrium changes represented by the cointegration vector.[37] More generally, each of the r non-zero columns of α contain information on which cointegration vector enters which short-run equation, and on the speed of the short-run response to disequilibrium.

β : columns
      intercept
α : columns of
α' are zero

Taking things a step further, the presence of *all* zeros in row i of $\alpha_{ij}, j = 1, \dots, r$, indicates that the cointegration vectors in β do not enter the equation determining Δz_{it}. As is shown in Box 5.4, this means when estimating the parameters of the model (i.e., the $\Gamma_i, \Pi, \alpha, \beta$) there is no loss of information from *not* modelling the determinants of Δz_{it}; thus, this variable is weakly exogenous *to the system* and can enter on the right-hand side of the VECM. For example, suppose $z_t = [y_{1t}, y_{2t}, x_t]'$, and $r = 2$ (and for ease of exposition let $k = 2$); then repeating (4.16) by writing out the VECM in full gives:

3 × 2   say

$$
\begin{bmatrix} \Delta y_{1t} \\ \Delta y_{2t} \\ \Delta x_t \end{bmatrix} = \Gamma_1 \begin{bmatrix} \Delta y_{1t-1} \\ \Delta y_{2t-1} \\ \Delta x_{t-1} \end{bmatrix} + \begin{bmatrix} \alpha_{11} & \alpha_{12} \\ \alpha_{21} & \alpha_{22} \\ \alpha_{31} & \alpha_{32} \end{bmatrix} \begin{bmatrix} \beta_{11} & \beta_{21} & \beta_{31} \\ \beta_{12} & \beta_{22} & \beta_{32} \end{bmatrix} \begin{bmatrix} y_{1t-1} \\ y_{2t-1} \\ x_{t-1} \end{bmatrix}
\tag{5.7}
$$

If $\alpha_{3j} = 0$, $j = 1, 2$, then the equation for Δx_t contains no information about the long-run β since the cointegration relationships do not enter into this equation, and it is therefore valid to condition on the weakly exogenous variable x_t and proceed with the following partial version of the VECM:

$$
\Delta y_t = \Gamma_0 \Delta x_t + \tilde{\Gamma}_1 \Delta z_{t-1} + \alpha_1 \beta' z_{t-2} + \tilde{u}_t
\tag{5.8}
$$

where $y_t = [y_{1t}, y_{2t}]'$, and α_1 is equal to α with $\alpha_{31} = \alpha_{32} = 0$. Note, the weakly exogenous variable, x_t, remains in the long-run model (i.e., the cointegration vectors) although its short-run behaviour is not modelled because of its exclusion from the vector on the left-hand side of the equation.[38]

There are at least two potential advantages from estimating the multivariate model having conditioned on the weakly exogenous variables. In particular, if the weakly exogenous variables exhibit all the 'problematic' data features (see the earlier section

Box 5.4 Conditional and marginal models

If the vector $\mathbf{z}_t = [y_{1t}, y_{2t}, x_t]'$ is decomposed into $\mathbf{y}_t = [y_{1t}, y_{2t}]'$ and x_t, Johansen (1992b) shows that (5.3), ignoring $\mathbf{D}_t$, can be decomposed into the conditional model for $\mathbf{y}_t$ given x_t:

$$\Delta \mathbf{y}_t = \boldsymbol{\omega}\Delta x_t + (\boldsymbol{\Gamma}_{y1} - \boldsymbol{\omega}\boldsymbol{\Gamma}_{x1})\Delta \mathbf{z}_{t-1} + (\boldsymbol{\alpha}_y - \boldsymbol{\omega}\boldsymbol{\alpha}_x)\boldsymbol{\beta}'\mathbf{z}_{t-2} + \mathbf{u}_{yt} - \boldsymbol{\omega}\mathbf{u}_{xt} \tag{5.4.1}$$

and the marginal model for x_t:

$$\Delta x_t = \boldsymbol{\Gamma}_{x1}\Delta \mathbf{z}_{t-1} + \boldsymbol{\alpha}_x\boldsymbol{\beta}'\mathbf{z}_{t-2} + \mathbf{u}_{xt} \tag{5.4.2}$$

where $\boldsymbol{\omega} = \boldsymbol{\Omega}_{yx}\boldsymbol{\Omega}_{yx}^{-1}$. Note, estimating this model *as a system* is equivalent to estimating the full model, as can be seen by simply substituting (5.4.2) into (5.4.1). Also, all the cointegration relations $\boldsymbol{\beta}'\mathbf{z}_t$ enter into the marginal as well as the conditional models.

If $\boldsymbol{\alpha}_x = 0$ (i.e., the rows of $\boldsymbol{\alpha}$ corresponding to x_t are zero: $\alpha_{3j} = 0$ for $j = 1, 2$), then (5.4.1) and (5.4.2) reduce to:

$$\Delta \mathbf{y}_t = \omega\Delta x_t + (\boldsymbol{\Gamma}_{y1} - \boldsymbol{\omega}\boldsymbol{\Gamma}_{x1})\Delta \mathbf{z}_{t-1} + \boldsymbol{\alpha}_y\boldsymbol{\beta}'\mathbf{z}_{t-2} + \mathbf{u}_{yt} - \boldsymbol{\omega}\mathbf{u}_{xt} \tag{5.4.3}$$

and:

$$\Delta x_t = \boldsymbol{\Gamma}_{x1}\Delta \mathbf{z}_{t-1} + \mathbf{u}_{xt} \tag{5.4.4}$$

When this holds, x_t is said to be weakly exogenous with respect to $\boldsymbol{\beta}$ since, by the definition of weak exogeneity due to Engle, Hendry and Richard (1983), two necessary conditions are fulfilled. First, the parameters of interest (here $\boldsymbol{\beta}$) are functions only of the parameters in the conditional model, because $\boldsymbol{\beta}$ now only enters (5.4.3). Second, the parameters in the conditional and marginal models must be variation-free in that they do not have joint restrictions, and this is guaranteed by the properties of the Gaussian distribution.

Lastly, note that (5.4.4) shows that both $\Delta \mathbf{y}_{t-1}$ and Δx_{t-1} determine Δx_t, since $\Delta \mathbf{z}_{t-1}$ features on the right hand side of the equation. Thus, x_t is only weakly exogenous with respect to $\boldsymbol{\beta}$. However, if x_t is not Granger-caused by $\mathbf{y}_t$, then x_t is strongly exogenous with respect to $\boldsymbol{\beta}$. This is true if the coefficients of $\Delta \mathbf{y}_{t-1}$ are zero such that we can replace $\Delta \mathbf{z}_{t-1}$ with Δx_{t-1} in (5.4.4).

on determining the elements in $\mathbf{D}_t$), then conditioning on these variables will usually ensure that the rest of the system determining $\Delta \mathbf{y}_t$ has better stochastic properties (in terms of the residuals of the short-run equations being free of problems). This is linked to the second advantage, which becomes apparent when the short-run model is also of interest, since the number of short-run variables in the VECM will be reduced. However, it is not prudent to start with the modelling of a conditional system. Although the estimates of $\boldsymbol{\alpha}$ and $\boldsymbol{\beta}$ are the same as when estimating the full model with weak exogeneity restrictions on $\boldsymbol{\alpha}$, the asymptotic distributions of the rank test statistics are different and as yet are not as widely available as are those for the full model.[39] More importantly, though, we will usually want to test for weak exogeneity in the full model rather than to assume it. Thus, conditional models are usually estimated after determining the restrictions to be placed on $\boldsymbol{\alpha}$ (and $\boldsymbol{\beta}$).

So far, weak exogeneity has been discussed in terms of $\mathbf{x}_t$ being weakly exogenous in every cointegration vector. This is the usual way in which exogeneity and endogeneity are established, with variables classified on the basis of their role in all the equations in the system. However, it is possible to consider whether $\mathbf{x}_t$ is weakly exogenous with respect to the parameters of a particular cointegration vector. Thus, for instance, there may be two cointegration vectors, and tests for weak exogeneity may involve hypotheses that some vector $\mathbf{x}_{1t}$ is weakly exogenous with respect to the parameters of the first cointegration vector, while a second vector $\mathbf{x}_{2t}$ (which may or may not be the same as $\mathbf{x}_{1t}$) is weakly exogenous with respect to the parameters of the second cointegration vector. Indeed, it is possible to test each α_{ij} $(i=1, \ldots, n;\ j=1, \ldots, r)$ separately and to talk about the corresponding variable x_{it} being weakly exogenous with respect to the cointegration vector j. This is valid, as long as weak exogeneity is clearly defined with respect to a single cointegration vector (and not to the full model which may comprise more than one long-run relationship among the variables in the model), since accepting the hypothesis that some $\alpha_{ij}=0$ amounts to finding that the particular cointegration vector j does not enter into the short-run equation determining the associated variable Δx_{it}.[40]

It is also important to stress that testing for weak exogeneity in a particular cointegration vector presumes that this vector represents a structural long-run relationship between the variables in the model and not a linear combination,[41] in which case $\boldsymbol{\alpha}$ will also be a linear combination of the speed-of-adjustment coefficients, and testing for weak exogeneity in this context is not particularly meaningful. This suggests that in practice testing for restrictions involving $\boldsymbol{\alpha}$ should ideally be done alongside testing for restrictions that identify $\boldsymbol{\beta}$. We shall return to this later.

It is usually not valid to condition the VECM on x_{it} unless this variable is weakly exogenous in the full system, although there are exceptions to this rule. For instance, suppose $n=4$ and that one of the cointegration vectors, say the first one, has associated with it the following: $\boldsymbol{\alpha}'_{i1}=[*, 0, 0, 0]$, where the $*$ denotes an unrestricted parameter. Then all the variables in the cointegration vector (except the first, y_{1t}) are weakly exogenous with respect to $\boldsymbol{\beta}_1$ and if we are only interested in this first cointegration relationship, then it is valid to abandon the multivariate model and move to a single equation approach and condition on the weakly exogenous variables (i.e., they move to the right-hand side of the equation and are contemporaneous with the dependent variable).[42] If the other cointegration vectors do not enter the short-run model determining Δy_{1t} (which will be true when $\boldsymbol{\alpha}'_{i.j}=[0, *, *, *]$ for $j \neq 1$) then y_{1t} can be said to be weakly exogenous in these other cointegration vectors, and it is appropriate to concentrate on the first vector of interest only. However, if other cointegration vectors *do* enter the model determining Δy_{1t} we might not want to move to the single equation approach if modelling the system might be appropriate (see the discussion of structural VAR modelling in the next chapter).

To test for weak exogeneity in the system as a whole requires a test of the hypothesis that H: $\alpha_{ij}=0$ for $j=1, \ldots, r$, that is, row i contains zeros. This test is conducted by placing row restrictions on $\boldsymbol{\alpha}$, to give a new restricted model, and then using a likelihood ratio test involving the restricted and unrestricted models to ascertain whether the restrictions are valid (see the earlier discussion of testing for reduced rank for details). The form of the restrictions is determined by specifying an $(n \times m)$ matrix $\mathbf{A}$ of linear restrictions[43] where $(n-m)$ equals the number of row restrictions imposed on $\boldsymbol{\alpha}$, such that the null hypothesis amounts to testing whether $\boldsymbol{\alpha}=\mathbf{A}\boldsymbol{\alpha}_0$. Imposing the restrictions reduces $\boldsymbol{\alpha}$ to an $(m \times n)$ matrix $\boldsymbol{\alpha}_0$. It is also useful to note that these same restrictions in $\mathbf{A}$ could be imposed by specifying an $(n \times (n-m))$ matrix $\mathbf{B}$ such that $\mathbf{B}'\boldsymbol{\alpha}=0$. Clearly, $\mathbf{B}$ must be orthogonal to $\mathbf{A}$, that is, $\mathbf{B}'\mathbf{A}=\mathbf{A}_{\perp}'\mathbf{A}=0$. Both the matrices $\mathbf{A}$ and $\mathbf{B}$ are used in the mechanics of restricting the Johansen reduced rank regression model, thereby obtaining $(n-1)$ new eigenvalues $\hat{\lambda}_i^*$ for the restricted model which are used in the following LR test statistic:[44]

$$-2 \log (Q) = T\sum_{i=1}^{r} \log \left\{ \frac{(1-\hat{\lambda}_i^*)}{(1-\hat{\lambda}_i)} \right\} \tag{5.9}$$

This test statistic is compared with the χ^2-distribution with $(r \times (n-m))$ degrees of freedom in order to obtain the significance level for rejecting the null hypothesis. As with the testing procedure for reduced rank, it has been suggested that the above LR statistic should be corrected for degrees of freedom, which involves replacing T, the sample size, by $T-(l/n)$, where l is the number of parameters estimated in the reduced rank regression model.[45] Psaradakis (1994) found, on the basis of Monte Carlo testing, that such a modification improved the small-sample behaviour of the LR statistics.

The first example of testing for weak exogeneity to be considered is the UK money-demand model, with seasonally unadjusted data ($k=4$ and seasonal dummies are included in $\mathbf{D}_t$). It has already been established (Table 5.5 above) that it is possible to accept that there is one cointegration vector (and deterministic trends in the levels of the data). The estimates of $\boldsymbol{\alpha}$ and $\boldsymbol{\beta}$ obtained from applying the Johansen technique (using the *Cats* program) are presented in Box 5.5; note, only the normalised $\boldsymbol{\beta}$ (and consequently $\boldsymbol{\alpha}$) corresponding to $r=1$ is presented. Since three row restrictions are imposed on $\boldsymbol{\alpha}$, the dimensions of the matrices are $\mathbf{A}(4 \times 1)$ and $\mathbf{B}(4 \times 3)$. The test of H: $\alpha_{i.1}=0$ for $i=2, 3, 4$, that is y, Δp and R are weakly exogenous, requires:

$$\mathbf{A} = \begin{bmatrix} 1 \\ 0 \\ 0 \\ 0 \end{bmatrix} \quad \mathbf{B} = \begin{bmatrix} 0 & 0 & 0 \\ 1 & 0 & 0 \\ 0 & 1 & 0 \\ 0 & 0 & 1 \end{bmatrix} \tag{5.10}$$

Box 5.5 Output from *Cats* for the UK money-demand model

Eigenv.	λ-max	Trace	H_0: r=	n−r=
0.5369	77.74	98.51	0	4
0.1243	13.41	20.77	1	3
0.0691	7.23	7.36	2	2
0.0013	0.13	0.13	3	1

<u>*Normalised*</u> (The matrices based on 1 cointegration vector)

β′

m−p	y	Δp	R
1.000	−1.073	7.325	6.808

α	T-VALUES FOR **α**
−0.160	−9.367
−0.019	−1.205
0.011	1.433
0.005	0.337

<u>Testing Restrictions on α</u>

The LR test, $\chi^2(3) = 4.05$, p-value = 0.26

β′

m−p	y	Δp	R
1.000	−1.097	7.780	6.835

α	T-VALUES FOR **α**
−0.150	−8.992
0.000	0.000
0.000	0.000
0.000	0.000

The largest new eigenvalue $\hat{\lambda}_1^*$ for the restricted model, along with $\hat{\lambda}_1$ from the unrestricted model, are used to compute:

$$-2\log(Q) = 101\log\left\{\frac{(1-0.5179)}{(1-0.5369)}\right\} = 4.05 \tag{5.11}$$

which does not exceed $\chi^2(3) = 7.81$. If the LR statistic is corrected for degrees of freedom, which involves replacing T by $T - (l/n)$ in (5.9), then LR = 3.30, which again does not reject the null.

Separate tests on each of the adjustment parameters could also be conducted; for instance, testing H: $\alpha_{41}=0$ requires

$$\mathbf{A}=\begin{bmatrix}1&0&0\\0&1&0\\0&0&1\\0&0&0\end{bmatrix}\qquad \mathbf{B}=\begin{bmatrix}0\\0\\0\\1\end{bmatrix} \tag{5.12}$$

since there is only one restriction imposed on $\boldsymbol{\alpha}$. With the *Cats* program, it is not necessary to conduct these individual tests, which are distributed under the χ^2-distribution with one degree of freedom, since t-values associated with each α_{ij} are automatically reported (see Box 5.5).[46] Initially, before testing any restrictions on $\boldsymbol{\alpha}$, the t-values would have suggested that weak exogeneity for y, Δp and R was likely to hold. Since it does, this confirms that it is valid to condition on these variables and use a single equation estimator of the cointegration vector. Comparison of the Johansen multivariate estimator of $\boldsymbol{\beta}'_{\text{full}}=[-1.0, 1.097, -7.780, -6.835]$ with the estimate in (4.13) of $\boldsymbol{\beta}'_{\text{part}}=[-1.0, 1.052, -7.332, -6.871]$ shows that the two approaches are equivalent.

As a second example of testing for weak exogeneity, consider the PPP and UIP model of Johansen and Juselius (1992), where $n=5$ and $r=2$. Looking at the results in Box 5.2, the t-values on the α_{ij} when $r=2$ (i.e., the first two columns of $\boldsymbol{\alpha}$) suggest that either or both of the following hypotheses might be valid: H: $\alpha_{2.j}=0$ for $j=1,2$, and H: $\alpha_{3.j}=0$ for $j=1,2$. The first test involves:

$$\mathbf{A}=\begin{bmatrix}1&0&0&0\\0&0&0&0\\0&1&0&0\\0&0&1&0\\0&0&0&1\end{bmatrix}\qquad \mathbf{B}=\begin{bmatrix}0\\1\\0\\0\\0\end{bmatrix} \tag{5.13}$$

since only one *row* restriction is imposed on $\boldsymbol{\alpha}$, although $r=2$. The largest new eigenvalues for the restricted model along with $\hat{\lambda}_i$ from the unrestricted model are used to compute:

$$-2\log(Q)=60\log\left\{\frac{(1-0.4002)(1-0.2854)}{(1-0.4067)(1-0.2854)}\right\}=0.658 \tag{5.14}$$

which does not exceed $\chi^2(2)$.[47] If the LR statistic is corrected for degrees of freedom, which involves replacing T by $T-(l/n)$ in (5.14), then LR $=0.49$, which again does not reject the null. The second test is very similar and simply requires swapping around the second and third rows in (5.13). The joint test that H: $\alpha_{2.j}=\alpha_{3.j}=0$ for $j=1,2$ imposes two row restrictions on $\boldsymbol{\alpha}$:

$$\mathbf{A}=\begin{bmatrix}1&0&0\\0&0&0\\0&0&0\\0&1&0\\0&0&1\end{bmatrix}\qquad \mathbf{B}=\begin{bmatrix}0&0\\1&0\\0&1\\0&0\\0&0\end{bmatrix} \tag{5.15}$$

and results in the two new eigenvalues for this version of the restricted model along with λ_i from the unrestricted model, giving a value for *LR*:

$$-2\log(Q) = 60\log\left\{\frac{(1-0.3743)(1-0.2853)}{(1-0.4067)(1-0.2854)}\right\} = 3.201 \quad (5.16)$$

which does not exceed $\chi^2(4)$. Thus, on the basis of these tests, both p_2 (trade weighted foreign wholesale price index) and e (the UK effective exchange rate), are weakly exogenous.

Finally, if we wish to test restrictions on each α_{ij} $(i = 1, \ldots, n;\ j = 1, \ldots, r)$ separately when $r > 1$, or only a subset of $\boldsymbol{\alpha}$ which does not involve the restriction that row i contains all zeros, then the above formulation of the **A**- and **B**-matrices is not general enough. To impose more general restrictions requires the use of a testing procedure such as H: $\{\boldsymbol{\alpha} = f(\boldsymbol{\alpha}^{u})\}$ where $\boldsymbol{\alpha}$ is expressed as a function of the unrestricted elements in $\boldsymbol{\alpha}$. This function may even be non-linear. The software package *PcFiml* (version 8) makes use of a switching algorithm that can solve this kind of problem using a numerical optimisation procedure (see Doornik and Hendry, 1994, for further details).[48]

Testing for linear hypotheses on cointegration relations

Earlier it was stated that having determined how many cointegration vectors there are, it is necessary to consider whether these are unique and consequently whether they tell us anything about the structural economic relationships underlying the long-run model. Since the Johansen reduced rank regression procedure only determines how many unique cointegration vectors *span* the cointegration space, and since any linear combination of the stationary vectors is also a stationary vector, the estimates produced for any particular column in $\boldsymbol{\beta}$ are not necessarily unique. Therefore, it will be necessary to impose restrictions motivated by economic arguments (e.g., that some of the β_{ij} are zero, or that homogeneity restrictions are needed such as $\beta_{1j} = -\beta_{2j}$) and then test whether the columns of $\boldsymbol{\beta}$ are identified. Testing for identification will be followed up in the next section.

Hypotheses about $\boldsymbol{\beta}$ can be formulated as follows:

$$H_{\beta}: \boldsymbol{\beta} = (\mathbf{H}_1\boldsymbol{\varphi}_1, \mathbf{H}_2\boldsymbol{\varphi}_2, \ldots, \mathbf{H}_r\boldsymbol{\varphi}_r) \quad (5.17)$$

where the matrices $\mathbf{H}_1, \ldots, \mathbf{H}_r$, expressing the linear economic hypotheses to be tested on each of the r cointegration relations, are $(n \times s_i)$ matrices, and each $\boldsymbol{\varphi}_i$ is an $(s_i \times 1)$ vector of parameters to be estimated in the ith cointegration relation. Since there are s_i unrestricted parameters in $\boldsymbol{\beta}_i$, then $\mathbf{H}_i$ imposes k_i restrictions such that $(k_i + s_i = n)$. Note that, in a similar fashion to testing restrictions on $\boldsymbol{\alpha}$, it is possible to impose the same restrictions in $\mathbf{H}_i$ by specifying an $(n \times k_i)$ matrix $\mathbf{R}_i$ such that $\mathbf{R}_i'\boldsymbol{\beta}_i = 0$. Since this is equivalent to $\boldsymbol{\beta}_i = \mathbf{H}_i\boldsymbol{\varphi}_i$, this implies that $\mathbf{R}_i$ is orthogonal to $\mathbf{H}_i$ and consequently $\mathbf{R}_i'\mathbf{H}_i = \mathbf{R}_i'\mathbf{R}_{i\perp} = 0$. In practice, it is only necessary to use one of the forms for imposing restrictions,[49] although both will be needed when testing uniqueness since identification depends upon finding the rank of $(\mathbf{R}_i'\mathbf{H}_j)$ for $i \neq j$. To illustrate the way in which $\mathbf{R}_i$ and $\mathbf{H}_i$ are formulated, Table 5.6 presents examples from Johansen and Juselius (1994) associated with the following two versions of $\boldsymbol{\beta}$ of dimension (6×3), involving various homogeneity and zero restrictions:

$$\boldsymbol{\beta}^1 = \begin{bmatrix} a & 0 & 0 \\ * & * & * \\ -a & * & * \\ 1 & 1 & 0 \\ 0 & -1 & 1 \\ * & * & * \end{bmatrix} \qquad \boldsymbol{\beta}^2 = \begin{bmatrix} a & 0 & 0 \\ 1 & 0 & 0 \\ -a & 0 & * \\ 0 & 1 & 0 \\ 0 & -1 & 1 \\ * & 0 & * \end{bmatrix} \tag{5.18}$$

The restrictions placed on the vectors in the first example are as follows: the two restrictions on $\boldsymbol{\beta}_1$ comprise a homogeneity constraint $(\beta_{11} = -\beta_{31})$ and $\beta_{51} = 0$. The cointegration vector is normalised by setting $\beta_{41} = 1$ which is not a constraint. Since

Table 5.6 Specifying restriction on β

$\boldsymbol{\beta}1 = (\mathbf{H}_1\boldsymbol{\varphi}_1, \mathbf{H}_2\boldsymbol{\varphi}_2, \mathbf{H}_3\boldsymbol{\varphi}_3)$

$$\mathbf{H}_1 = \begin{bmatrix} 0 & 0 & 0 & 0 \\ 0 & 1 & 0 & 0 \\ -1 & 0 & 0 & 0 \\ 0 & 0 & 1 & 0 \\ 0 & 0 & 0 & 0 \\ 0 & 0 & 0 & 1 \end{bmatrix} \qquad \mathbf{H}_2 = \begin{bmatrix} 0 & 0 & 0 & 0 \\ 1 & 0 & 0 & 0 \\ 0 & 1 & 0 & 0 \\ 0 & 0 & 1 & 0 \\ 0 & 0 & -1 & 0 \\ 0 & 0 & 0 & 1 \end{bmatrix} \qquad \mathbf{H}_3 = \begin{bmatrix} 0 & 0 & 0 & 0 \\ 1 & 0 & 0 & 0 \\ 0 & 1 & 0 & 0 \\ 0 & 0 & 0 & 0 \\ 0 & 0 & 1 & 0 \\ 0 & 0 & 0 & 1 \end{bmatrix}$$

$$\mathbf{R}_1 = \begin{bmatrix} 1 & 0 \\ 0 & 0 \\ 1 & 0 \\ 0 & 0 \\ 0 & 1 \\ 0 & 0 \end{bmatrix} \qquad \mathbf{R}_2 = \begin{bmatrix} 0 & 1 \\ 0 & 0 \\ 0 & 0 \\ 1 & 0 \\ 1 & 0 \\ 0 & 0 \end{bmatrix} \qquad \mathbf{R}_3 = \begin{bmatrix} 1 & 0 \\ 0 & 0 \\ 0 & 0 \\ 0 & 1 \\ 0 & 0 \\ 0 & 0 \end{bmatrix}$$

$\boldsymbol{\beta}^2 = (\mathbf{H}_1\boldsymbol{\varphi}_1, \mathbf{H}_2\boldsymbol{\varphi}_2, \mathbf{H}_3\boldsymbol{\varphi}_3)$

$$\mathbf{H}_1 = \begin{bmatrix} 1 & 0 & 0 \\ 0 & 1 & 0 \\ -1 & 0 & 0 \\ 0 & 0 & 0 \\ 0 & 0 & 0 \\ 0 & 0 & 1 \end{bmatrix} \qquad \mathbf{H}_2 = \begin{bmatrix} 0 \\ 0 \\ 0 \\ 1 \\ -1 \\ 0 \end{bmatrix} \qquad \mathbf{H}_3 = \begin{bmatrix} 0 & 0 & 0 \\ 0 & 0 & 0 \\ 1 & 0 & 0 \\ 0 & 0 & 0 \\ 0 & 1 & 0 \\ 0 & 0 & 1 \end{bmatrix}$$

$$\mathbf{R}_1 = \begin{bmatrix} 1 & 0 & 0 \\ 0 & 0 & 0 \\ 1 & 0 & 0 \\ 0 & 1 & 0 \\ 0 & 0 & 1 \\ 0 & 0 & 0 \end{bmatrix} \qquad \mathbf{R}_2 = \begin{bmatrix} 0 & 1 & 0 & 0 & 0 \\ 0 & 0 & 1 & 0 & 0 \\ 0 & 0 & 0 & 1 & 0 \\ 1 & 0 & 0 & 0 & 0 \\ 1 & 0 & 0 & 0 & 0 \\ 0 & 0 & 0 & 0 & 1 \end{bmatrix} \qquad \mathbf{R}_3 = \begin{bmatrix} 1 & 0 & 0 \\ 0 & 1 & 0 \\ 0 & 0 & 0 \\ 0 & 0 & 1 \\ 0 & 0 & 0 \\ 0 & 0 & 0 \end{bmatrix}$$

$(k_i + s_i = 2 + 4 = 6)$, this results in the following dimensions $\mathbf{R}_1\,(6\times 2)$ and $\mathbf{H}_1\,(6\times 4)$. $\mathbf{H}_1$ expresses the linear economic hypothesis to be tested on $\boldsymbol{\beta}_1$, its first column imposing the homogeneity constraint, while the second to the fourth columns in turn locate the unrestricted elements of the cointegration vector (i.e., β_{21}, β_{41} and β_{61}). In contrast, the first column of $\mathbf{R}_1$ imposes the homogeneity constraint while the second column imposes the zero restriction. There are also two restrictions, each placed on $\boldsymbol{\beta}_2$ and $\boldsymbol{\beta}_3$ so that $\mathbf{R}_2$ and $\mathbf{R}_3$ have the same dimensions as $\mathbf{R}_1$. The fact that all three cointegration vectors have exactly two restrictions has implications for identification, as explained below. Determining the elements of $\mathbf{R}_2$ and $\mathbf{R}_3$, and their counterparts $\mathbf{H}_2$ and $\mathbf{H}_3$, proceeds in a similar fashion. Formulating the restrictions on the vectors in $\boldsymbol{\beta}_2$ is equally straightforward: it is useful to write out the restricted $\boldsymbol{\beta}$ and then determine the dimensions of k_i and s_i.

All the restrictions on $\boldsymbol{\beta}$ due to the hypotheses in H_β will be tested jointly, that is, all the restricted cointegration vectors are estimated together comprising one joint test of their validity.[50] The outcome, assuming identification, will be unique cointegration vectors. However, testing joint restrictions involving all of the separate $\boldsymbol{\beta}_i$ spanning the entire cointegration space is often not the best way to start when testing restrictions, unless economic theory is particularly informative on the hypotheses that should be tested. Instead, Johansen and Juselius (1992) suggested (three) more general tests of hypotheses, which are in fact special cases of (5.17):

1. The same restrictions are placed on all the cointegration vectors spanning $\boldsymbol{\beta}$. This hypothesis, depicted $\mathcal{H}_4$ in Johansen and Juselius (op. cit.), amounts to specifying $\mathcal{H}_4\!: \boldsymbol{\beta} = \mathbf{H}\boldsymbol{\varphi}$; this it is the special case of H_β when $\mathbf{H}_1 = \mathbf{H}_2 = \ldots = \mathbf{H}_r$. Given that $\mathbf{H}$ imposes k restrictions it will be of dimension $(n\times s)$, since $(s = n - k)$, while $\boldsymbol{\varphi}$ is an $(s\times r)$ matrix of parameters to be estimated involving all r cointegration vectors. Thus, this general hypothesis can be used to test whether a particular structure holds in all the cointegration relations.
2. If r_1 cointegration vectors are assumed to be known, while the remaining r_2 vectors are unrestricted then we have $\mathcal{H}_5\!: \boldsymbol{\beta} = (\mathbf{H}, \boldsymbol{\varphi})$, where $\mathbf{H}$ is $(n\times r_1)$, $\boldsymbol{\varphi}$ is the $(n\times r_2)$ matrix of unrestricted parameters involving the r_2 cointegration vectors and $(r_1 + r_2 = r)$. Another way of looking at the problem, which is particularly useful when implementing the procedure, is to reformulate the test as $H\!: \boldsymbol{\beta} = (\mathbf{H}_1\boldsymbol{\varphi}_1, \mathbf{H}_2\boldsymbol{\varphi}_2)$, where $\mathbf{H}_1$ and $\mathbf{H}_2$ now cover two groups, the first group comprising the $r_1 = 1$ 'known' vector and the second comprising $r_2\ (= r - r_1)$ unrestricted vectors. There are $(n-1)$ restrictions imposed on the vector in the first group,[51] and thus $\mathbf{H}_1$ will be of dimension $(n\times 1)$, and since no restrictions have been placed on the second group $\mathbf{H}_2$ becomes the identity matrix $\mathbf{I}_n$ with dimension $(n\times n)$. Consequently, $\boldsymbol{\varphi}_1$ is a $(1\times r_1)$ matrix of parameters to be estimated involving the 'known' cointegration vector, while $\boldsymbol{\varphi}_2$ is an $(n\times r_2)$ matrix of parameters to be estimated involving the r_2 cointegration vectors. If there is more than one 'known' cointegration vector (so that $r_1 > 1$ in the first group), then the test can be expanded to cover each 'known' vector plus the remaining 'unknown' vectors. In the limit, when all cointegration vectors are

Box 5.6 Testing for unit roots with the Johansen procedure

The general test $\mathcal{H}_5: \boldsymbol{\beta} = (\mathbf{H}, \boldsymbol{\varphi})$ formulated by Johansen and Juselius (1992) can be used to test whether each of the individual variables in the model are stationary by themselves for differing values of r. This is a particular type of unit root test using a multivariate form of the augmented Dickey–Fuller test with the null hypothesis of stationarity rather than the usual non-stationary null. Using the PPP and UIP model where $\mathbf{z}_t = [p_1, p_2, e, i_1, i_2]'$, tests of type $\mathcal{H}_5$ are performed for each variable, where $\mathbf{H}_5$ is a vector from the identity matrix $\mathbf{I}_n$ with element i as unity. That is, the following tests of hypotheses are conducted:

$$\mathbf{H}_{5.1} = \begin{bmatrix} 1 \\ 0 \\ 0 \\ 0 \\ 0 \end{bmatrix} \quad \mathbf{H}_{5.2} = \begin{bmatrix} 0 \\ 1 \\ 0 \\ 0 \\ 0 \end{bmatrix} \quad \mathbf{H}_{5.3} = \begin{bmatrix} 0 \\ 0 \\ 1 \\ 0 \\ 0 \end{bmatrix} \quad \mathbf{H}_{5.4} = \begin{bmatrix} 0 \\ 0 \\ 0 \\ 1 \\ 0 \end{bmatrix} \quad \mathbf{H}_{5.5} = \begin{bmatrix} 0 \\ 0 \\ 0 \\ 0 \\ 1 \end{bmatrix}$$

The resulting LR statistics are distributed as χ^2 with $(n - r)$ degrees of freedom. To test for trend-stationarity, the model has to allow for a linear trend in the cointegration space (i.e., Model 4 as discussed in the section in this chapter on deterministic components in the multivariate model). Then the general test $\mathcal{H}_6: \boldsymbol{\beta} = (\mathbf{H}\boldsymbol{\varphi}_1, \boldsymbol{\varphi}_2)$ is used with each $\mathbf{H}_6$-matrix having a dimension of $(n \times 2)$, the second column bringing the time trend into the test, namely:

$$\mathbf{H}_{6.1} = \begin{bmatrix} 1 & 0 \\ 0 & 0 \\ 0 & 0 \\ 0 & 0 \\ 0 & 0 \\ 0 & 1 \end{bmatrix} \quad \mathbf{H}_{6.2} = \begin{bmatrix} 0 & 0 \\ 1 & 0 \\ 0 & 0 \\ 0 & 0 \\ 0 & 0 \\ 0 & 1 \end{bmatrix} \quad \mathbf{H}_{6.3} = \begin{bmatrix} 0 & 0 \\ 0 & 0 \\ 1 & 0 \\ 0 & 0 \\ 0 & 0 \\ 0 & 1 \end{bmatrix} \quad \mathbf{H}_{6.4} = \begin{bmatrix} 0 & 0 \\ 0 & 0 \\ 0 & 0 \\ 1 & 0 \\ 0 & 0 \\ 0 & 1 \end{bmatrix} \quad \mathbf{H}_{6.5} = \begin{bmatrix} 0 & 0 \\ 0 & 0 \\ 0 & 0 \\ 0 & 0 \\ 1 & 0 \\ 0 & 1 \end{bmatrix}$$

The resulting LR test statistics are distributed under the χ^2-distribution with $(r_1 \times (n - s - r_2))$ degrees of freedom.

Using this testing procedure for unit roots with the two models considered in this chapter (the UK money-demand model with $r = 1$, and the PPP/UIP model with $r = 2$), provides the following results:

Table 5.6.1 Testing for unit roots using the Johansen procedure

Hypothesis and 5% critical value	Variable tested:				
	p_1	p_2	e	i_1	i_2
Stationarity $\chi^2(3)$=7.82	5.87	6.22	3.16	12.87	10.58
Trend-stationarity $\chi^2(3)$=7.82	9.86	10.11	7.09	9.24	10.20
	$m-p$	Δp	y	R	
Stationarity $\chi^2(3)$=7.82	74.61	64.25	60.56	66.08	
Trend-stationarity $\chi^2(3)$=7.82	62.31	59.84	51.00	55.35	

→

> Surprisingly, the null of stationarity is not rejected for the PPP variables, although trend stationarity is. The time series graphs of the variables in the model show that p_1 and p_2 are strongly upward trending, but the other three variables are less so (especially the interest rate variables). Either we can conclude that the null of trend-stationarity is more appropriate in such situations, or that the test has poor power properties.[52] In contrast, the money-demand variables are clearly non-stationary.

'known' this reformulated version of the $\mathcal{H}_5$-test would be equivalent to the hypotheses tested using (5.17), with all of the $\mathbf{H}_i$ as $(n \times 1)$ vectors.

3. The same k restrictions are placed on r_1 of the cointegration vectors spanning $\boldsymbol{\beta}$, and the remaining r_2 vectors are unrestricted, giving $\mathcal{H}_6$: $\boldsymbol{\beta} = (\mathbf{H}\varphi_1, \varphi_2)$, where $\mathbf{H}$ is $(n \times s)$, φ_1 is the $(s \times r_1)$ matrix of unrestricted parameters involving the r_1 cointegration vectors, and φ_2 is the $(n \times r_2)$ matrix of parameters involving the r_2 cointegration vectors, with $(r_1 + r_2 = r)$. The major difference between $\mathcal{H}_6$ and $\mathcal{H}_5$ is that the former is used when we wish to test if there exists *some* vector in the cointegration space that linearly combines the variables in a particular hypothesised stationary relationship (which is less restrictive than testing whether this vector is present in all r cointegration vectors, that is, $\mathcal{H}_4$, and less restrictive than testing that all the elements in this vector are 'known' to exist in a particular column of $\boldsymbol{\beta}$, that is, $\mathcal{H}_5$). Again, it is useful to reformulate this general test as H: $\boldsymbol{\beta} = (\mathbf{H}_1\varphi_1, \mathbf{H}_2\varphi_2)$. Given that $\mathbf{H}_1$ imposes k restrictions it will be of dimension $(n \times s)$, since $(s = n - k)$, while φ_1 is an $(s \times r_1)$ matrix of parameters to be estimated involving the r_1 cointegration vectors. As $\mathbf{H}_2$ imposes no restrictions it will be an identity matrix of dimension $(n \times n)$, while φ_2 is an $(n \times r_2)$ matrix of parameters to be estimated involving the r_2 cointegration vectors.

These three general tests of hypotheses are now illustrated using the PPP and UIP model estimated by Johansen and Juselius (1992). The results given in Table 5.4 indicate that it is plausible to set $r = 2$, with the first cointegration vector seeming to contain the PPP relation among the first three variables and the second to contain the interest rate differential among the last two variables. Thus, the first general hypothesis is that the PPP relationship $[a_{1j}, -a_{2j}, -a_{3j}, *, *]$, for $j = 1, \ldots, r$, holds in both vectors. This requires specifying the $\mathcal{H}_4$-test with two restrictions (i.e. $a_{1j} = -a_{2j}$, and $a_{1j} = -a_{3j}$) thus $\mathbf{H}_{4.1}$ is of dimension (5×3). A second form of the $\mathcal{H}_4$-test is for only the UIP relationship $[*, *, *, a_{4j}, -a_{5j}]$ to enter all cointegration vectors, thus imposing one restriction (i.e., $a_{4j} = -a_{5j}$) and thus $\mathbf{H}_{4.2}$ is of dimension (5×4).

$$\mathbf{H}_{4.1} = \begin{bmatrix} 1 & 0 & 0 \\ -1 & 0 & 0 \\ -1 & 0 & 0 \\ 0 & 1 & 0 \\ 0 & 0 & 1 \end{bmatrix} \qquad \mathbf{H}_{4.2} = \begin{bmatrix} 1 & 0 & 0 & 0 \\ 0 & 1 & 0 & 0 \\ 0 & 0 & 1 & 0 \\ 0 & 0 & 0 & 1 \\ 0 & 0 & 0 & -1 \end{bmatrix}$$

Table 5.7 Testing some general restrictions on cointegration vectors in the PPP and UIP model[a]

Test		Restricted $\boldsymbol{\beta}$					LR statistic	Probability of accepting null
		p_1	p_2	e	i_1	i_2		
$\mathbf{H}_{4.1}$	$\boldsymbol{\beta}_1$	1.000	−1.000	−1.000	−2.614	−2.095	$\chi^2(4)=2.76$	0.60
	$\boldsymbol{\beta}_2$	0.035	−0.035	−0.035	1.000	−0.914		
$\mathbf{H}_{4.2}$	$\boldsymbol{\beta}_1$	1.000	−1.127	−2.341	20.715	−20.715	$\chi^2(2)=13.71$	0.00
	$\boldsymbol{\beta}_2$	0.344	−0.439	0.400	1.000	−1.000		
$\mathbf{H}_{5.1}$	$\boldsymbol{\beta}_1$	1.000	−1.000	−1.000	0.000	0.000	$\chi^2(3)=14.52$	0.00
	$\boldsymbol{\beta}_2$	−0.015	−0.012	−0.003	1.00	0.626		
$\mathbf{H}_{5.2}$	$\boldsymbol{\beta}_1$	1.000	−0.910	−0.933	−2.616	−2.616	$\chi^2(3)=1.89$	0.59
	$\boldsymbol{\beta}_2$	0.000	0.000	0.000	1.000	1.000		
$\mathbf{H}_{6}$	$\boldsymbol{\beta}_1$	1.000	−1.269	1.745	0.000	0.000	$\chi^2(1)=2.43$	0.12
	$\boldsymbol{\beta}_2$	−0.268	0.234	0.324	1.000	0.559		

[a]The first vector is always normalised on p_1 and the other vector is normalised on i_1.

These **H**-matrices restrict the Johansen reduced rank regression model, thereby obtaining $(n-s)$ new eigenvalues λ_i^* for the restricted model which are then used to obtain the LR test statistic given by (5.9), with $(r \times (n-s))$ degrees of freedom.[53] The results for the above two hypotheses, together with the restricted $\boldsymbol{\beta}$, are given in Table 5.7. The PPP relationship appears to hold in both cointegration relationships but the hypothesis that only the interest rate differential enters both vectors is strongly rejected.

On the basis of these results, Johansen and Juselius (op. cit.) went on to test if the PPP and UIP relationships were stationary by themselves, that is, whether one cointegration vector can be specified as $\mathbf{H}_{5.1} = [1, -1, -1, 0, 0]'$, and the other as $\mathbf{H}_{5.2} = [0, 0, 0, 1, -1]'$.[54] Testing for a 'known' cointegration vector, with the other vector unrestricted, involves the $\mathcal{H}_5$-test with four restrictions on the unrestricted Johansen reduced rank regression model, resulting in $(n-r_1)$ new eigenvalues λ_i^* for the restricted model plus an additional eigenvalue ρ corresponding to a two-stage reduced rank problem involving the known r_1.[55] The LR statistic is more complicated in this instance, being based on (5.9) but with an additional term involving $\log(1-\rho)$. The resulting test is based on the χ^2-distribution with $(r_1 \times (n-r))$ degrees of freedom. The results for the $\mathcal{H}_5$-test are also given in Table 5.7, and the hypothesis that one of the cointegration vectors represents only the PPP relationship is rejected, while there is support for the idea that one of the vectors contains a stationary relationship between just the interest rate variables.

The results obtained so far suggest that the PPP relationship exists in both cointegration vectors but not on its own, while the opposite is true for the UIP relationship. This might at first seem contradictory, since hypothesis $\mathbf{H}_{5.2}$ would suggest that the PPP relationship does not exist in the cointegration vector containing the UIP relationship and yet $\mathbf{H}_{4.1}$ was not rejected. A reconciliation of the apparent contradiction requires the PPP relationship to be insignificant in the UIP cointegration relationship, and this seems to be supported by the estimate of $\boldsymbol{\beta}_2$ in $\mathbf{H}_{4.1}$. These results are informative from the point of view of formulating hypotheses about whether there are unique vectors in the cointegration space, and we take this up again in the next section. For completeness, the final general hypothesis tested by Johansen and Juselius is reported, although given the support for $\mathbf{H}_{4.1}$ it seems somewhat redundant to ask whether any stationary linear combination between p_1, p_2 and e exists. This is tested by imposing two restrictions so that $\mathbf{H}$ is of dimension (5×3):

$$\mathbf{H}_6 = \begin{bmatrix} 1 & 0 & 0 \\ 0 & 1 & 0 \\ 0 & 0 & 1 \\ 0 & 0 & 0 \\ 0 & 0 & 0 \end{bmatrix}$$

The resulting LR test[56] is based on the χ^2-distribution with $(r_1 \times (n - s - r_2))$ degrees of freedom, and the results are given in Table 5.7. The test provides weak support for the existence of a linear combination involving the PPP variables, but the values obtained for the β_{ij} again call into question the usefulness of this test in the present context, given that the PPP relationship appears to hold in both cointegration relationships.

Testing for unique cointegration vectors

It has already been pointed out that since the Johansen approach only provides information on the uniqueness of the cointegration *space*, it is necessary to impose restrictions motivated by economic arguments to obtain unique *vectors* lying within that space, and then test whether the columns of $\boldsymbol{\beta}$ are identified.[57] Identification here is defined in Johansen (1992d) and Johansen and Juselius (1994) with respect to the linear restrictions specified in $\mathbf{R}_i$ and $\mathbf{H}_i$ (see equation (5.17)). The first vector in the cointegration space is identified if:

$$\text{rank}\,(\mathbf{R}_1'\boldsymbol{\beta}_1, \mathbf{R}_1'\boldsymbol{\beta}_2, \ldots, \mathbf{R}_1'\boldsymbol{\beta}_r) = \text{rank}\,(\mathbf{R}_1'\mathbf{H}_1\boldsymbol{\varphi}_1, \mathbf{R}_1'\mathbf{H}_2\boldsymbol{\varphi}_2, \ldots, \mathbf{R}_1'\mathbf{H}_r\boldsymbol{\varphi}_r) = r - 1 \quad (5.19)$$

Thus identification is achieved if when applying the restrictions of the first vector to the other $r - 1$ vectors the result is a matrix of rank $r - 1$, that is, a matrix with $r - 1$ independent columns. Put another way, '... it is not possible by taking linear combinations of for instance $\boldsymbol{\beta}_2, \ldots, \boldsymbol{\beta}_r$ to construct a vector and hence an equation which is restricted in the same way as $\boldsymbol{\beta}_1$ and in this sense could be confused with the equation defined by $\boldsymbol{\beta}_1$. Hence, $\boldsymbol{\beta}_1$ can be recognised among all linear combinations of $\boldsymbol{\beta}_1, \ldots, \boldsymbol{\beta}_r$ as the only one that is in sp($\mathbf{H}_1$), the space spanned by the columns in $\mathbf{H}_1$ or the only one that satisfies the restrictions $\mathbf{R}_1$' (Johansen, 1992d).

Johansen (op. cit.) generalises (5.19) to provide a definition for a set of restrictions which identify the unique vectors. Specifically, his theorem 3 states that the restrictions $\mathbf{R}_1, \ldots, \mathbf{R}_r$ are identifying if (and only if) for $k=1, \ldots, r-1$ and for any set of indices $1 \leqslant i_1 < \ldots < i_k \leqslant r$ not containing i, it holds that

$$\text{rank}\,(\mathbf{R}_i'\mathbf{H}_{i_1}, \ldots, \mathbf{R}_i'\mathbf{H}_{j_k}) \geqslant k \tag{5.20}$$

If (5.20) is satisfied for a particular value of i, then the restrictions $\mathbf{R}_i$ identify vector i. When $r=2$, so that hypotheses about $\boldsymbol{\beta}$ can be formulated as $\mathbf{H}_\beta: \boldsymbol{\beta} = (\mathbf{H}_1\varphi_1, \mathbf{H}_2\varphi_2)$, then (5.20) is satisfied and $\mathbf{R}_1$ and $\mathbf{R}_2$ identify the vectors in $\boldsymbol{\beta}$ if:

$$\text{rank}\,(\mathbf{R}_1'\mathbf{H}_2) \geqslant 1 \quad \text{and} \quad \text{rank}\,(\mathbf{R}_2'\mathbf{H}_1) \geqslant 1 \tag{5.21}$$

As a simple illustration, Johansen (op. cit.) considered the following model:

$$\boldsymbol{\beta} = \begin{bmatrix} a & c \\ -a & 0 \\ b & -c \\ 0 & d \end{bmatrix} \quad \mathbf{R}_1 = \begin{bmatrix} 1 & 0 \\ 1 & 0 \\ 0 & 0 \\ 0 & 1 \end{bmatrix} \quad \mathbf{H}_1 = \begin{bmatrix} 1 & 0 \\ -1 & 0 \\ 0 & 1 \\ 0 & 0 \end{bmatrix} \quad \mathbf{R}_2 = \begin{bmatrix} 1 & 0 \\ 0 & 1 \\ 1 & 0 \\ 0 & 0 \end{bmatrix} \quad \mathbf{H}_1 = \begin{bmatrix} 1 & 0 \\ 0 & 0 \\ -1 & 0 \\ 0 & 1 \end{bmatrix}$$

Applying (5.21), the rank of both matrices is found to equal 2 ($\geqslant 1$), and thus $\boldsymbol{\beta}$ is identified by the two vectors considered.

When $r=3$, things are more complicated because there are more linear combinations of the $\mathbf{R}_i'\mathbf{H}_i$ to be considered. Hypotheses about $\boldsymbol{\beta}$ can be formulated as $H_\beta: \boldsymbol{\beta} = (\mathbf{H}_1\varphi_1, \mathbf{H}_2\varphi_2, \mathbf{H}_3\varphi_3)$, and $\mathbf{R}_1$, $\mathbf{R}_2$ and $\mathbf{R}_3$ identify the *first* vector in $\boldsymbol{\beta}$ if:

$$\text{rank}\,(\mathbf{R}_1'\mathbf{H}_2) \geqslant 1 \quad \text{and} \quad \text{rank}\,(\mathbf{R}_1'\mathbf{H}_3) \geqslant 1 \quad \text{and} \quad \text{rank}\,(\mathbf{R}_1'(\mathbf{H}_2{:}\mathbf{H}_3)) \geqslant 2 \tag{5.22}$$

where $\mathbf{H}_2{:}\mathbf{H}_3$ denotes the concatenation of these two matrices. For ease of computation, the problem is reformulated in terms of equivalent symmetric matrices; thus define:

$$\mathbf{M}_{i.jm} = \mathbf{H}_j'\mathbf{H}_m - \mathbf{H}_j'\mathbf{H}_i(\mathbf{H}_i'\mathbf{H}_i)^{-1}\mathbf{H}_i'\mathbf{H}_m \quad \text{for } i, j, m = 1, 2, 3$$

and in terms of (5.22) we now have:

$$\text{rank}\,(\mathbf{M}_{1.22}) \geqslant 1 \quad \text{rank}\,(\mathbf{M}_{1.33}) \geqslant 1 \quad \text{rank}\begin{bmatrix} \mathbf{M}_{1.22} & \mathbf{M}_{1.23} \\ \mathbf{M}_{1.32} & \mathbf{M}_{1.33} \end{bmatrix} \geqslant 2 \tag{5.23}$$

Similar expressions can be used to check if $\mathbf{R}_1$, $\mathbf{R}_2$ and $\mathbf{R}_3$ identify the other vectors, $i=2, 3$, in $\boldsymbol{\beta}$.[58]

A discussion of the identification problem relating to the IS/LM model is provided in Johansen and Juselius (1994) and four of their examples are reproduced here, that is, the two examples in (5.18) and two new examples as set out in (5.24) and Table 5.8:

Table 5.8 Specifying restrictions on $\boldsymbol{\beta}$

$\boldsymbol{\beta}^3=(\mathbf{H}_1\varphi_1,\mathbf{H}_2\varphi_2,\mathbf{H}_3\varphi_3)$

$$\mathbf{H}_1=\begin{bmatrix}1&0&0&0\\-1&0&0&0\\-1&0&0&0\\0&1&0&0\\0&0&1&1\\0&0&0&1\end{bmatrix}\quad \mathbf{H}_2=\begin{bmatrix}0\\0\\0\\1\\-1\\0\end{bmatrix}\quad \mathbf{H}_3=\begin{bmatrix}0&0&0\\0&0&0\\1&0&0\\0&0&0\\0&1&0\\0&0&1\end{bmatrix}$$

$$\mathbf{R}_1=\begin{bmatrix}1&1\\1&0\\0&1\\0&0\\0&0\\0&0\end{bmatrix}\quad \mathbf{R}_2=\begin{bmatrix}1&0&0&0&0\\0&1&0&0&0\\0&0&1&0&0\\0&0&0&1&0\\0&0&0&1&0\\0&0&0&0&1\end{bmatrix}\quad \mathbf{R}_3=\begin{bmatrix}1&0&0\\0&1&0\\0&0&0\\0&0&1\\0&0&0\\0&0&0\end{bmatrix}$$

$\boldsymbol{\beta}^4=(\mathbf{H}_1\varphi_1,\mathbf{H}_2\varphi_2,\mathbf{H}_3\varphi_3)$

$$\mathbf{H}_1=\begin{bmatrix}1&0&0\\-1&0&0\\-1&0&0\\0&1&0\\0&0&0\\0&0&1\end{bmatrix}\quad \mathbf{H}_2=\begin{bmatrix}0\\0\\0\\1\\-1\\0\end{bmatrix}\quad \mathbf{H}_3=\begin{bmatrix}0&0&0\\0&0&0\\1&0&0\\0&0&0\\0&1&0\\0&0&1\end{bmatrix}$$

$$\mathbf{R}_1=\begin{bmatrix}1&1&0\\1&0&0\\0&1&0\\0&0&0\\0&0&1\\0&0&0\end{bmatrix}\quad \mathbf{R}_2=\begin{bmatrix}1&0&0&0&0\\0&1&0&0&0\\0&0&1&0&0\\0&0&0&1&0\\0&0&0&1&0\\0&0&0&0&1\end{bmatrix}\quad \mathbf{R}_3=\begin{bmatrix}1&0&0\\0&1&0\\0&0&0\\0&0&1\\0&0&0\\0&0&0\end{bmatrix}$$

$$\boldsymbol{\beta}^3=\begin{bmatrix}1&0&0\\-1&0&0\\-1&0&*\\*&1&0\\*&-1&1\\*&0&*\end{bmatrix}\qquad \boldsymbol{\beta}^4=\begin{bmatrix}1&0&0\\-1&0&0\\-1&0&*\\*&1&0\\0&-1&1\\*&0&*\end{bmatrix} \tag{5.24}$$

The results from applying the test of identification in (5.23) for each vector are reported in Table 5.9. The cointegration space represented by $\boldsymbol{\beta}^1$ is identified since the necessary conditions are satisfied. However, this is a special case in that exactly $r-1=2$ restrictions have been imposed, through $\mathbf{H}_1$, $\mathbf{H}_2$ and $\mathbf{H}_3$, on each cointegration vector. Thus, given that these restrictions are identifying, it can be said that the model is just identified. Since the likelihood function for the exactly identified model is not changed, no testing of the hypotheses is involved. The second

Table 5.9 Rank conditions (equation (5.20)) for identifying cointegration vectors

Rank $\mathbf{M}_{i.jm}$	$\boldsymbol{\beta}^1$	$\boldsymbol{\beta}^2$	$\boldsymbol{\beta}^3$	$\boldsymbol{\beta}^4$
Hypothesis $\boldsymbol{\beta}_1=\mathbf{H}_1\boldsymbol{\varphi}_1$				
1.22	2	1	0	1
1.33	2	2	1	2
1.23	2	3	2	2
Hypothesis $\boldsymbol{\beta}_2=\mathbf{H}_2\boldsymbol{\varphi}_2$				
2.11	2	3	3	3
2.33	1	3	3	3
2.13	2	5	4	4
Hypothesis $\boldsymbol{\beta}_3=\mathbf{H}_3\boldsymbol{\varphi}_3$				
3.11	2	2	2	2
3.22	1	2	1	1
3.12	2	3	2	2

example involves over-identification, since the number of restrictions $k_i > r-1$. Again the cointegration space represented by $\boldsymbol{\beta}^2$ is identified since the necessary conditions are satisfied (cf. Table 5.9). The test of whether restrictions are valid is based on an LR test[59] involving $\nu = \Sigma_i(n-r+1-s_i)$ degrees of freedom. In this case, where $(n-r+1)=4$, then $\nu = (4-3)+(4-1)+(4-3)=5$, and thus the test statistic is distributed as $\chi^2(5)$.

In the next example involving $\boldsymbol{\beta}^3$ the rank condition involving $\mathbf{H}_1$ is not satisfied since the rank of $\mathbf{M}_{1.22}=0$. This occurs because it is possible to take a linear combination of $\mathbf{H}_1$ and $\mathbf{H}_2$ which would remove either β_{41} or β_{51} from $\boldsymbol{\beta}_1^3$ and yet *jointly* the restricted $\boldsymbol{\beta}_1^3$ and $\boldsymbol{\beta}_2^3$ are a valid representation of the first two cointegration vectors in $\boldsymbol{\beta}^3$. To see this clearly, consider the following linear combinations of the first two vectors

$$\begin{bmatrix} 1.000 \\ -1.000 \\ -1.000 \\ 1.893 \\ 1.893 \\ -0.005 \end{bmatrix} + 1.893 \times \begin{bmatrix} 0.000 \\ 0.000 \\ 0.000 \\ 1.000 \\ -1.000 \\ 0.000 \end{bmatrix} = \begin{bmatrix} 1.000 \\ -1.000 \\ -1.000 \\ 3.786 \\ 0.000 \\ -0.005 \end{bmatrix}$$

In effect, as Johansen and Juselius (op. cit.) point out: '... the space spanned by $\mathbf{H}_2$ is contained in the space spanned by $\mathbf{H}_1$ ... and within this set-up we can only estimate uniquely the impact of a linear combination of $(\beta_{41}$ or $\beta_{51})$ in the first relation'. Lastly, although $\boldsymbol{\beta}^3 = (\mathbf{H}_1\boldsymbol{\varphi}_1, \mathbf{H}_2\boldsymbol{\varphi}_2, \mathbf{H}_3\boldsymbol{\varphi}_3)$ is not identified, the restrictions on the cointegration space are valid and can be tested using an LR test. Note, however, that in this instance $\nu = (4-3)+(4-1)+(4-3)=5$ rather than $\nu = (4-4)+(4-1)+(4-3)=4$, that is, $s_i = 3$ in $\mathbf{H}_1$ since three, and not two, restrictions are imposed because of the lack of identification.

The last example, involving $\boldsymbol{\beta}^4$, is the same as the previous example except that the additional restriction that $\beta_{51}=0$ is imposed to achieve an identified model. Thus, when the system is not identified, the rank condition tests often provide information to suggest what needs to be done to identify the model. As an example, consider the PPP and UIP model and the tests of restrictions undertaken in the last section. The general hypotheses tested using $\mathcal{H}_4$ and $\mathcal{H}_5$ suggest that the PPP relationship is significant in one-vector, while the UIP relationship exists on its own in the other vector. Thus, it would appear valid to specify the following:

$$\boldsymbol{\beta} = \begin{bmatrix} 1 & 0 \\ -1 & 0 \\ -1 & 0 \\ * & 1 \\ * & -1 \end{bmatrix} \quad \mathbf{R}_1 = \begin{bmatrix} 1 & 1 \\ 1 & 0 \\ 0 & 1 \\ 0 & 0 \\ 0 & 0 \end{bmatrix} \quad \mathbf{H}_1 = \begin{bmatrix} 1 & 0 & 0 \\ -1 & 0 & 0 \\ -1 & 0 & 0 \\ 0 & 1 & 0 \\ 0 & 0 & 1 \end{bmatrix}$$

$$\mathbf{R}_2 = \begin{bmatrix} 1 & 0 & 0 & 0 \\ 0 & 1 & 0 & 0 \\ 0 & 0 & 1 & 0 \\ 0 & 0 & 0 & 1 \\ 0 & 0 & 0 & 1 \end{bmatrix} \quad \mathbf{H}_2 = \begin{bmatrix} 0 \\ 0 \\ 0 \\ 1 \\ -1 \end{bmatrix}$$

So the first vector is not identified for exactly the same reasons given when discussing $\boldsymbol{\beta}^3$. The LR test of these restrictions gives a test statistic of 3.97, which is not very significant under the $\chi^2(5)$-distribution,[60] lending support to the general hypotheses. Reformulating the problem as:

$$\boldsymbol{\beta} = \begin{bmatrix} 1 & 0 \\ -1 & 0 \\ -1 & 0 \\ 0 & 1 \\ 0 & -1 \end{bmatrix} \quad \mathbf{R}_1 = \begin{bmatrix} 1 & 1 & 0 & 0 \\ 1 & 0 & 0 & 0 \\ 0 & 1 & 0 & 0 \\ 0 & 0 & 1 & 0 \\ 0 & 0 & 0 & 1 \end{bmatrix} \quad \mathbf{H}_1 = \begin{bmatrix} 1 \\ -1 \\ -1 \\ 0 \\ 0 \end{bmatrix}$$

$$\mathbf{R}_2 = \begin{bmatrix} 1 & 0 & 0 & 0 \\ 0 & 1 & 0 & 0 \\ 0 & 0 & 1 & 0 \\ 0 & 0 & 0 & 1 \\ 0 & 0 & 0 & 1 \end{bmatrix} \quad \mathbf{H}_2 = \begin{bmatrix} 0 \\ 0 \\ 0 \\ 1 \\ -1 \end{bmatrix}$$

means that the model is clearly identified (rank $(\mathbf{R}_1'\mathbf{H}_2)=1$ and rank $(\mathbf{R}_2'\mathbf{H}_1)=1$), but the test of these restrictions results in an LR test statistic of 25.38, which is highly

Box 5.7 Testing joint restrictions on $\boldsymbol{\alpha}$ and $\boldsymbol{\beta}$: *Cats* output for the PPP and UIP model

Testing restrictions on $\boldsymbol{\alpha}$ and $\boldsymbol{\beta}$

The LR test, $\chi^2(9) = 10.20$, p-value = 0.33

$\boldsymbol{\beta}'$

p_1	p_2	e	i_1	i_2
1.000	−1.000	−1.000	−4.331	0.000
0.000	0.000	0.000	1.000	−1.000

"STANDARD ERRORS" FOR $\boldsymbol{\beta}'$

0.000	0.000	0.000	0.487	0.000
0.000	0.000	0.000	0.000	0.000

$\boldsymbol{\alpha}$		T-VALUES FOR ALPHA	
−0.071	−0.076	−4.578	−1.311
0.000	0.000	0.000	0.000
0.000	0.000	0.000	0.000
−0.000	−0.076	−0.013	−0.812
0.077	0.419	2.748	4.029

<u>Conditional Model: p_2 and e exogenous</u>

The LR test, $\chi^2(5) = 7.00$, p-value = 0.22

$\boldsymbol{\beta}'$

p_1	i_1	i_2	p_2	e
1.000	−4.331	0.000	−1.000	−1.000
0.000	1.000	−1.000	0.000	0.000

"STANDARD ERRORS" FOR $\boldsymbol{\beta}'$

0.000	0.515	0.000	0.000	0.000
0.000	0.000	0.000	0.000	0.000

$\boldsymbol{\alpha}$		T-VALUES FOR ALPHA	
−0.071	−0.076	−4.681	−1.363
−0.000	−0.076	−0.016	−1.009
0.077	0.419	2.709	4.040

significant under the $\chi^2(6)$-distribution. The compromise position is to specify:

$$\boldsymbol{\beta} = \begin{bmatrix} 1 & 0 \\ -1 & 0 \\ -1 & 0 \\ * & 1 \\ 0 & -1 \end{bmatrix} \quad \mathbf{R}_1 = \begin{bmatrix} 1 & 1 & 0 \\ 1 & 0 & 0 \\ 0 & 1 & 0 \\ 0 & 0 & 0 \\ 0 & 0 & 1 \end{bmatrix} \quad \mathbf{H}_1 = \begin{bmatrix} 1 & 0 \\ -1 & 0 \\ -1 & 0 \\ 0 & 1 \\ 0 & 0 \end{bmatrix} \tag{1}$$

$$\mathbf{R}_2 = \begin{bmatrix} 1 & 0 & 0 & 0 \\ 0 & 1 & 0 & 0 \\ 0 & 0 & 1 & 0 \\ 0 & 0 & 0 & 1 \\ 0 & 0 & 0 & 1 \end{bmatrix} \quad \mathbf{H}_2 = \begin{bmatrix} 0 \\ 0 \\ 0 \\ 1 \\ -1 \end{bmatrix}$$

which is identified (rank $(\mathbf{R}_1'\mathbf{H}_2) = 1$ and rank $(\mathbf{R}_2'\mathbf{H}_1) = 2$), with an LR test statistic of 3.97, which is not very significant under the $\chi^2(5)$-distribution, lending support to the general hypotheses. Thus, imposing a structure on the PPP and UIP model suggests that the PPP relationship exists in one vector along with the UK interest rate (but not as covered interest parity), while the UIP relationship uniquely forms the second cointegration vector.

When the cointegration space is uniquely identified the *Cats* program will calculate the 'standard errors' associated with each freely estimated β_{ij}. In the last model estimated there is only one such parameter, and it has a coefficient value of −4.710 and standard error of 0.489. The standard errors can be used to calculate Wald tests of hypotheses about the β_{ij} which are asymptotically distributed as $\chi^2(1)$. Thus, if it is meaningful to test that the interest rate variable in the PPP cointegration vector is −5, then we can use the following Wald test:

$$\left(\frac{-4.710 - (-5)^2}{0.489} \right) = 0.35$$

which does not reject this hypothesis since $\chi^2_{0.95}(1) = 3.84$.

Joint tests of restrictions on α and β

It is now possible jointly to test restrictions on both the cointegration vectors and the speed-of-adjustment parameters. However, care is needed when doing this since some forms of constraint on $\boldsymbol{\alpha}$ can induce a failure of identification of $\boldsymbol{\beta}$, and vice versa.[61] Having obtained results in the PPP and UIP model for the hypotheses that H: $\alpha_{2,j} = \alpha_{3,j} = 0$ for $j = 1, 2$, and that $\boldsymbol{\beta} = (\mathbf{H}_1\boldsymbol{\varphi}_1, \mathbf{H}_2\boldsymbol{\varphi}_2)$, where $\mathbf{H}_1' = [1, -1, -1, *, 0]$ and $\mathbf{H}_2' = [0, 0, 0, 1, -1]$, pooling the various restrictions gives the results reported in Box 5.7. The overall LR test does not significantly reject the null and therefore these joint restrictions are satisfied.[62]

On the basis of these results, the last step is to condition on the weakly exogenous variables and then check that imposing the various restrictions has not altered the model's underlying properties. The conditional estimates, when p_2 and e are exogenous, are also reported in Box 5.7, and these indicate that there is little overall change in the model after applying the conditioning, and little improvement in the (not reported) diagnostic tests of the residuals (primarily because we cannot validly condition on the non-normal Euro-interest rate i_2). Plots of the restricted cointegration relations and recursive eigenvalues (again not shown), suggest that the model performs as well as in its unrestricted form, and indeed the first cointegration vector now looks more stationary.

Conclusions

The Johansen approach to testing for cointegration has only recently become widely accessible to applied economists. Although users of the *Microfit* (version 3.0) software package have been able to estimate cointegration vectors for a number of years, there have been several developments limiting the *Microfit* user (see the appendix chapter, which provides a review of the *Cats*, *PcFiml* and *Microfit* programs). In particular, it is important to spend some time in formulating the dynamic model in terms of which deterministic components (intercept, trend and dummy variables) should enter, setting the correct lag-length of the VAR, and using all the information available when testing for the reduced rank and thus the number of cointegration vectors in the system. There is also the issue of modelling the $I(2)$ system, when there are $I(2)$ variables in the model.

Testing for weak exogeneity is now fairly standard, and the more general tests of linear hypotheses on cointegration vectors are also relatively straightforward. The most important recent development is the ability to formulate unique cointegration vectors, which involves testing for identification. This is very important, since the unrestricted estimates of $\boldsymbol{\beta}$ are often difficult to interpret in terms of their economic information. In fact, what is becoming increasingly obvious is the need to ensure that prior information motivated by economic arguments forms the basis for imposing restrictions, and not the other way around. To give just a single example of this, Clements and Mizon (1991) estimated a model of the UK labour market involving real average earnings per person-hour (w), the inflation rate (Δp), productivity (y), average hours (a), and the unemployment rate (u). The unrestricted model which they obtained from the Johansen approach was:

$$\boldsymbol{\beta} = \begin{bmatrix} w & \Delta p & y & a & u \\ 1 & -0.740 & -0.643 & 6.017 & -9.822 \\ 8.801 & 1 & -0.495 & -7.289 & 14.553 \\ -2.031 & 1.298 & 1 & -5.897 & 7.828 \\ 0.765 & 2.128 & -0.383 & 1 & 12.837 \\ 0.344 & -0.093 & -0.101 & 0.259 & 1 \end{bmatrix}$$

On the basis of testing for reduced rank, they found that there were probably three stationary relationships in the model. In terms of their unrestricted results it is difficult to make immediate sense of all but perhaps the first vector, which seems to be a fairly standard wage equation. Although they do not test for unique cointegration vectors or formally test for identification, they do (on the basis of prior economic information) transform the unrestricted space into the following:

$$\boldsymbol{\beta}' = \begin{bmatrix} w & \Delta p & y & a & u \\ 1 & 0.000 & -1.000 & 5.983 & 0.112 \\ 0.037 & 0.000 & 0.037 & 1 & 0.001 \\ 0.100 & -1 & -0.100 & -0.050 & -0.009 \end{bmatrix}$$

These restrictions[63] define a system that is quite different to the original, with the average hours and inflation vectors essentially containing nothing but these $I(0)$ variables, while the wage equation remains (minus the inflation variable). This seems more reasonable than the unrestricted estimates, and probably would not have been apparent from a more general *ad hoc* approach to imposing restrictions on $\boldsymbol{\beta}$.

But this is a difficult area since on the one hand the practitioner justifiably wants to limit the number of variables that can enter the model in order to simplify the cointegration relationships, but economic theory may suggest a plethora of relevant variables. Economic models are also subject to debate, and part of the role of applied work is to test competing hypotheses. These problems are not new, but the relative newness and difficulty of implementing the Johansen approach gives them a renewed emphasis.

Appendix 1: Programming in *SHAZAM*: testing identification restrictions in β

```
* See Table 6, Johansen and Juselius (1994)
read h1 / rows=6 cols=3 list
  1  0  0
  0  1  0
 -1  0  0
  0  0  0
  0  0  0
  0  0  1
read h2 / rows=6 cols=1 list
  0
  0
  0
  1
 -1
  0
read h3 / rows=6 cols=3 list
```

```
0  0  0
0  0  0
1  0  0
0  0  0
0  1  0
0  0  1

*****************
* First equation*
*****************
*defining equation 14 in Johansen 1992
matrix m1_22=(h2'h2) - (h2'h1*inv(h1'h1)*h1'h2)
matrix m1_33=(h3'h3) - (h3'h1*inv(h1'h1)*h1'h3)
matrix m1_23=(h2'h3) - (h2'h1*inv(h1'h1)*h1'h3)
matrix m1_32=(h3'h2) - (h3'h1*inv(h1'h1)*h1'h2)
matrix s1=m1_22|m1_23
matrix s2=m1_m32|m1_33
matrix m1=(s1'|s2')'

matrix rm1_22=rank(m1_22)'
matrix rm1_33=rank(m1_33)'
matrix rm1_23=rank(m1)'
print rm1_22 rm1_33 rm1_23

*****************
* Second equation*
*****************
matrix m2_11=(h1'h1) - (h1'h2*inv(h2'h2)*h2'h1)
matrix m2_33=(h3'h3) - (h3'h2*inv(h2'h2)*h2'h3)
matrix m2_13=(h1'h3) - (h1'h2*inv(h2'h2)*h1'h3)
matrix m2_31=(h3'h1) - (h3'h2*inv(h2'h2)*h2'h1)
matrix s1=m2_11|m2_13
matrix s2=m2_31|m2_33
matrix m1=(s1'|s2')'
matrix rm2_11=rank(m2_11)'
matrix rm2_33=rank(m2_33)'
matrix rm2_13=rank(m1)'
print rm2_11 rm2_33 rm2_13

*****************
* Third equation*
*****************
matrix m3_11=(h1'h1) - (h1'h3*inv(h3'h3)*h3'h1)
matrix m3_22=(h2'h2) - (h2'h3*inv(h3'h3)*h3'h2)
```

```
matrix m3_12=(hl'h2) - (hl'h3*inv(h3'h3)*h3'h2)
matrix m3_21=(h2'hl) - (h2'h3*inv(h3'h3)*h3'hl)
matrix sl=m3_11|m3_12
matrix s2=m3_21|m23_2
matrix ml=(sl'|s2')'
matrix rm3_11=rank(m3_11)'
matrix rm3_22=rank(m3_22)'
matrix rm3_12=rank(ml)'
print rm3_11 rm3_22 rm3_12
stop
```

Notes

1. *PcFiml (version 8), Interactive Econometric Modelling of Dynamic Systems*, developed by Jurgen A. Doornik and David F. Hendry, distributed as part of *PcGive Professional* by Chapman-Hall; and *Cointegration Analysis of Times Series (Cats in* Rats*)*, Henrik Hansen and Katrina Juselius, distributed by Estima.
2. Note, $\hat{\mathbf{V}}$ is normalised such that $\hat{\mathbf{V}}'\hat{\mathbf{S}}_{kk}\hat{\mathbf{V}} = \mathbf{I}$.
3. Each of the r cointegration vectors in $\boldsymbol{\beta}$ is associated with a particular column in $\boldsymbol{\alpha}$ which must contain at least one non-zero element. See (4.16) for a simple example.
4. Note that once we know how many r linearly independent columns there are in $\boldsymbol{\Pi}$ (i.e., once we know its rank), we then know that the last $(n - r)$ columns of $\boldsymbol{\alpha}$ are (effectively) zero and thus that the last $(n - r)$ columns of $\boldsymbol{\beta}$ are non-stationary and do not enter (5.2). Thus, it is in this sense that we can then reduce the dimensions of $\boldsymbol{\alpha}$ and $\boldsymbol{\beta}$ to $(n \times r)$.
5. That is, even if, say, the last $(n - r)$ columns of $\boldsymbol{\alpha}$ are insignificantly small, such that there are only r columns in $\boldsymbol{\alpha}$ which are *significantly* different from zero, estimates of $\boldsymbol{\Pi}$ $(= \boldsymbol{\alpha\beta}')$ obtained using standard regression techniques are likely to be of full rank $(n \times n)$ in any practical situation (given that the last $(n - r)$ columns in $\boldsymbol{\beta}$ representing the common trends will be non-zero and these will combine with the last $(n - r)$ columns of $\boldsymbol{\alpha}$ which are insignificantly small but nevertheless are likely to be non-zero). Thus, an inability to factorise $\boldsymbol{\Pi}$ would mean that we could not carry out tests of the rank of $\boldsymbol{\Pi}$ based on testing the number of non-zero columns in $\boldsymbol{\alpha}$ directly. Factorisation is achieved by a procedure based on reduced rank regression involving canonical correlations (see Box 5.1).
6. Kleibergen and van Dijk (1994) have recently developed an approach based on estimating $\boldsymbol{\Pi}$ directly using OLS and then decomposing it. However, it is yet to be seen whether this new approach has any particular advantages over Johansen's, given that the procedure is not straightforward.
7. In Box 2.4 it was stated that for cointegration to exist, a subset of the higher-order series must cointegrate to the order of the lower-order series. So, if $y_t \sim I(1)$, $x_t \sim I(2)$, and $z_t \sim I(2)$ then as long as we can find a cointegration relationship between x_t and z_t such that v_t $(= x_t - \lambda z_t) \sim I(1)$, then v_t can potentially cointegrate with y_t to obtain w_t $(= y_t - \xi v_t) \sim I(0)$. Note that this presupposes that there are in fact two cointegration relationships, suggesting that unbalanced equations should always be estimated in a multivariate framework.

8. E.g., if wages and labour market variables are $I(1)$, it might be necessary to include the relationship between wage inflation and the unemployment rate – the Phillips Curve – to obtain cointegration relations.
9. Recall, that in the extreme if $\boldsymbol{\Pi}$ has full rank (i.e., there are $r = n$ linearly independent columns) then all the variables in $\mathbf{z}_t$ are $I(0)$. Note, this points to a problem regarding what is meant by cointegration between $I(0)$ variables, since there are potentially an infinite number of ways we can combine these variables and each time (by definition) the relationship formed is $I(0)$. This is not a problem when the variables are $I(1)$, since Engle–Granger (1987) have shown that linear combinations of non-stationary variables are in general also non-stationary unless we can find some $\boldsymbol{\beta}_i$ that results in a cointegration relationship.
10. Johansen (1994) shows that if the number of cointegration relations exceeds the number of $I(2)$ common trends in $\boldsymbol{\beta}$ then combinations of the variables in $\mathbf{z}_t$ can be stationary by themselves. If this condition is not met then it should still be possible to combine some of the $I(1)$ vectors in $\boldsymbol{\beta}$ with suitable combinations of the $I(2)$ variables to form stationary vectors. However, there will of course still remain $I(1)$ and/or $I(2)$ vectors which are non-stationary 'common trends'.
11. Indeed, if residual autocorrelation is due to omitted conditioning variables, increasing the value of k results in potentially harmful over-parameterisation which affects the estimates of cointegration rank (including the $\boldsymbol{\beta}$), making it difficult to interpret economically the cointegration relations present.
12. Note, however, that in the general case of setting the value of k, Monte Carlo evidence suggests that tests of cointegration rank (see below) are relatively robust to over-parameterisation, while setting too small a value of k severely distorts the size of the tests (Cheung and Lai, 1993).
13. For example, the usual quarterly (0, 1) dummies for each period (S_{1t}, S_{2t}, S_{3t} and S_{4t}) are entered as $(S_{it} - S_{1t})$, $i = 1, \dots, 4$.
14. Johansen and Nielsen (1993) derive the asymptotic distributions for some models with dummy variables which can be simulated via a program called *DisCo* (written in Pascal).
15. Note, *PcFiml* actually estimates the VAR model in levels (see equation (5.1)) rather than the equivalent VECM in first differences with the lagged $\mathbf{z}_{t-k}$ (see equation (5.2)). This needs to be borne in mind when conducting any hypothesis tests with respect to the regressors in the model, since the usual t- and F-tests are not normally distributed in a system containing non-stationary $I(1)$ variables in levels (see Chapter 2).
16. Most of these were considered in the last chapter. Note, hypothesis tests with respect to the residuals of the model are valid since these are stationary $I(0)$ on the presumption that there are cointegration relationships in the data-set. The F-tests that the i-period lag ($F_{k=i}$) is zero are only indicative (see the previous footnote).
17. The variable Δpo_t is highly significant in the equation determining p_2.
18. Note again the comments in previous footnotes about hypothesis testing with respect to non-stationary variables.
19. It is fairly common for conditional heteroscedasticity to lead to heavy-tailed distributions.
20. Hendry and Doornik (1994) estimated a similar model to the present one, using seasonally adjusted data, and they introduced two extra dummies into $\mathbf{D}_t$, one to account for the two oil price shocks in the 1970s, and the other to account for the Barber boom in 1973 and the tight monetary policy introduced in 1979 (see Hendry and Doornik, op cit., footnote 1). These dummies are significant in the model estimated here but their inclusion has little impact on the short-run model other than to introduce mild autocorrelation into

the real output equation. This points to a potential trade-off that often occurs in terms of setting the value of k and introducing $I(0)$ variables into $\mathbf{D}_t$.

21. Note, the last row of results is not relevant and does not indicate that we should accept the possibility that there are four cointegration vectors since we fail to reject the previous null hypotheses. This type of 'quirky result' can occur in finite samples when the critical values are based upon asymptotic distributions.
22. Cheung and Lai (1993) note that '... an equivalent way to make finite-sample corrections is to adjust the critical values and not the test statistics'. The scaling factor used to adjust the critical values is $T/(T-nk)$.
23. Recall that the roots of the characteristic equation used to solve for the eigenvalues (or characteristic roots) can be complex (i.e., contain a real and an imaginary part, $h \pm vi$, where h and v are two real numbers and i is an imaginary number), and the modulus is the absolute value of the complex root and is calculated as $\sqrt{(h^2+v^2)}$.
24. Formal testing of the $I(2)$ model is considered in Box 5.3.
25. Note, for simplicity and in line with common practice, the full rank (5×5) matrices are labelled $\boldsymbol{\alpha}$ and $\boldsymbol{\beta}$ in Box 5.2, although it might be more appropriate to label them as $\hat{\mathbf{V}} = (\hat{v}_1, \ldots, \hat{v}_n)$ and $\hat{\mathbf{W}} = (\hat{w}_1, \ldots, \hat{w}_n)$ where the v_i are the eigenvectors obtained from the Johansen procedure with associated weights, w_i. Only the first r elements in $\hat{\mathbf{W}}$ and $\hat{\mathbf{V}}$ which are associated with stationary relationships should be labelled $\boldsymbol{\alpha}$ and $\boldsymbol{\beta}$, with the latter having reduced rank.
26. The *PcFiml* package automatically normalises along the diagonal of the $\boldsymbol{\beta}$-matrix, so that each column is normalised by a different variable in $\mathbf{z}_t$. The *Microfit* package normalises all columns by the same element (i.e., the first variable $\times -1$) and *Cats* asks the user to choose which variable in each column of $\boldsymbol{\beta}$ to use as the normalising variable.
27. Including centred seasonal dummies and a constant in $\mathbf{D}_t$.
28. Note, Paruolo (1993) has developed a joint test of s_1 and r.
29. Note, $*$ denotes an unrestricted value.
30. Note, in the *Cats* program this is referred to as Model 1.
31. Model 1 is when $\boldsymbol{\delta}_1 = \boldsymbol{\delta}_2 = \boldsymbol{\mu}_1 = \boldsymbol{\mu}_2 = 0$.
32. Note, one of the other variables in $\mathbf{z}_t$ may also be trend-stationary and form a cointegration relationship with time, so adding the trend to the cointegration space is necessary.
33. Note, in this form of the deterministic model, the constant in the cointegration space again cancels out with the intercept in the short-run model.
34. In *Cats*, it is possible to test for Models 1 and 5, but it is not possible to then use Model 5 when analysing the $I(1)$ model, because it is not considered a plausible alternative.
35. Recall that each of the r cointegration vectors in $\boldsymbol{\beta}$ is associated with a particular column in $\boldsymbol{\alpha}$ which must contain at least one non-zero element. See (4.16) for a simple example.
36. As shown in the last chapter, when discussing the problems of using a single equation approach to cointegration.
37. See the discussion in Chapter 2 on short-run models for more information on the role of the speed-of-adjustment parameter.
38. Note, if x_t is both weakly exogenous and insignificant in the long-run cointegration space (the latter can be tested when imposing restrictions on the $\boldsymbol{\beta}$), then we can condition on x_t by confining it to lie within the short-run model. Then (5.8) can be reformulated as:

$$\Delta \mathrm{y}_t = \Gamma_0 \Delta \mathrm{x}_t + \tilde{\Gamma}_1 \Delta \mathrm{z}_{t-1} + \alpha\beta' \mathrm{y}_{t-2} + \mathrm{u}_t$$

where x_{t-2} has been removed from the vector determining the long-run relations.

39. Of course, the estimates of the short-run parameters are different, as are t-values associated with each of the α_{ij}, since the conditional model includes $\Delta\mathbf{x}_t$ on the right-hand side of the system determining the Δy_t.
40. The next chapter will illustrate the role of testing individual α_{ij} and show up the potential confusion that arises from labelling these as tests of 'weak exogeneity'.
41. Recall, the reduced rank regression procedure provides information on how many unique cointegration vectors *span* the cointegration space, while any linear combination of the stationary vectors is itself a stationary vector and thus the estimates produced for any particular column in $\boldsymbol{\beta}$ are not necessarily unique.
42. See the discussion in the last chapter about the appropriateness of the single equation model.
43. Note, it is common practice to denote the linear restrictions on the α as matrix $\mathbf{A}$, even though $\mathbf{A}$ is also used (perhaps confusingly) to indicate the companion matrix.
44. Although both are used to solve the reduced rank regression, the user will only have to specify either $\mathbf{A}$ or $\mathbf{B}$ (e.g., *PcFiml* uses $\mathbf{A}$ while *Cats* uses $\mathbf{B}$).
45. I.e., $l = ((k \times n) + \text{number of deterministic components}) \times n$.
46. The *Cats* manual reports how such t-values are calculated.
47. Note, the degrees of freedom were calculated using $(r \times (n - m)) = 2$.
48. Implementation of the testing procedure is easy for the user, since all that is required is to specify the constraint using a 'constraints editor' built into *PcFiml*. More will be said regarding this when testing for unique cointegration vectors.
49. *Cats* allows either form to be used, although using $\mathbf{H}_i$ has the advantage that if the cointegration vector is identified then the program will supply 'standard errors' for each β_{ij}.
50. More exactly, the parameters of the model are estimated under the restrictions using an iterative procedure which (in *Cats*) involves successive reduced rank regressions. Each iteration solves sequentially for $\boldsymbol{\beta}_1$ then $\boldsymbol{\beta}_2$, and so on, up to $\boldsymbol{\beta}_r$, with each step involving a reduced rank regression. This then gives the restricted log-likelihood function which can be compared to the unrestricted model's log-likelihood function (based on a single reduced rank regression), so allowing LR test statistics to be computed. Details are given in Johansen and Juselius (1994, p. 16).
51. Only the 'normalised' parameter is unrestricted.
52. The possibility that p_1 and p_2 could be $I(2)$ may also be a factor affecting this test in so far as the $r = 2$ cointegration vectors would then not be stationary.
53. Note, Podivinsky (1992) provided an alternative F-type test to Johansen's LR test, which adjusts for degrees of freedom (see the discussion above of similar adjustments that can be applied to reduced rank tests and tests of restrictions on α). However, the Monte-Carlo work of Psaradakis (1994) suggests that overall such small-sample corrections of the $\mathcal{H}_4$-test do not have particularly desirable properties. Moreover, as yet they have not been applied to other tests of restrictions on $\boldsymbol{\beta}$.
54. It would obviously be feasible (even desirable) to test for these jointly by specifying restrictions on both cointegration vectors (see below).
55. Details are given in Johansen and Juselius (1992, section 5.2).
56. This is calculated in the same way as for the $\mathbf{H}_{5.1}$.
57. Of course, when $r = 1$, then the space is uniquely defined by a single vector. Note also, it may not be possible to identify unique vectors, and this does not invalidate the long-run stationary relationships between the variables in the cointegration space.
58. Most statistical software programs can handle these types of calculation with ease. An

example using *SHAZAM*, based on the second example in Table 5.6, can be found in the appendix to this chapter.

59. This test is not computed in the same way as the more general tests since the solution of the reduced rank regression now involves numerical optimisation based on a switching algorithm that concentrates the likelihood function on $\boldsymbol{\alpha}$ and $\boldsymbol{\beta}$, respectively.
60. Note, the degrees of freedom are, as above, calculated as $\nu = (5-2+1-2) + (5-2+1-1) = 5$, since $s_1 = 2$ and not 3.
61. Restrictions on $\boldsymbol{\alpha}$ can also have implications for the dynamic stability of the short-run model, as Fischer (1993) shows.
62. Note, deriving the degrees of freedom in this test is not straightforward, although in this instance adding together the degrees of freedom from the separate tests provides the appropriate value. When the model is not identified, then ν is only approximate.
63. It is difficult to be conclusive, because of a lack of information on the restrictions actually imposed (they were arrived at by choosing $\boldsymbol{\xi}$ such that $\boldsymbol{\alpha\beta}' = \boldsymbol{\alpha\xi}^{-1}\boldsymbol{\xi\beta}' = \boldsymbol{\alpha}^*\boldsymbol{\beta}'^*$, where $\boldsymbol{\xi}$ is any $r \times r$ non-singular matrix). However, it appears from applying the test given in (5.20) that the third vector is not identified due to the fact that the space spanned by the second vector is contained in the space spanned by this third vector.

6

Modelling the short-run and other extensions

Important terms and concepts

Short-run VAR Dynamic modelling Parsimonious VAR (or VECM) Conditional VAR-modelling Structural modelling Simultaneous effects FIML Non-linear constraints Identification of the short-run structural model

Introduction

Obtaining long-run estimates of the cointegration relationships is only a first step to estimating the complete model. The short-run structure of the model is also important in terms of the information it conveys on the short-run adjustment behaviour of economic variables, and this is likely to be at least as interesting from a policy viewpoint as estimates of the long-run. Another important aspect of modelling both the short- and long-run structures of the system is that we can attempt to model the contemporaneous interactions between variables, that is, we can estimate a simultaneous system, and this then provides an additional layer of valuable information (see Hendry and Doornik, 1994, for a full discussion of this and related issues). The approach adopted here amounts to the following steps, and is greatly influenced by the Hendry approach of general-to-specific modelling:

- Use the Johansen approach to obtain the long-run cointegration relationships between the variables in the system.
- Estimate the short-run VAR in error-correction form (hence VECM) with the cointegration relationships explicitly included and obtain a parsimonious

representation of the system. This is by custom denoted the PVAR, but it seems more aptly designated a PVECM.

- Condition on any (weakly) exogenous variables thus obtaining a conditional PVECM model.
- Model any simultaneous effects between the variables in the (conditional) model and test to ensure that the resulting restricted model parsimoniously encompasses the PVECM.

To illustrate these steps the small UK monetary model presented in Hendry and Doornik (op. cit.) is used (with seasonally *un*adjusted data). Although the final version estimated is different, the purpose here is to illustrate the methodology involved, rather than to argue with their model of the money-demand function.[1] It will also become apparent that no attempt is made to discuss the full implications and procedures of dynamic modelling in depth. That is beyond the scope of this book, so what follows is by way of an introduction to (and illustration of) the topic.

Finally, we conclude the chapter with a few general comments on some current issues and developments in cointegration analysis which seem likely to feature more prominently in future applications of the overall approach.

Estimating the long-run cointegration relationships

The Johansen approach for obtaining estimates of the long-run relationships between the variables ($\mathbf{z}_t$) in the multivariate model was discussed extensively in the last chapter. Here we present a slightly different version of the UK money-demand model that was used to illustrate the approach, as a first step towards estimating the short-run dynamic model.

In the last chapter, it was possible to identify a single cointegration vector describing the stationary relationship between the following $I(1)$ variables: $m-p$, y, Δp and R. Hendry and Mizon (1993) allow for a time trend in the cointegration vectors to take account of long-run exogenous growth not already included in the model.[2] Taking a similar approach with a seasonally unadjusted data-set produced the results in Table 6.1 (note *PcFiml* was used and all the test statistics reported were

Table 6.1 Tests of the cointegration rank[a] for the UK money-demand data (1963:1–1989:2)

$H_0: r$	$n-r$	$\hat{\lambda}_i$	$-T\log(1-\hat{\lambda}_{r+1})$	λ_{max} (0.95)	$-T\Sigma\log(1-\hat{\lambda}_i)$	λ_{trace} (0.95)
0	4	0.586	89.01**	31.5	130.80**	63.0
1	3	0.221	25.24*	25.5	41.76*	42.4
2	2	0.105	11.20	19.0	16.52	25.3
3	1	0.051	5.32	12.2	5.32	12.2

[a] See the discussion of Table 5.4.

** Denotes rejection at the 5 per cent significance level; * denotes rejection at the 10 per cent significance level.

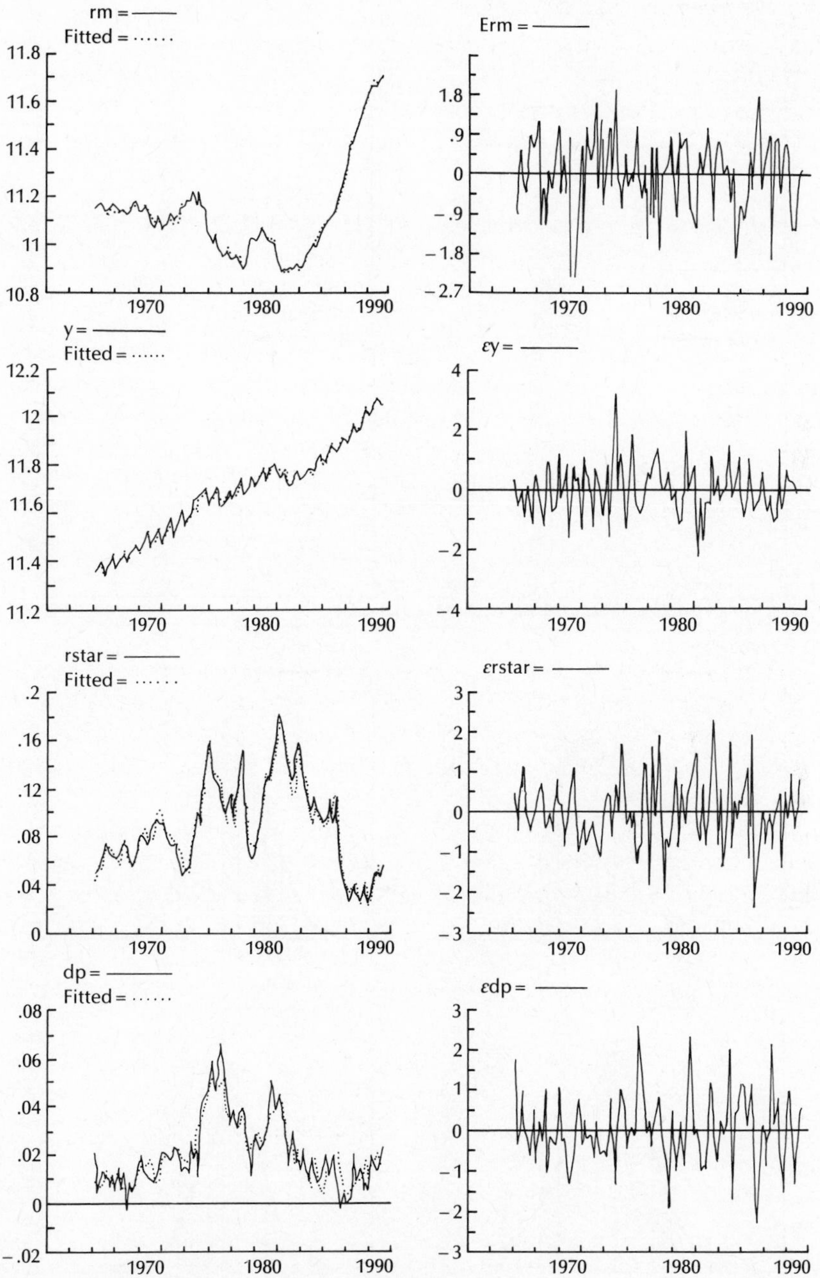

Figure 6.1 Actual and fitted values and scaled residuals

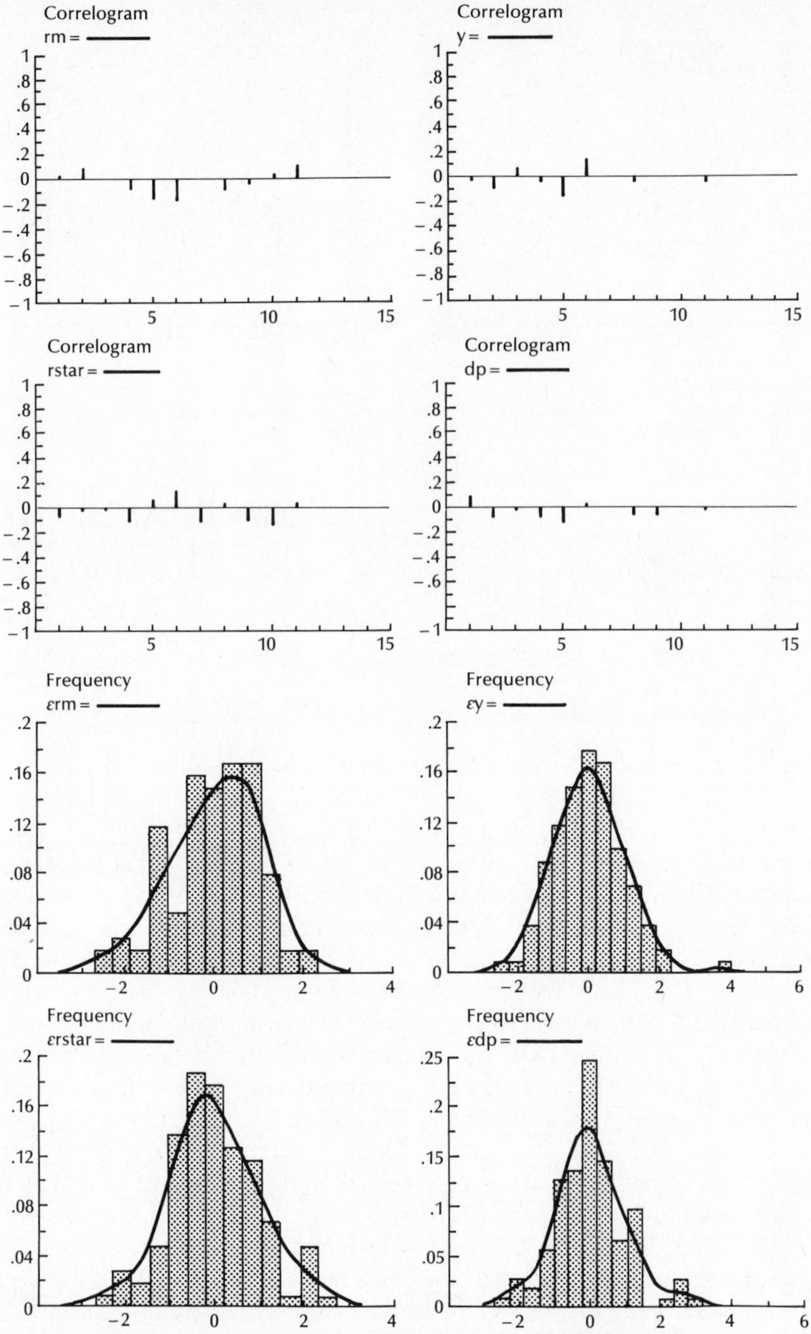

Figure 6.2 Diagnostic graphs of the residuals: correlogram and distribution

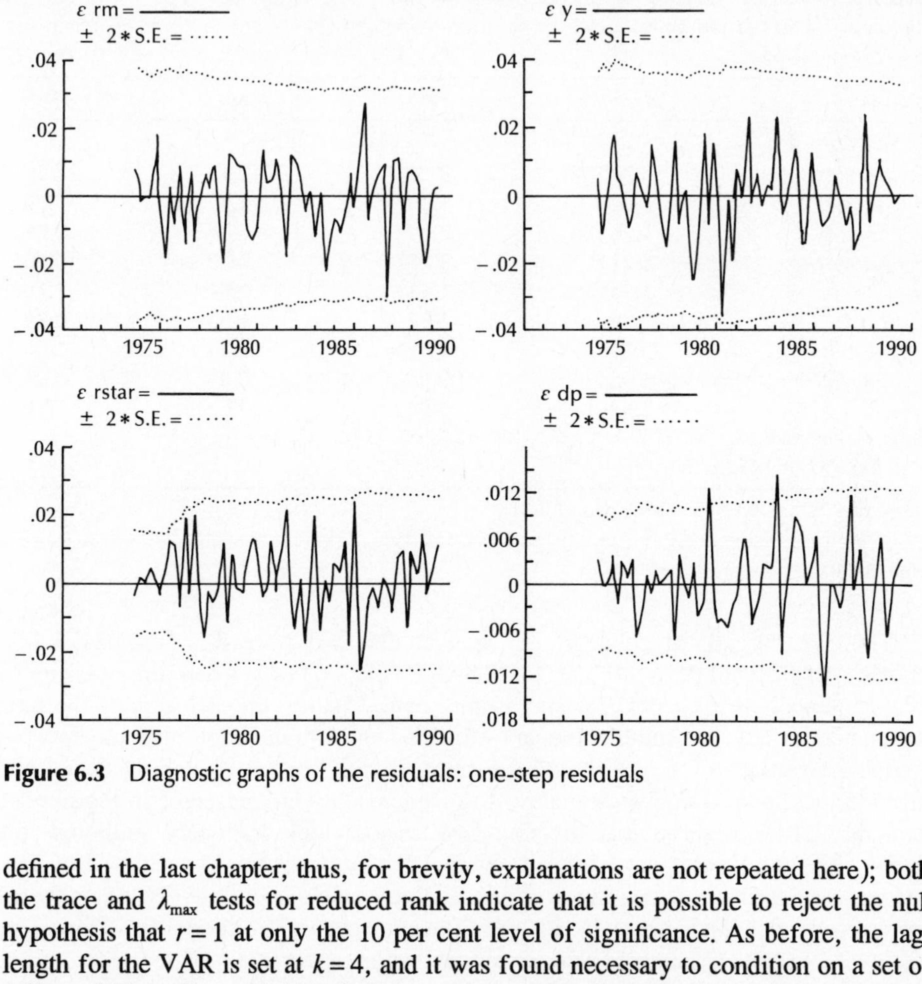

Figure 6.3 Diagnostic graphs of the residuals: one-step residuals

defined in the last chapter; thus, for brevity, explanations are not repeated here); both the trace and λ_{max} tests for reduced rank indicate that it is possible to reject the null hypothesis that $r=1$ at only the 10 per cent level of significance. As before, the lag-length for the VAR is set at $k=4$, and it was found necessary to condition on a set of $I(0)$ variables, $\mathbf{D}_t$, which included centred seasonal dummy variables and three (impulse) dummies that take account of outliers in the data. Hendry and Mizon include dummies labelled DOIL and DOUT to account for the 'Barber boom' and the two oil price shocks in the 1970s. Here it was found necessary to include three separate dummies that took on a value of one in 1973:3, 1974:2 and 1977:1. The first two (denoted D_1 and D_2) were necessary to 'induce' normal residuals in the equation determining Δp, while the third dummy (denoted D_3) was sufficient to account for an outlier in the interest rate equation.[3] The model evaluation diagnostic tests are provided in Table 6.2, and these show that the residuals can generally be considered to be Gaussian (the only remaining system problem is the rejection of normality at the 5 per cent level). Actual and fitted values for each equation are given in Figure 6.1, while Figures 6.2 and 6.3 present various plots associated with diagnostic testing of the residuals, confirming that the performance of the VECM is generally satisfactory.

Table 6.2 Model evaluation diagnostics:[a] the UK money-demand data (1963:1–1989:2) (an intercept, seasonal dummies, and three impulse dummies in $\mathbf{D}_t$; a time trend in the cointegration space)

Statistic	$m-p$	y	Δp	R
Lag-length = 4				
$F_{k=1}(4, 74)$	8.74**	8.99**	2.12	27.09**
$F_{k=2}(4, 74)$	2.02	1.00	2.82*	2.10
$F_{k=3}(4, 74)$	1.56	2.87*	0.54	0.05
$F_{k=4}(4, 74)$	6.21**	3.28*	0.89	0.66
$\hat{\sigma}$	1.54%	1.61%	0.61%	1.26%
$F_{ar}(5, 72)$	1.29	1.97	1.05	0.98
$F_{arch}(4, 69)$	0.76	1.12	0.73	1.68
$F_{het}(34, 42)$	0.35	0.65	0.88	0.94
$\chi^2_{nd}(2)$	3.52	5.02	4.62	1.10
Multivariate tests: $F_{ar}(80, 215) = 0.93$; $F_{het}(340, 345) = 0.53$; $\chi^2_{nd}(8) = 16.42$*; $F_{ur}(68,292) = 127.58$**				

[a] See the discussion of Tables 5.1 and 5.3.

** Denotes rejection at the 1 per cent significance level; * denotes rejection at the 5 per cent significance level.

The two normalised cointegration vectors obtained were $\boldsymbol{\beta}_1' = [1, 0.029, 4.440, 8.063, -0.007]$ and $\boldsymbol{\beta}_2' = [-0.113, 1, -2.893, 0.208, -0.006]$, where the ordering of the elements is $m-p$, y, Δp, R and a time trend. Clearly, the inclusion of the time trend has an adverse (multicollinear) effect on the estimate for y in the money-demand function (cf. $\boldsymbol{\beta}_1$). Plots of the cointegration vectors (including actual and fitted values) and recursive estimates of the eigenvalues are presented in Figures 6.4 and 6.5. These indicate that the first two vectors look stationary (although the money-demand vector is less so), while the common-trend vectors are non-stationary. Estimates of these vectors are relatively stable over time (as shown by the recursively obtained eigenvalues which were generally constant). Thus, the following tests of hypotheses were conducted with respect to $\boldsymbol{\beta} = (\mathbf{H}_1\boldsymbol{\varphi}_1, \mathbf{H}_2\boldsymbol{\varphi}_2)$:

$$\boldsymbol{\beta} = \begin{bmatrix} 1 & 0 \\ -1 & 1 \\ * & * \\ * & * \\ 0 & * \end{bmatrix} \quad \mathbf{R}_1 = \begin{bmatrix} 1 & 0 \\ 1 & 0 \\ 0 & 0 \\ 0 & 0 \\ 0 & 1 \end{bmatrix} \quad \mathbf{H}_1 = \begin{bmatrix} 1 & 0 & 0 \\ -1 & 0 & 0 \\ 0 & 1 & 0 \\ 0 & 0 & 1 \\ 0 & 0 & 0 \end{bmatrix}$$

$$\mathbf{R}_2 = \begin{bmatrix} 1 \\ 0 \\ 0 \\ 0 \\ 0 \end{bmatrix} \quad \mathbf{H}_2 = \begin{bmatrix} 0 & 0 & 0 & 0 \\ 1 & 0 & 0 & 0 \\ 0 & 1 & 0 & 0 \\ 0 & 0 & 1 & 0 \\ 0 & 0 & 0 & 1 \end{bmatrix}$$

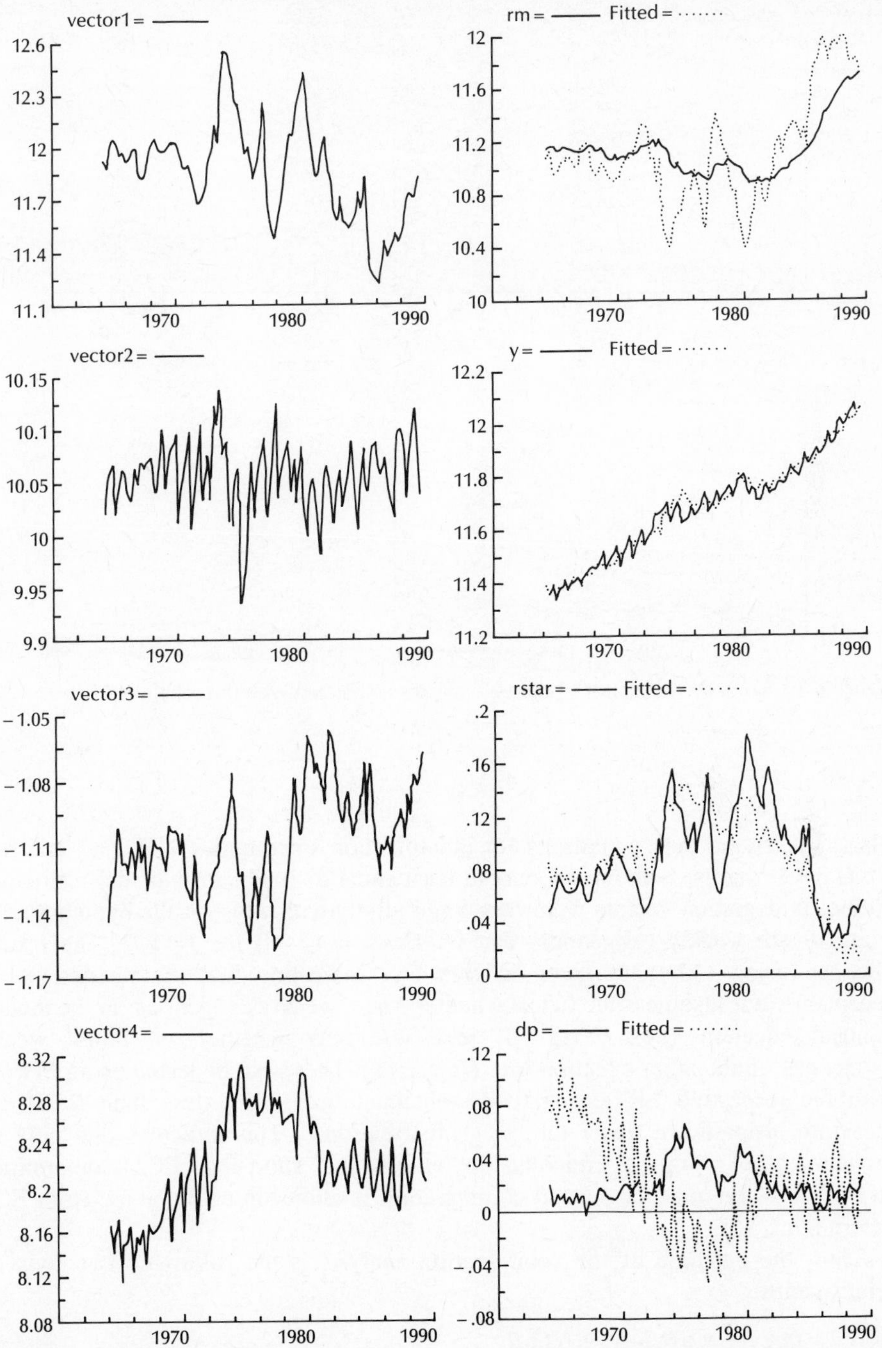

Figure 6.4 Plots of the relations $\hat{\mathbf{v}}_i'\mathbf{z}_t$ (those which cointegrate can be denoted as $\hat{\boldsymbol{\beta}}_i'\mathbf{z}_t$)

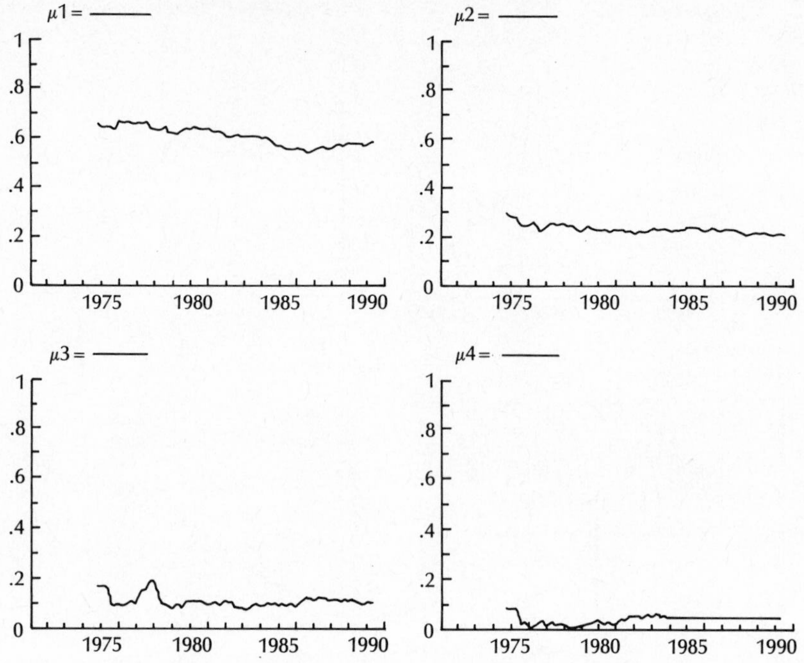

Figure 6.5 Recursive estimates of the eigenvalues associated with the relations $\hat{\mathbf{v}}_i'\mathbf{z}_t$

These satisfy the rank conditions for identification since rank $(\mathbf{R}_1'\mathbf{H}_2)=2$ and rank $(\mathbf{R}_2'\mathbf{H}_1)=1$, that is, both have a rank at least equal to 1. The tests of the restrictions on the cointegration vectors were conducted jointly with a test of the hypothesis that y and R are weakly exogenous, that is, H: $\alpha_{2j}=\alpha_{4j}=0$ for $j=1,2$. The results, obtained using *Cats*, are given in Box 6.1, indicating that the restrictions are acceptable. It is also possible to test whether Δp is 'weakly exogenous' in the money-demand equation (i.e. H: $\alpha_{31}=0$) and separately whether $m-p$ is 'weakly exogenous' in the other equation (i.e. H: $\alpha_{12}=0$). These can be tested using *PcFiml*, with the respective LR test statistics obtained both being less than 0.001 and therefore insignificant under the $\chi^2(1)$ distribution.[4,5] This indicates that only the money-demand long-run relationship enters the short-run ECM determining $\Delta(m-p)$, while only the second cointegration relationship enters a short-run ECM determining $\Delta^2 p$.

Thus, the outcome of the cointegration analysis is the following two long-run relationships:

$$\hat{\boldsymbol{\beta}}_1'\tilde{\mathbf{z}} = m - p - y + 6.54\Delta p + 6.66R$$

$$\hat{\boldsymbol{\beta}}_2'\tilde{\mathbf{z}} = y - 0.007t - 2.81\Delta p + 1.14R \tag{6.1}$$

Box 6.1 Testing joint restrictions on $\boldsymbol{\alpha}$ and $\boldsymbol{\beta}$: *Cats* output for the UK money-demand model

```
Testing Restrictions on α and β

The LR test, χ²(5) = 3.60, p-value = 0.61

β'
  m-p          y           Δp          R          time
 1.000      -1.000       6.541       6.657       0.000
 0.000       1.000      -2.810       1.136      -0.007

"STANDARD ERRORS" FOR β'
 0.000       0.000       0.788       0.301       0.000
 0.000       0.000       0.414       0.172       0.000

α           T-VALUES FOR ALPHA
-0.179      -0.083      -9.293      -1.081
 0.000       0.000       0.000       0.000
 0.012       0.152       1.556       5.109
 0.000       0.000       0.000       0.000
```

which define the error-correction terms to be included when estimating the VECM. Note $\tilde{\mathbf{z}}_t = [(m-p)_t, y_t, \Delta p_t, R_t, t]'$ while $\mathbf{z}_t$ has no time trend in the vector.

To reiterate, the first relationship is the standard money-demand relationship, while the second vector is deemed to represent 'excess demand', with the deviation of output from trend having a significant positive relationship to inflation and a negative one to the interest rate. Note, Figure 6.4 shows that disequilibrium is large in the money-demand equation (as can be seen by comparing the actual and fitted values), but less so in the 'excess demand' relation, although since all the speed-of-adjustment parameters are small in value (cf. the estimates of $\boldsymbol{\alpha}$ in Box 6.1) both the money supply and inflation adjust relatively slowly to changes to the underlying equilibrium relationship.

Parsimonious VECM

Having obtained the long-run cointegration relations using the Johansen approach, it is now possible to reformulate the above model and estimate the VECM with the error-correction terms explicitly included:

$$\Delta\mathbf{z}_t = \boldsymbol{\Gamma}_1\Delta\mathbf{z}_{t-1} + \boldsymbol{\Gamma}_2\Delta\mathbf{z}_{t-2} + \boldsymbol{\Gamma}_3\Delta\mathbf{z}_{t-3} + \boldsymbol{\alpha}(\hat{\boldsymbol{\beta}}_1'\tilde{\mathbf{z}}_{t-1} + \hat{\boldsymbol{\beta}}_2'\tilde{\mathbf{z}}_{t-1}) + \boldsymbol{\Psi}\mathbf{D}_t + \mathbf{u}_t \tag{6.2}$$

Table 6.3 Certain model evaluation diagnostics relating to equation (6.2) (an intercept, seasonal dummies, and three impulse dummies in $\mathbf{D}_t$)

Statistic	$\Delta(m-p)$	Δy	$\Delta^2 p$	ΔR
Lag-length = 3				
$F_{k=1}(4, 77)$	4.88**	2.28	3.39*	1.85
$F_{k=2}(4, 77)$	4.57**	0.83	1.59	0.15
$F_{k=3}(4, 77)$	4.19**	3.84**	1.23	0.20
t-tests of significance				
$\hat{\boldsymbol{\beta}}_1'\tilde{\mathbf{z}}_{t-1}$	5.95**	0.07	1.72	0.76
$\hat{\boldsymbol{\beta}}_2'\tilde{\mathbf{z}}_{t-1}$	0.73	0.61	4.12**	0.75

** Denotes rejection at the 1 per cent significance level; * denotes rejection at the 5 per cent significance level.

It makes no difference whether $\tilde{\mathbf{z}}_t$ enters the error-correction term with a lag of $t-1$ or $t-k$, since these two forms of (6.2) can be shown to be equivalent. At this stage no separate restrictions are placed on each α_{ij} (even though the above testing of weak exogeneity in the long-run model indicates that only one cointegration relationship is present in each equation and therefore it is appropriate to place restrictions on $\boldsymbol{\alpha}$). Thus OLS is still an efficient way to estimate each equation comprising (6.2) given that each has a common set of (lagged) regressors. Since all the variables in the model are now $I(0)$, statistical inference using standard t- and F-tests is valid.

Estimating the multivariate system denoted by (6.2) confirms the above tests of weak exogeneity and also tests whether all the (common) lagged $\Delta\mathbf{z}_{t-i}$ are significant in every equation (see Table 6.3). Thus, parsimony can be achieved by removing the insignificant regressors and testing whether this reduction in the model is supported by an F-test. In fact retaining Δy_{t-1} in the system, while dropping all other non-significant lagged terms in Table 6.3 gave a test statistic of $F(24, 269) = 1.37$, which results in an acceptance of the null hypothesis that the omitted regressors have zero coefficients. Finally, the resultant model was checked in terms of diagnostic tests on the residuals (cf. Table 6.2), together with checks that parameter constancy holds (involving graphs of the recursive properties of the model, such as one-step residuals and Chow F-tests for break points in the individual equations and in the system as a whole). Although these tests are not reported here, the parsimonious reduced-form system is congruent as defined by the Hendry general-to-specific approach to modelling.

Conditional PVECM

From tests involving the long-run model, as well as tests of the significance of the error-correction terms in the PVECM, it is possible to accept that y and R are weakly

Table 6.4 OLS estimates of the conditional model

Variable	$\Delta(m-p)_t$		$\Delta^2 p_t$	
	Coefficient	t-values	Coefficient	t-values
Δy_t	0.089	0.95	−0.015	0.43
ΔR_t	−0.514	4.04	0.137	2.90
$\Delta^2 p_{t-1}$	0.694	2.85	−0.332	3.69
$\Delta(m-p)_{t-1}$	−0.338	3.61	0.074	2.13
$\Delta(m-p)_{t-2}$	−0.292	3.41	0.089	2.82
$\Delta(m-p)_{t-3}$	−0.285	4.09	0.027	1.05
$\hat{\boldsymbol{\beta}}_1'\tilde{\mathbf{z}}_{t-1}$	−0.153	9.94	0.003	0.44
$\hat{\boldsymbol{\beta}}_2'\tilde{\mathbf{z}}_{t-1}$	−0.056	1.03	0.113	5.57
D_1	−0.010	0.61	0.016	2.61
D_2	0.059	3.47	−0.023	3.58
Constant	0.672	1.08	−1.284	5.59
SEAS	−0.020	2.54	−0.003	1.09
$SEAS_{t-1}$	−0.012	2.06	0.007	3.31
$SEAS_{t-2}$	−0.011	1.79	0.003	1.35
Diagnostics				
$\hat{\sigma}$	1.55%		0.57%	
$F_{ar}(5, 81)$	1.66		1.13	
$F_{arch}(4, 78)$	0.44		0.47	
$F_{het}(16, 69)$	0.84		0.89	
$\chi^2_{nd}(2)$	1.93		8.14*	

Multivariate tests: $F_{ar}(20, 150) = 1.06$; $F_{het}(48, 200) = 0.95$; $\chi^2_{nd}(4) = 8.27$; $F_{ur}(28, 164) = 12.66^{**}$

** Denotes rejection at the 1 per cent significance level; * denotes rejection at the 5 per cent significance level.

exogenous in the system under investigation. Therefore, we can condition on these two variables, assuming that we are more concerned with modelling money demand and inflation. Hendry and Doornik (1994) retain the full system, and thus continue to model the weakly exogenous variables.[6] Thus, our system is now defined as (see also equation (5.8)):

$$\Delta \mathbf{y}_t = \boldsymbol{\Gamma}_0 \Delta \mathbf{x}_t + \boldsymbol{\Gamma}_1 \Delta \mathbf{z}_{t-1} + \boldsymbol{\Gamma}_2 \Delta \mathbf{z}_{t-2} + \boldsymbol{\Gamma}_3 \Delta \mathbf{z}_{t-3} + \boldsymbol{\alpha}_1 (\hat{\boldsymbol{\beta}}_1' \tilde{\mathbf{z}}_{t-1} + \hat{\boldsymbol{\beta}}_2' \tilde{\mathbf{z}}_{t-1}) + \boldsymbol{\Psi} \mathbf{D}_t + \mathbf{u}_t \quad (6.3)$$

where $\mathbf{y}_t = [(m-p)_t, \Delta p_t]'$ and $\mathbf{x}_t = [y_t, R_t]'$ and $\boldsymbol{\alpha}_1$ is equal to $\boldsymbol{\alpha}$ with $\alpha_{2j} = \alpha_{4j} = 0$ for $j = 1, 2$. It is possible to test for a parsimonious version of (6.3), where non-significant (common) lagged $\Delta \mathbf{z}_{t-i}$ are removed and the resulting reduction in the model is supported by an F-test.

The results from estimating the parsimonious version of the conditional model are given in Table 6.4. The various diagnostic tests of the residuals indicate that the model has the desired properties for OLS estimation, other than an indication that the rate of inflation equation has non-normal errors. However, multivariate tests are satisfactory.[7] The correlation of actual and fitted values is 0.90 and 0.77, respectively, for the $\Delta(m-p)_t$ and $\Delta^2 p_t$ equations. As earlier tests have already indicated, the money-demand error-correction term (cointegration relationship) is only significant in the first equation, while the 'excess demand' ECM is only significant in the second equation. The coefficients attached to these terms (i.e., the speed of adjustment to disequilibrium) are not dissimilar to those obtained using the Johansen approach (see Box 6.1). The change in output, Δy_t, is not significant in either equation and could be dropped but it is retained in order to model the system.

Structural modelling

A major feature of the last model is the rather large correlation of −0.30 between the residuals of the two equations. This suggests that the money-demand and rate of inflation equations are not independent of each other, but rather that there are simultaneous effects between $\Delta(m-p)_t$ and $\Delta^2 p_t$ that could be modelled by imposing some structure on the conditional PVECM.[8] That is, it might seem reasonable to presume that $\Delta(m-p)_t$ contemporaneously depends on $\Delta^2 p_t$. To ignore this information, if it is correct, means that OLS estimation of the PVECM will be inconsistent.

Estimation of a structural model requires the inclusion of those endogenous variables that determine other endogenous variables, as additional right-hand-side regressors in the relevant equation (see Box 6.2 for a discussion of structural models and their identification). The model also requires to be identified, which among other requirements means that no more than $\ell = (n \times (k-1)) + r$ regressors can enter any equation and no more than $n \times \ell$ unknowns can enter the model (excluding intercepts and other deterministic components in $\mathbf{D}_t$).[9] Identification also requires that no equation can be a linear combination of other equations, and thus the actual location of the restrictions placed on an unrestricted structural VECM (which has $(n \times (n+\ell))$ potential regressors) is an important element in identifying unique short-run equations. As a very general guide, each equation in the model requires at least one unique predetermined variable (entering with a non-zero coefficient) to identify it, and in the example used here we know from earlier testing that the money-demand error-correction term enters only the equation determining $\Delta(m-p)_t$, while the 'excess demand' term only enters the $\Delta^2 p_t$ equation.

Before proceeding to estimate a simultaneous model, using the FIML procedure in *PcFiml*, it is necessary to discuss the status of the error-correction terms in each equation. These are not estimated by the short-run model since they have been previously obtained when the long-run model was estimated using the Johansen approach. Thus, they enter as identities which can be obtained by reformulating (6.1) as:

$$\hat{\boldsymbol{\beta}}_1'\tilde{\mathbf{z}}_t \equiv \hat{\boldsymbol{\beta}}_1'\tilde{\mathbf{z}}_{t-1} + \Delta(m-p)_t - \Delta y_t + 6.54\Delta^2 p_t + 6.66\Delta R_t$$
$$\hat{\boldsymbol{\beta}}_2'\tilde{\mathbf{z}}_t \equiv \hat{\boldsymbol{\beta}}_2'\tilde{\mathbf{z}}_{t-1} + \Delta(y_t - 0.007t) - 2.81\Delta^2 p_t + 1.14\Delta R_t \qquad (6.4)$$

Box 6.2 Structural models and identification

The structural VECM-counterpart of the example used here requires the reduced-form (6.2) to be reformulated as

$$\mathbf{A}_0\Delta\mathbf{z}_t = \mathbf{A}_1\Delta\mathbf{z}_{t-1} + \mathbf{A}_2\Delta\mathbf{z}_{t-2} + \mathbf{A}_3\Delta\mathbf{z}_{t-3} + \mathbf{a}(\hat{\boldsymbol{\beta}}_1'\tilde{\mathbf{z}}_{t-1} + \hat{\boldsymbol{\beta}}_2'\tilde{\mathbf{z}}_{t-1}) + \boldsymbol{\Psi}\mathbf{D}_t + \boldsymbol{\varepsilon}_t$$
$$\boldsymbol{\varepsilon}_t \sim \mathrm{NI}(0, \boldsymbol{\Omega}) \qquad (6.2.1)$$

where $\mathbf{A}_i = \mathbf{A}_0\boldsymbol{\Gamma}_i$, for $i = 1$, 2, and 3; $\mathbf{a} = \mathbf{A}_0\boldsymbol{\alpha}$, $\boldsymbol{\Psi} = \mathbf{A}_0\boldsymbol{\Psi}$, $\boldsymbol{\Omega} = \mathbf{A}_0\boldsymbol{\Sigma}\mathbf{A}_0'$, and $\boldsymbol{\varepsilon}_t = \mathbf{A}_0\mathbf{u}_t$. That is, (6.2.1) is obtained by premultiplying the reduced-form through by the $(n \times n)$ matrix $\mathbf{A}_0$, where the latter specifies the structure that links the endogenous variables in the model. To see this, assume for the moment that $k = 2$ (this will simplify notation by removing the terms involving $\mathbf{A}_2\Delta\mathbf{z}_{t-2}$ and $\mathbf{A}_3\Delta\mathbf{z}_{t-3}$), ignore the term $\boldsymbol{\Psi}\mathbf{D}_t$, and write out the left-hand side of the structural VECM given in (6.2.1):

$$\begin{bmatrix} 1 & A_{12} & A_{13} & A_{14} \\ A_{21} & 1 & A_{23} & A_{24} \\ A_{31} & A_{32} & 1 & A_{34} \\ A_{41} & A_{42} & A_{43} & 1 \end{bmatrix} \begin{bmatrix} \Delta(m-p)_t \\ \Delta y_t \\ \Delta^2 p_t \\ \Delta R_t \end{bmatrix} = \mathbf{A}_1\Delta\mathbf{z}_{t-1} + \mathbf{a}(\hat{\boldsymbol{\beta}}_1'\tilde{\mathbf{z}}_{t-1} + \hat{\boldsymbol{\beta}}_2'\tilde{\mathbf{z}}_{t-1}) + \boldsymbol{\varepsilon}_t \qquad (6.2.2)$$

As can be seen, the parameters A_{ij} contemporaneously link all the endogenous variables in $\mathbf{z}_t$. To proceed to the identification of the short-run dynamic model, (6.2.1) can be rewritten in compact notation as:

$$\mathbf{A}'\mathbf{X}_t = \boldsymbol{\Psi}\mathbf{D}_t + \boldsymbol{\varepsilon}_t \qquad (6.2.3)$$

where $\mathbf{A}' = [\mathbf{A}_0, \mathbf{A}_1, \mathbf{A}_2, \mathbf{A}_3, \mathbf{a}]$ is an $((n + \ell) \times n)$ matrix, with $\ell = (n \times (k-1)) + r$, and where $\mathbf{X}_t' = [\Delta\mathbf{z}_t', \Delta\mathbf{z}_{t-1}', \Delta\mathbf{z}_{t-2}', \Delta\mathbf{z}_{t-3}', \tilde{\mathbf{z}}_{t-1}'\hat{\boldsymbol{\beta}}]$. Identification in the short-run model requires restrictions on the structural equations and in particular restrictions on $\mathbf{A}$. These restrictions are typically determined by economic theory, and, as Johnston (1984, p. 453) explains '...the most common restrictions are *exclusion* restrictions, which specify that certain variables do *not* appear in certain equations'. However, homogeneity restrictions are also fairly common, and in general Johansen and Juselius (1994) show that identifying restrictions on the columns of $\mathbf{A}$, denoted as $(\mathbf{A}_1, \ldots, \mathbf{A}_{n+\ell})$, take the form:

$$\mathbf{A} = (\mathbf{H}_1\varphi_1, \mathbf{H}_2\varphi_2, \ldots, \mathbf{H}_{n+\ell}\varphi_{n+\ell}) \qquad (6.2.4)$$

which can be checked by the rank order condition as set out in (5.20), with $k = n - 1$, together with the computational procedure they suggest for obtaining the rank orders (see the discussion in the last chapter surrounding equation (5.20)).

It can now be seen why Δy_t, despite its insignificance in the conditional PVECM, has been retained, since a feature of the *PcFiml* program is that dropping it from the latter would have necessitated dropping it from (6.4).

Estimating the structural model and then dropping insignificant regressors gave

Table 6.5 FIML estimates of the conditional model

Variable	$\Delta(m-p)_t$		$\Delta^2 p_t$	
	Coefficient	*t*-values	Coefficient	*t*-values
$\Delta^2 p_t$	−0.980	3.18	—	—
ΔR_t	−0.321	2.55	0.140	3.08
$\Delta^2 p_{t-1}$			−0.314	3.82
$\Delta(m-p)_{t-1}$	−0.299	3.23	0.071	2.72
$\Delta(m-p)_{t-2}$	−0.140	2.02	0.083	3.30
$\Delta(m-p)_{t-3}$	−0.243	3.78	—	—
$\hat{\boldsymbol{\beta}}_1'\tilde{\mathbf{z}}_{t-1}$	−0.141	10.65	—	—
$\hat{\boldsymbol{\beta}}_2'\tilde{\mathbf{z}}_{t-1}$	—	—	0.117	6.57
D_1	—	—	0.015	2.46
D_2	0.040	2.57	−0.023	3.73
Constant	0.032	9.90	−1.330	6.57
SEAS	−0.026	5.40	−0.002	0.85
$SEAS_{t-1}$	−0.008	1.44	0.008	4.54
$SEAS_{t-2}$	−0.007	1.29	0.004	2.07
Diagnostics				
$\hat{\sigma}$	1.48%		0.57%	

Multivariate tests: $F_{\text{ar}}(140, 36) = 1.26$; $F_{\text{het}}(54, 203) = 1.01$; $\chi^2_{\text{nd}}(4) = 9.02$

**Denotes rejection at the 1 per cent significance level; * denotes rejection at the 5 per cent significance level.

the estimates reported in Table 6.5. The χ^2-test of the null hypothesis that these regressors are zero resulted in a test statistic of 2.31 (with five degrees of freedom), and the null is consequently accepted. More importantly, since the structural model has 22 parameters against 28 in the conditional PVECM (Table 6.4) the LR test of over-identifying restrictions is given by $\chi^2(6) = 5.25$, which does not reject. So the structural model can be said to encompass parsimoniously the conditional PVECM. Other tests of whether the model is congruent with the data evidence are provided in Table 6.5 and in Figures 6.6–6.9. The model has generally constant coefficients (Figure 6.7 shows one-step residuals and Figure 6.8 shows Chow tests for breaks in the series) and approximately 'white-noise', normally distributed errors (cf. the test statistics in Table 6.5). The model appears to 'fit' the data quite well (Figure 6.6), and the parameter estimates are generally sensible (and not very different to those in Hendry and Doornik, 1994). In economic terms the model supports the contention that causality is from output, interest rates and prices to money.[10,11] Moreover, the correlation between the structural residuals obtained from the FIML model is 0.06, indicating some success in modelling the structure underlying the data evidence that is available. Figure 6.9 shows one-step static (ex-post) forecasts for the last two years of the data (together with a small sample of the preforecast data); none of the forecasts lie outside their individual confidence bars, and therefore constancy of the model is readily accepted (this is confirmed by the final graph, which shows the

Chow tests of stability, with all χ^2-values lying below the 5 per cent significance line – see Doornik and Hendry, 1994, for details).

Finally, estimates of the coefficients attached to error-correction terms again confirm that the speed of adjustment to long-run changes in the variables is slow but significant.

Some current issues and developments

The $I(2)$ model was discussed in Chapter 5 (see especially Box 5.3), which showed how to test the null hypothesis that there are at most s_1 common $I(1)$ trends (and thus $s_2 = (n - r - s_1)$ common $I(2)$ trends) using a likelihood ratio test statistic equivalent to the trace statistic in the standard $I(1)$ approach. However, the Johansen (1994) approach for the $I(2)$ model goes much further than this in that he shows how it is possible to decompose $\boldsymbol{\Pi}$ into the r stationary relations, $\boldsymbol{\beta}$, and the $n-r$ non-stationary relations, $\boldsymbol{\beta}_{\perp}$, and $\boldsymbol{\beta}_{\perp}$ into the $I(1)$ and $I(2)$ 'common trends'. Various outcomes are possible in the model, including cointegration relationships which are stationary by themselves, those which are stationary when combined with a suitable combination of differenced $I(2)$ processes, and those which remain non-stationary relationships (with the possibility that some of the $I(1)$ relationships, while not stationary, can none the less be considered as cointegration relationships since they combine $I(2)$ variables down to a lower order of integration). Clearly, when software programs incorporating these various $I(2)$ features are available, more flexible applied modelling will emerge (e.g., Juselius, 1994).

Another likely development will be a movement away from the *linear* nature of restrictions placed on the $\boldsymbol{\alpha}$- and $\boldsymbol{\beta}$-matrices of speeds of adjustment and cointegration vectors. This will be useful for a number of reasons, including obviously when the underlying economic theory suggests that cointegration vectors include certain non-linear constraints both within and across equations. Factor demand models (for labour and capital) are an obvious example (cf. Harris, 1985). The *PcFiml* (version 8.0) package already allows for non-linear restrictions to be placed on these matrices, and it is likely that this will soon be reflected in applied econometrics analysis.

Other developments continue to appear, which improve the ability of applied researchers to undertake further tests, usually by offering alternative approaches. For instance, Leybourne (1994) offers an alternative to unit root testing which, it is claimed, avoids many of the problems associated with the size and power properties of the standard ADF test. His approach is to note that an $I(1)$ process exhibits autocorrelations which persist over time (see (2.1.1)), while the autocorrelations in an $I(0)$ process decrease much more rapidly (see (2.1.2)). He suggests a test statistic based on regressing the variable under consideration against a simple time trend to ascertain the length of the lag of the (positive values of the) autocorrelation function. Variables with lag-lengths that exceed a certain critical value(s) can be categorised as non-stationary. His Monte Carlo experiments suggest that this new procedure is fairly robust.

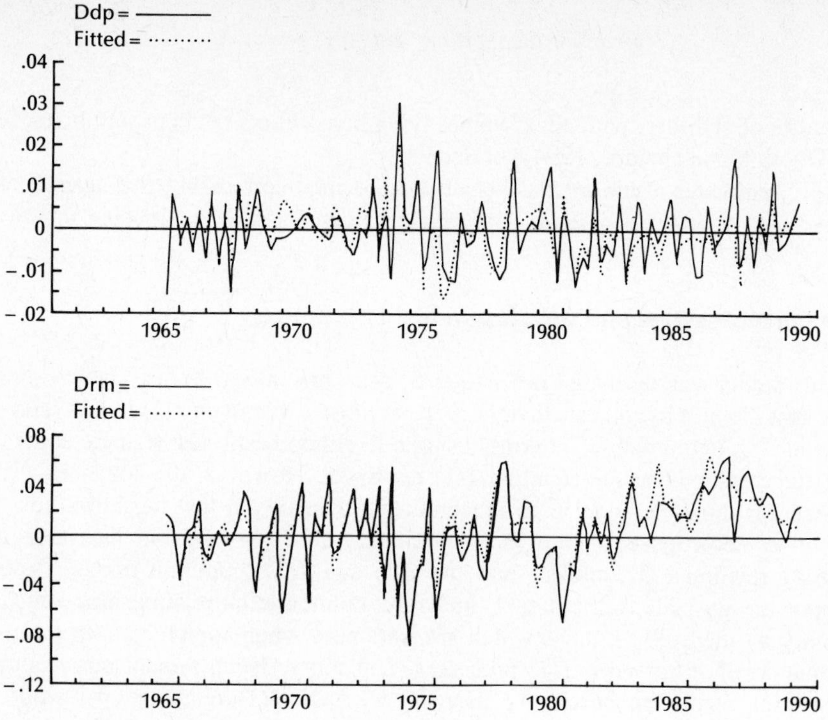

Figure 6.6 Actual and fitted values: short-run model

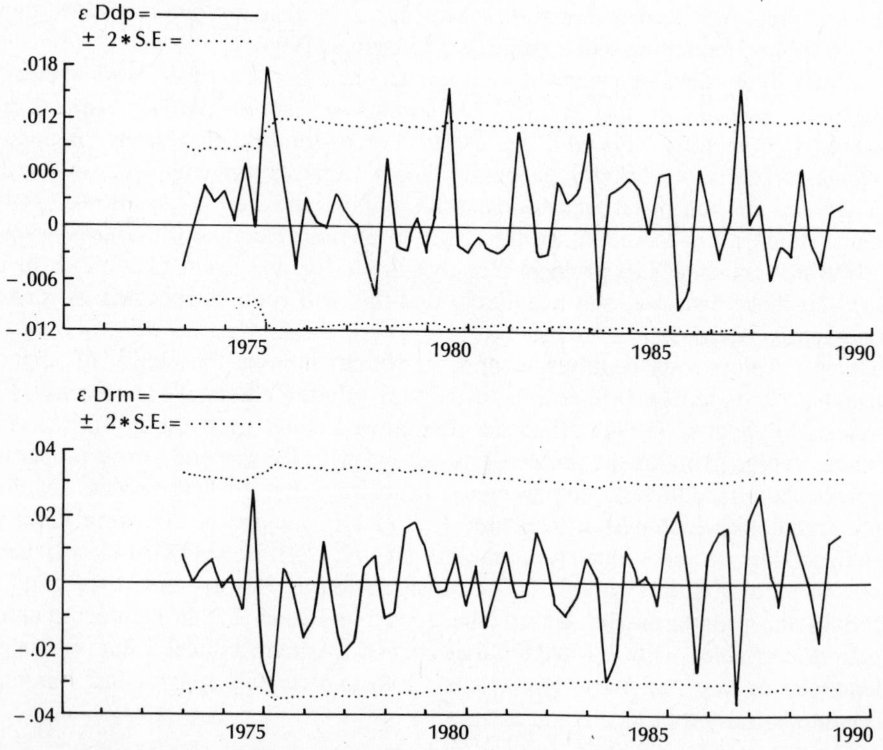

Figure 6.7 Diagnostic one-step residuals: short-run model

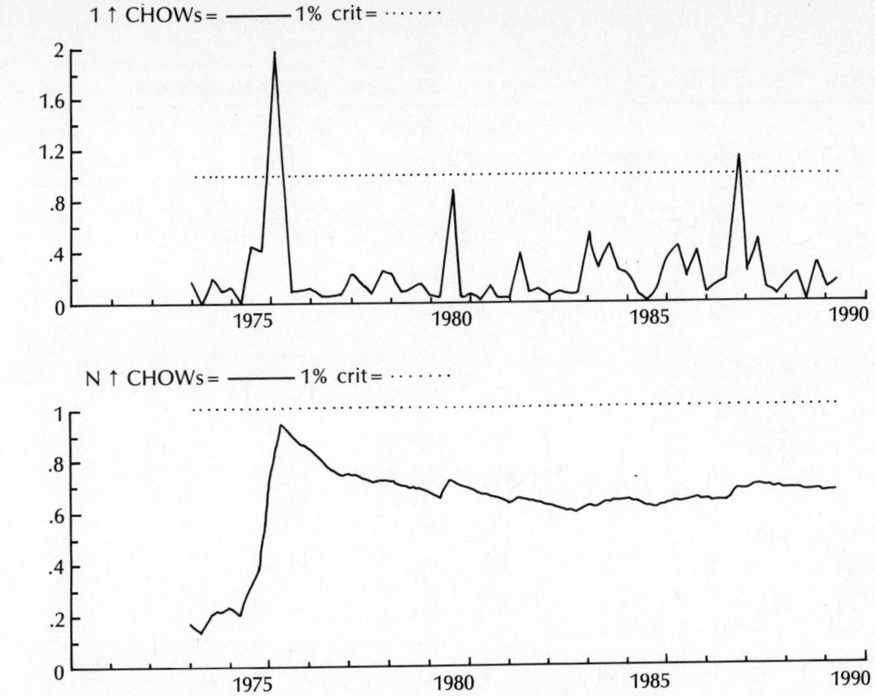

Figure 6.8 Diagnostic Chow tests of parameter stability: short-run model

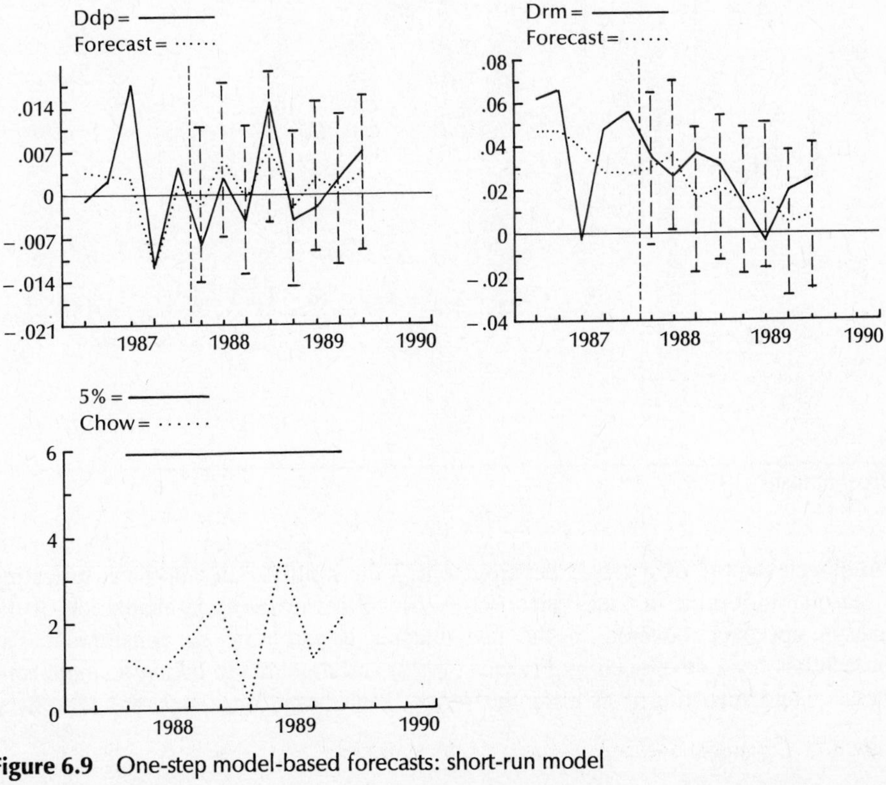

Figure 6.9 One-step model-based forecasts: short-run model

Table 6.6 Testing for (non-) seasonal unit roots using the Johansen approach

Rank of Π	Restrictions matrix	Cointegration vectors	Differencing filter	(non-) seasonal unit roots
3	$\mathbf{H}_{31} = \begin{bmatrix} -1 & 0 & 0 \\ 1 & -1 & 0 \\ 0 & 1 & -1 \\ 0 & 0 & 1 \end{bmatrix}$	$X_{2T} - X_{1T}$ $X_{3T} - X_{2T}$ $X_{4T} - X_{3T}$	$(1 - L)$	1
3	$\mathbf{H}_{32} = \begin{bmatrix} 1 & 0 & 0 \\ 1 & 1 & 0 \\ 0 & 1 & 1 \\ 0 & 0 & 1 \end{bmatrix}$	$X_{2T} + X_{1T}$ $X_{3T} + X_{2T}$ $X_{4T} + X_{3T}$	$(1 + L)$	-1
2	$\mathbf{H}_{21} = \begin{bmatrix} -1 & 0 \\ 0 & -1 \\ 1 & 0 \\ 0 & 1 \end{bmatrix}$	$X_{3T} - X_{1T}$ $X_{4T} - X_{2T}$	$(1 - L^2)$	$1, -1$
2	$\mathbf{H}_{22} = \begin{bmatrix} 1 & 0 \\ 0 & 1 \\ 1 & 0 \\ 0 & 1 \end{bmatrix}$	$X_{3T} + X_{1T}$ $X_{4T} + X_{2T}$	$(1 + L^2)$	$i, -i$
1	$\mathbf{H}_{11} = \begin{bmatrix} -1 \\ 1 \\ -1 \\ 1 \end{bmatrix}$	$X_{4T} - X_{3T} + X_{2T} - X_{1T}$	$(1 - L)(1 + L^2)$	$1, i, -i$
1	$\mathbf{H}_{12} = \begin{bmatrix} -1 \\ 1 \\ 1 \\ 1 \end{bmatrix}$	$X_{4T} + X_{3T} + X_{2T} + X_{1T}$	$(1 + L)(1 + L^2)$	$-1, i, -i$
0			$(1 - L^4)$	$1, -1, i, -i$

Source: Franses (1994).

Another example of a recent development is the multivariate approach to testing for seasonal unit roots in a univariate series. Since this involves an adaptation of the Johansen approach covered in the last chapter it can now be considered. The approach has been developed by Franses (1994) and amounts to taking a single time series, x_t, and rewriting it as s annual series, each based on a separate season, s.

When dealing with quarterly data, we obtain the vector $\mathbf{X}_T = [X_{1T}, X_{2T}, X_{3T}, X_{4T}]'$, where X_{iT} contains all the observations from quarter i for $t = 1, \ldots, T$. Writing this as a VECM (cf. 5.2) gives:

$$\Delta\mathbf{X}_T = \mathbf{\Gamma}_1 \Delta\mathbf{X}_{T-1} + \ldots + \mathbf{\Gamma}_{k-1}\Delta\mathbf{X}_{T-k+1} + \mathbf{\Pi}\mathbf{X}_{T-k} + \mathbf{\Psi}\mathbf{D}_t + \mathbf{u}_t \tag{6.5}$$

where $\mathbf{D}_t$ contains an intercept for each short-run equation, and in practice it is likely that $k = 1$. This model can be estimated in the usual way based on the Johansen reduced rank regression approach, and reduced rank tests (equations (5.4) and (5.5)) applied to determine the number of cointegration vectors contained in the model. If $r = 4$, there are no unit roots (seasonal or otherwise) in x_t, and hence the series (being stationary) does not require any differencing. If $r = 0$, then all the unit roots $(1, -1, i, -i)$ are contained in x_t (see the discussion of (3.7)), and this series needs to be differenced by $(1 - L^4)$. If $0 < r < 4$, then roots at different frequencies are present, and various tests of linear hypotheses can be conducted involving the cointegration vectors, which will determine the types of unit root present. These are summarised in Table 6.6 (Table 1 in Franses, 1994). Note, if the various tests of the rank of $\mathbf{\Pi}$ are accepted but the hypotheses concerning the form of the restrictions on the cointegration vectors in Table 6.6 are rejected, then this is evidence of the (as yet unmentioned) periodically integrated model with time varying seasonal parameters (see Osborn *et al.* 1988, for a discussion of this form of unit root).[12] Franses (op. cit.) provides the critical values of the tests for reduced rank when the sample is $T = 25$, 50, and when the constant term is restricted or unrestricted to lie in the cointegration space, since these are not the same as in the standard Johansen approach.[13] He also applies his approach to the Japanese consumption function data used in Engle *et al.* (1993), finding no evidence of seasonal unit roots in the data.

Other developments continue and it is hoped that, based on the discussions and exposition presented here, readers will be able to interpret the new literature as it appears, and make use of appropriate advances in their own applied work.

Notes

1. Of course, economic justification of the final model is usually necessary, but less attention is paid to this aspect of modelling in the example to be presented.
2. Recall, that on the basis of applying the Pantula principle to testing which version of the deterministic component should be used, it was possible to accept that there is only one cointegration vector and there are deterministic trends in the levels of the data (denoted Model 3). The Hendry and Mizon model includes two cointegration vectors and a linear trend in the cointegration space.
3. Note, there is little effect here from ignoring these outliers, but at other times 'factoring out' outliers can be important in terms of the estimates of the cointegration relations. When this occurs, and assuming that little prior knowledge is available to justify the dummy variables, it becomes a moot point whether conditioning in this fashion is valid. If there are genuine outliers, then it would seem justifiable to 'drop' such observations in terms of their influence on the model. The alternative would be to include other variables

that can explain the outliers.

4. The joint hypothesis that H: $\alpha_{21} = \alpha_{41} = \alpha_{22} = \alpha_{42} = \alpha_{31} = \alpha_{12} = 0$ results in an LR test statistic of 2.69, which is again insignificant under the $\chi^2(6)$-distribution.
5. This use of the term 'weakly exogenous' when testing the significance of a single element in α will be clarified when estimating the structural short-run model below, where we find evidence to suggest that in a system of simultaneous equations there is support for the notion that changes in prices 'cause' changes in the money supply.
6. In fact, their estimated equations for Δy_t and ΔR_t amount to marginal equations where each dependent variable is regressed on lags of itself, the DOIL dummy, and the 'excess demand' cointegration vector.
7. Plots and graphs including recursive statistics are also satisfactory, although not shown here.
8. Alternatively, as Doornik and Hendry (1994) state, the observed correlation between the residuals may result from other influences, such as cross-correlated random shocks or common omitted variables.
9. Recall that n is the number of variables in $\mathbf{z}_t$, while k is the lag-length of the VAR and r is the number of cointegration relationships that enter the short-run ECM.
10. Note, this highlights the care that needs to be taken when speaking of weak exogeneity with respect to variables in a single equation. Earlier tests involving the long-run model found that y and R were weakly exogenous to the system, while Δp is weakly exogenous in the money-demand equation and $m - p$ is weakly exogenous in the price equation. However, what the latter tests actually established was that the money-demand cointegration relationship does not enter the short-run model determining Δp and the 'excess-demand' long-run relationship does not enter the short-run equation determining $m - p$. Clearly, the FIML results suggest that changes in prices cause changes in the money supply.
11. Changing the simultaneous model around so that $\Delta(m-p)_t$ enters as a regressor in the equation determining $\Delta^2 p_t$ is unsuccessful. First, the test of over-identifying restrictions is $\chi^2(6) = 14.67$, which rejects at the 5 per cent level. Thus, this form of the structural model can*not* be said to encompass parsimoniously the conditional PVECM. Moreover, the coefficient on $\Delta(m-p)_t$ is not significantly different from zero in the $\Delta^2 p_t$ equation and the correlation between the structural residuals obtained from the FIML model is now -0.29, indicating a failure to model the structure underlying the data evidence that is available.
12. In simple terms, periodic cointegration which involves periodically integrated data can be formulated as an ECM in which parameters are allowed to vary over the seasons. This would require reformulating (4.28), the seasonal cointegration model, as:

$$(1 - L^4)c_t = \Delta_4 c_t = \sum_{j=0}^{q} a_j \Delta_4 y_{t-j} + \sum_{i=0}^{p} b_i \Delta_4 c_{t-i} + \sum_{i=1}^{4} \beta_s D_{st}(c - \mu_s - \phi_s y)_{t-1} + u_t \qquad (6.6)$$

where the D_{st} denote the seasonal dummies. It is clear that this model has varying cointegration relations per quarter (see Franses, 1993, for further details).

13. These are reproduced as Tables A.13–A.16 in the Statistical Appendix.

APPENDIX

Cointegration analysis using the Johansen technique: A practitioner's guide to the software[1]

This appendix seeks to replicate the tests (and results) provided in Johansen and Juselius (1992), which considered the issue of purchasing power parity and uncovered interest rate parity for the UK.[2,3] The aim is to see how easy it is for an applied economist to implement the Johansen technique using:

1. *Microfit ver 3.0, An Interactive Econometric Software Package*, developed by Hashem Pesaran and Bahram Pesaran and distributed by Oxford University Press (27-3-92).
2. *Cointegration Analysis of Times Series (Cats in* Rats*)*, a beta version developed by Henrik Hansen and Katrina Juselius, to be distributed by Estima (22-3-94).
3. *PcFiml ver 8, Interactive Econometric Modelling of Dynamic Systems*, developed by Jurgen A. Doornik and David F. Hendry, distributed as part of *PcGive Professional* by Chapman-Hall.

Using the same data-set, the purpose of replicating the steps taken in the Johansen and Juselius (JJ) paper is to provide a benchmark. Thus, the ease with which each of the above packages allows the user to do the following is considered:

- Testing the order of integration of each variable that enters the multivariate model.
- Whether there are trends in the data and therefore whether or not deterministic variables (a constant and trend) should be restricted to enter the cointegration space.
- What should be the lag-length of the VAR model (in order to ensure Gaussian error terms in the VECM) and thus whether the system should be conditioning on any predetermined $I(0)$ variables (including dummies to take account of policy interventions perhaps).
- Testing for reduced rank.
- Testing for weak exogeneity (which leads to the modelling of a partial system with exogenous variables).
- Testing for linear hypothesis on cointegration relations.
- Joint tests involving restrictions on $\boldsymbol{\alpha}$ and $\boldsymbol{\beta}$.

Microfit

This package operates in interactive mode, and the system of moving through the menus is generally helpful.[4] The major drawback of such an approach is that it offers little (if any) scope for the user to modify the procedures that are available, and this limits the usefulness of the program as new developments have occurred in cointegration analysis. The ADF command provides standard augmented Dickey–Fuller tests up to a user specified lag k. Thus, in principle,[5] it is easy to test the various null hypotheses that each series is non-stationary and thus establish the order of integration. Only three models representing alternative ways of including deterministic components are available: if there are no trends in the data, then the user can choose menu Option 2 to restrict the intercept to lie within the cointegration space. If there are linear trends but they are assumed to cancel in the cointegration relations, then two further options are available. Option 3 is a rather special case where linear trends exist in the data but there is no trend term in the d.g.p., while Option 4 allows for trends in both. The only difference in terms of the models estimated is in the need to use different critical values when conducting tests of rank order, and thus *Microfit* really only offers two alternatives for dealing with deterministic trends. It does not allow the user to specify a model with linear trends in the variables *and* in the cointegration space (unlike the other packages being considered). Since the λ-max and trace statistics are available, it is possible to follow the procedure suggested in Johansen (1992c) to test the joint hypothesis of both the rank order and the deterministic components, based on the Pantula principle. However, the user would need to know how to do this in advance, since (given the earlier date of the package) no guidance is available in the manual.

After choosing the lag-length for the VAR, there are no facilities for directly testing the adequacy of the VECM model in terms of the Gaussian assumption of the stochastic nature of the process. Instead, each equation has to be formulated separately and tested using the univariate diagnostic tests available in the linear regression menu. Thus, it is possible to undertake tests, although this is somewhat messy. Additional $I(0)$ variables (including centred seasonal dummy variables), necessary to account for short-run effects which could otherwise violate the Gaussian assumption, can be included in the VAR under the assumption that they are both weakly exogenous and do not have any long-run impact (and so do not enter the cointegration relations).

Microfit provides good displays of both the λ-max and trace statistics for deciding cointegration rank r, along with 95 per cent and 90 per cent critical values (obtained from Ostewald-Lenum, 1992). No statistics corrected for degrees of freedom are presented and it is not possible to compute the eigenvalues of the companion matrix as a check when deciding the value of r (this is useful given the probable poor size and power properties of the λ-max and trace statistics, especially when additional $I(0)$ variables are included to 'whiten' the VECM residuals). Once r has been set (note, two cointegration relationships are indicated in JJ), the estimated cointegration vectors (unnormalised and normalised for the first variable on the left-hand side of the equation) and adjustment matrix (based on both unnormalised and normalised $\boldsymbol{\beta}$) are available, together with displays of the long-run $\boldsymbol{\Pi}$ matrix, and graphs of the residuals of the cointegration vectors (including corrections for short-run dynamics).

There is no procedure to test for restrictions on the $\boldsymbol{\alpha}$, and thus weak exogeneity. Consequently, it is not possible to model a partial system with weakly exogenous variables included in levels in the cointegration space and in first-differences in the short-run dynamic VAR. This is a major drawback. The package provides a separate menu for testing linear hypotheses on cointegration vectors. The first test considered here is that all r cointegration vectors are subject to the same s homogeneous linear restrictions. The manual explains that this is the hypothesis depicted $\mathcal{H}_4$ in JJ, and it requires the user to type in the number of restrictions to be imposed. $\mathbf{H}_{4.1}$ in JJ tests if the purchasing power parity restriction is valid in both cointegration vectors:

$$\mathbf{H}_{4.1} = \begin{bmatrix} 1 & 0 & 0 \\ -1 & 0 & 0 \\ -1 & 0 & 0 \\ 0 & 1 & 0 \\ 0 & 0 & 1 \end{bmatrix}$$

This meant imposing two restrictions in *Microfit*, that is, B1 = −B2 and B2 = −B3. The restricted cointegration relations were printed together with the LR test statistic $\chi^2(4) = 2.76$ (the test reported in JJ is $\chi^2(4) = 2.68$). The new adjustment matrix resulting from the imposition of restrictions on $\boldsymbol{\beta}$ is not available.

The second test is $\mathcal{H}_5$ in JJ, that $r_1 \leqslant r$ of the cointegration relations are known. In *Microfit*, the user has to state how many cointegration vectors are to be fixed (i.e., r_1) and then type in the restricted matrix corresponding to these cointegration vectors. One of the hypotheses considered in JJ was whether the PPP relation is stationary on its own: that is, $\mathbf{H}_{5.1} = [1, -1, -1, 0, 0]'$. This same vector is entered directly into *Microfit*. As above, the restricted cointegration relations are then given together with the LR test statistic $\chi^2(3) = 14.52$ (the test reported in JJ is $\chi^2(3) = 14.52$).

The final test available is a restricted version of $\mathcal{H}_6$ in JJ (which tests the same restriction on one or more of the cointegration relations). The test carried out in JJ is whether there exists a vector in the cointegration space that linearly combines the variables in the PPP in a stationary relationship:

$$\mathbf{H}_6 = \begin{bmatrix} 1 & 0 & 0 \\ 0 & 1 & 0 \\ 0 & 0 & 1 \\ 0 & 0 & 0 \\ 0 & 0 & 0 \end{bmatrix}$$

This test was performed in *Microfit* by imposing two restrictions, that is, B4 = 0 and B5 = 0. The restricted cointegration relations were printed together with the LR test statistic $\chi^2(1) = 2.43$ (the test reported in JJ is $\chi^2(1) = 2.4$). The new adjustment matrix that results from imposing restrictions on $\boldsymbol{\beta}$ is not available. Joint tests involving restrictions on $\boldsymbol{\alpha}$ and $\boldsymbol{\beta}$ are not available.

Cats

Not surprisingly, this program can perform all the tasks required of it here. It is called as a sub-routine within Rats, and needs (ideally) to be run in batch mode using a Rats source file.[6] An example source file UK.CAT is provided (based on an adaptation of the JJ paper) which can be modified for the user's own work. This is very easy, and includes setting the lag-length of the VAR model and deciding which form of the deterministic component should be used (see below); which frequency of centred seasonal dummies should be added to the deterministic component of the short-run model; which basic option of *Cats* should be run (three are available as explained below); whether a partial system is to be modelled with weakly exogenous variables which must then be specified; which additional $I(0)$ variables, particularly dummies, need to be specified to enter the model in the short-run dynamics but not in the cointegration space; and whether the user wants recursive analysis of the $I(1)$ model to test for parameter constancy.

At the initial stage one of three basic options is available: (i) to run the $I(1)$ model (which performs the bulk of the cointegration analysis);[7] (ii) to run the RANK option, which calculates the rank statistics for models with different assumptions about the deterministic component; or (iii) to run TSP, which provides univariate tests of exclusion, weak exogeneity and stationarity on the variables in the model. Choosing to run the TSP option at this stage gives the user an overall view of the variables to be included in the cointegration vectors; for example, if a variable passes tests for exclusion and weak exogeneity it might only need to be entered as a predetermined $I(0)$ variable in the VAR. Even if restrictions are not imposed at the outset, possible testing strategies might be suggested. Stationarity tests are based on estimating the model and setting $r = 1, \ldots, (n-1)$. Then for each value of r, tests of type $\mathcal{H}_5$ in JJ (that $r_1 \leq r$ of the cointegration relations are known) are performed for each variable, where $\mathbf{H}_5$ is a vector from $\mathbf{I}_n$ with element i as unity. This amounts to testing (based on the null of stationarity) whether the individual series are stationary by themselves for differing values of r.[8]

The RANK option automatically calculates eigenvalues, λ-max and trace statistics for up to five different ways of including deterministic components (from none, up to intercepts in the cointegration relations with quadratic trends in the levels[9]), so it is possible to test the joint hypothesis of both the rank order and the deterministic components. The manual provides clear guidelines of how to proceed. Once this has been done, the appropriate VECM can be used to obtain estimates of $\boldsymbol{\alpha}$ and $\boldsymbol{\beta}$ for the subsequent testing of restrictions.

When the main module (the $I(1)$ model) is chosen, *Cats* presents the eigenvalues, standard reduced rank test statistics (plus 90 per cent critical values if requested) and estimates of $\boldsymbol{\alpha}$, $\boldsymbol{\beta}$ and $\boldsymbol{\Pi}$. A main-menu is then available offering various procedures starting with the user setting the rank of $\boldsymbol{\Pi}$ (which can be checked by calculating the companion matrix which helps to verify the number of unit roots at or close to unity corresponding to the $I(1)$ common trends).[10] Before setting r, other options can be chosen to test the adequacy of the model.[11] Graphical analysis of the $\boldsymbol{\beta}$-vectors (unadjusted and adjusted for short-run dynamics) are available to provide a visual test of which vectors are stationary.[12] Plots of the residuals from each equation in the VECM are also useful as an indication of the presence (or otherwise) of Gaussian processes, while plots of the correlogram and autocorrelograms can help to identify any problems with autocorrelation. In addition to graphical analysis of the residuals, descriptive statistics and misspecification tests are available from the main-menu. These comprise the correlation matrix of residuals and standard deviations, multivariate tests for autocorrelation and normality and univariate statistics for autocorrelation, ARCH(2) processes, skewness, kurtosis and normality. Generally, the tests in the latest version of *Cats* are either new (e.g., the multivariate tests) or different to those undertaken in earlier versions (and reported in Table 1 in JJ). They also indicate more precisely that the assumption of Gaussian errors in the JJ paper may be inappropriate (this has implications for the LR test statistics used throughout).

Once a value of $r \leq n$ has been chosen, the user is asked to identify the column elements used to normalise the cointegration vectors, which is more flexible than always having the cointegration relations normalised by the same variable. New estimates of $\boldsymbol{\alpha}$, $\boldsymbol{\beta}$ and $\boldsymbol{\Pi}$ are presented based on the $n \times r$ cointegration vectors, together with t-values for the $\boldsymbol{\alpha}$ and $\boldsymbol{\Pi}$. The latter are useful (assuming that meaningful $\boldsymbol{\beta}$-vectors have been obtained) in that they indicate whether the cointegration relations are significant in all or only a subset of the equations in the system. Although this is not in itself an alternative to (manually) testing for weak exogeneity, it is very likely to help in the formulation of models as the analysis proceeds.

To test for weak exogeneity (e.g., in JJ the hypothesis $\mathbf{H}_2$: $\alpha_{2j} = 0$ for $j = 1, 2$ — the second row of the adjustment matrix is zero for the situation where $r = 2$), requires restricting $\boldsymbol{\alpha}$ by $\boldsymbol{\alpha} = \mathbf{A}\boldsymbol{\Psi}$, where $\mathbf{A}$ is an $(n \times m)$ matrix and $(n - m)$ equals the number of restrictions imposed on $\boldsymbol{\alpha}$. Defining $\mathbf{A}_{\perp} = \mathbf{B}(n \times (n - m))$, such that $\mathbf{B}'\mathbf{A} = 0$, then $\mathbf{H}_2$ in JJ amounts to the following:

$$\mathbf{A} = \begin{bmatrix} 1 & 0 & 0 & 0 \\ 0 & 0 & 0 & 0 \\ 0 & 1 & 0 & 0 \\ 0 & 0 & 1 & 0 \\ 0 & 0 & 0 & 1 \end{bmatrix} \qquad \mathbf{B} = \begin{bmatrix} 0 \\ 1 \\ 0 \\ 0 \\ 0 \end{bmatrix}$$

To perform this test in *Cats* requires specifying $\mathbf{B}'$ when choosing the main-menu option for testing restrictions on $\boldsymbol{\alpha}$, obtaining an LR test statistic $\chi^2(2) = 0.66$ (the test reported in JJ is incorrectly $\chi^2(2) = 1.31$). The new values of $\boldsymbol{\alpha}$, $\boldsymbol{\beta}$ and $\boldsymbol{\Pi}$ are then presented corresponding to the restriction imposed on $\boldsymbol{\alpha}$,and this model stays in effect until superseded.

The current version of *Cats* does not provide options in the main-menu that are explicitly matched to the $\mathcal{H}_4$, $\mathcal{H}_5$, and $\mathcal{H}_6$ testing of linear hypotheses on cointegration vectors as set out in JJ (an earlier version developed for their 1992 paper obviously did follow such a test procedure). Instead, the approach is based around the more general $\mathcal{H}_6$-test (encompassing $\mathcal{H}_4$ and $\mathcal{H}_5$) and there are three options: (i) where the user is prompted to divide $\boldsymbol{\beta}$ into groups where the groups can include more than one vector (and subsequently the user has to formulate restrictions on each of the groups); (ii) another option automatically divides the cointegration space into the r vectors and prompts for restrictions on each vector (the major difference between this and the previous option is that the rank condition for formal identification of the joint hypotheses concerning the restrictions placed on the entire cointegration space is checked); and (iii) the user can choose to formulate restrictions on the cointegration vectors either by specifying $\mathbf{H}$ (e.g., $\boldsymbol{\beta} = \mathbf{H}\boldsymbol{\varphi}$) or by specifying $\mathbf{R}$ such that $\mathbf{R}'\boldsymbol{\beta} = 0$. Using the default formulation for restrictions ($\boldsymbol{\beta} = \mathbf{H}\boldsymbol{\varphi}$) and option (i), to test $\mathbf{H}_{4.1}$ in JJ the user must specify that the number of different groups equals 1 (i.e., all cointegration vectors are to be restricted) and that there are two restrictions to be imposed. This leads straightforwardly to typing in $\mathbf{H}'_{4.1}$ and obtaining an LR test statistic $\chi^2(4) = 2.76$, as well as the new values of $\boldsymbol{\alpha}$, $\boldsymbol{\beta}$ and $\boldsymbol{\pi}$ corresponding to the restrictions imposed on $\boldsymbol{\beta}$. To test $\mathbf{H}_{5.1}$ in JJ that the vector $[1, -1, -1, 0, 0]'$ is in the cointegration space, *Cats* requires this problem to be parameterised as $\boldsymbol{\beta} = (\mathbf{H}_1\boldsymbol{\varphi}_1, \mathbf{H}_2\boldsymbol{\varphi}_2)$, where $\mathbf{H}_1 = [1, -1, -1, 0, 0]'$ and $\mathbf{H}_2 = \boldsymbol{I}_5$. That is, the number of different groups is now equal to 2 (since $r = r_1 + r_2$, and $r_1 = 1$ given that only one cointegration vector is assumed to be known) and the user specifies that there is one vector in the first group. In order to obtain a 5×1 vector for $\mathbf{H}_1$ the number of restrictions must be set equal to four. Then after typing in $\mathbf{H}_1$, the user specifies that the number of vectors in the second group equals 1 and there are no restrictions (hence, the identity matrix is imposed). The result is an LR test statistic $\chi^2(3) = 14.52$, as well as the new values of $\boldsymbol{\alpha}$, $\boldsymbol{\beta}$ and $\boldsymbol{\Pi}$ corresponding to the restrictions imposed on $\boldsymbol{\beta}$. Finally, to test $\mathbf{H}_6$ in JJ, the number of different groups is set to two with a single vector in the first group with two restrictions. This then allows the user to type in $\mathbf{H}_6$ followed again by the information that the number of vectors in the second group equals one and there are no restrictions. The result is an LR test statistic $\chi^2(1) = 2.43$ as well as the new values of $\boldsymbol{\alpha}$, $\boldsymbol{\beta}$ and $\boldsymbol{\Pi}$ corresponding to the restrictions imposed on $\boldsymbol{\beta}$. Finally, joint tests involving restrictions on $\boldsymbol{\alpha}$ and $\boldsymbol{\beta}$ are easily handled (although not conducted in JJ).

PcFiml

This latest version of *PcFiml* is very flexible, providing drop-down menus and an extensive range of modelling features for $I(1)$ and $I(0)$ systems.[13] Cointegration facilities are embedded in an overall modelling strategy leading through to structural VAR modelling. The model is first defined in (log-) levels, requiring the user to fix which deterministic variables should enter the cointegration space; the lag-length of the VAR; and whether $I(0)$ variables, particularly dummies, need to be specified to enter the model in the short-run dynamics but not in the cointegration space. In order to determine jointly the rank order and deterministic components of the model, several runs with different models would be needed, with the results then being compared in order to follow the Pantula principle. Testing the order of integration of each variable would require moving over to the companion module *PcGive* to run the ADF tests for unit roots, although it would be possible to set up the ADF test manually in *PcFiml* and/or run a series of tests for restrictions on the cointegration vectors (based on the null of stationarity) as to whether the individual series are stationary by themselves for differing values of r (as is done in *Cats* – see the above discussion). In general testing for unit roots in each variable requires the use of a little imagination.

Once the model has been defined, and estimated, it can automatically be subjected to diagnostic testing using both multivariate and univariate statistics (simply by choosing the relevant options in the menu labelled 'testing').[14] These are similar to those in *Cats*, although *PcFiml* is more flexible and includes systems and single equation tests for heteroscedasticity.[15] The 'cointegration' option can then be requested which provides the eigenvalues of the system (and log-likelihoods for each cointegration rank), standard reduced rank test statistics *and* those adjusted for degrees of freedom (plus 95 per cent critical values), and full-rank estimates of $\boldsymbol{\alpha}$, $\boldsymbol{\beta}$ and $\boldsymbol{\Pi}$ (the $\boldsymbol{\beta}$ are automatically normalised along the principal diagonal). Graphical analysis of the $\boldsymbol{\beta}$-vectors (unadjusted and adjusted for short-run dynamics) are available to provide a visual test of which vectors are stationary,[16] and graphs of the recursive eigenvalues associated with each eigenvector can be plotted to consider the stability of the cointegration vectors. After deciding on the value of $r \leqslant n$, it is possible to select a reduced rank system (under testing for cointegration restrictions) which will provide an estimate of the new value of $\boldsymbol{\Pi}$, together with the reduced form cointegration vectors.

To test for restrictions on $\boldsymbol{\alpha}$ and/or (known) $\boldsymbol{\beta}$, two general options are available under 'testing cointegration restrictions': first, it is possible to specify the **A**- and/or **H**-matrix of linear restrictions using an approach that is similar to JJ's and *Cats*. This presents a few problems in that once the value of r has been chosen it is often necessary to edit the null matrix presented in order to obtain the appropriate dimensions of **A** or **H** (see below). The second, and much more flexible, approach is the option 'general restrictions'. This produces a 'constraints editor' showing (for the rank chosen) the variables and elements associated with $\boldsymbol{\alpha}$ and $\boldsymbol{\beta}$, and constraints can be typed in using these elements (as such, this is similar to the approach used in *Microfit* except that the user can see the full model).

Thus, to test the hypothesis $\mathbf{H}_2$: $\alpha_{2j} = 0$ for $j = 1, 2$ in JJ (the second row of the adjustment matrix is zero for the situation where $r = 2$), if the option 'restricted $\boldsymbol{\alpha}$ and/or $\boldsymbol{\beta}$ ...' is chosen then the user must edit the 5×2 matrix presented in order to obtain the correct 5×4 dimension for **A**. This produces the correct new values of $\boldsymbol{\alpha}$, $\boldsymbol{\beta}$ and $\boldsymbol{\Pi}$ corresponding to the restriction imposed on $\boldsymbol{\alpha}$ (and the output also includes a print-out of **A** itself, which is useful), together with a test statistic of $\chi^2(2) = 0.66$. Since a need to edit the default matrix may not be obvious (especially since the manual does not guide the reader clearly through this situation), it is probably easier to choose the 'general restrictions' option, set $r=2$, and then set $\alpha_{2j}=0$ for $j=1,2$ using the constraints editor.

Similarly, to test $\mathbf{H}_{4.1}$ in JJ if the option 'restricted $\boldsymbol{\alpha}$ and/or $\boldsymbol{\beta}$ ...' is chosen and the rank is set equal to 2 the user must again edit the presented matrix in order to obtain a 5×3 dimension for $\mathbf{H}$ corresponding to $\mathbf{H}_{4.1}$. Alternatively, it may again be intuitively easier to use the 'general restrictions' option, set $r=2$, and then set $-\beta_{1j}=\beta_{2j}$ and $-\beta_{1j}=\beta_{3j}$ for $j=1,2$ using the constraints editor.

To test $\mathbf{H}_{5.1}$ in JJ, if the option 'restricted $\boldsymbol{\alpha}$ and/or known $\boldsymbol{\beta}$ ...' is chosen with the rank set equal to 2, then a 5×2 matrix for $\mathbf{H}$ is provided in the matrix editor, and this needs to be manually changed to a 5×1 matrix corresponding to $\mathbf{H}_{5.1}$. This produces the correct output and test statistic, but once again is not as straightforward as choosing the 'general restrictions' option, setting $r=2$, and then typing in the equivalent to $\mathbf{H}_{5.1}$ using the constraints editor. Finally, to test $\mathbf{H}_6$ in JJ, it is necessary to choose the 'general restrictions' option, set $r=2$, and then type in the two restrictions $\beta_{41}=0$ and $\beta_{51}=0$.

Using the 'general restrictions' option in *PcFiml* to test restrictions on the cointegration vectors (and thus to determine unique cointegration relations) is as flexible as the *Cats* option that divides the cointegration space into the *r* vectors and prompts for restrictions on each vector. The advantage is that the constraints editor in *PcFiml* is easier to work with (since the full model is seen by the user, while in *Cats* the user only sees one vector at a time); a possible disadvantage is that there is no direct test of whether the restrictions satisfy the rank conditions.

Conclusion

For the applied economist wishing to estimate cointegration relations and then to test for linear restrictions, the choice of which program to use would seem to preclude *Microfit* 3.0 for anything but the most basic analysis. As to which of the other two programs is preferable, *Cats* (in Rats) or *PcFiml*, both have strong features which recommend them to the general user. The *Cats* program is naturally closely linked to the JJ approach, and the various batch tests available are a useful aid to the (possibly less experienced) user. The manual provides a good overview of the Johansen approach, and covers most of the essential features clearly and concisely, and in readable terms for the non-specialist. In a tutorial, the user can work through the (updated) JJ analysis and learn about the method as (s)he proceeds, without needing to refer constantly to the original paper (in fact, it might have been better to stay with the original specification of the JJ paper for complete comparability).

Since *PcFiml* incorporates cointegration into a more general model building approach, it has other strengths. Cointegration is only part of the analysis, and therefore it is not as self-contained as *Cats*. However, it encourages the user to see cointegration in context (especially in the series of tutorials which lead the user through the various model building stages) and may be preferable in this respect. The non-specialist will probably find the manual less easy as a guide to the cointegration approach (especially the chapter on the econometric analysis of cointegration). This is not a criticism, rather an indication of the difference between the two packages.

Notes

1. The material presented here is a slightly abridged version of Harris (1994).
2. All analysis was carried out on an IBM-compatible 486 DX/2 with 20 megabytes of RAM; estimation time was very fast in all instances, including when using the more

intensive iterative subroutines in *Cats* and *PcFiml* (e.g., the 'switching routine' of the latter).

3. The variables used in the JJ paper comprised p_1 (log of UK wholesale price index), p_2 (log of trade weighted foreign wholesale price index), e_{12} (log of UK effective exchange rate), i_1 (three-month treasury bill rate in the UK) and i_2 (three-month Eurodollar interest rate). Throughout, matrices are expressed using this order of the variables.
4. For a full review of the package, see McAleer and Oxley (1993).
5. Notwithstanding the problems concerning the size and power of these tests.
6. Note, it was necessary to run the Rats386 version of the program to avoid memory problems.
7. The authors of *Cats* have indicated that they will be adding an $I(2)$ model to the procedure at some future date.
8. The TSP procedure does all the tests in a batch run but they could be performed manually using the $I(1)$ option in the *Cats* procedure, setting the rank r and then choosing the option that tests restrictions on subsets of the $\boldsymbol{\beta}$-vectors. As a check, this was done to confirm the batch results.
9. Although the latter is tested for using the RANK procedure, it is not an option when proceeding with the $I(1)$ main module.
10. If any of the eigenvalues are outside the unit root this indicates an explosive model and the probable presence of $I(2)$ variables.
11. The main-menu also provides for an inspection of the short-run parameters and associated t-values (the dynamic component of the VECM), as well as calculating the MA representation of the model.
12. This 'testing' can be repeated each time linear restrictions to the $\boldsymbol{\beta}_i$ are imposed. Note also, as pointed out in the *Cats* manual, differences between the adjusted and unadjusted series in terms of whether they look stationary can indicate whether $I(2)$ common trends enter the model.
13. Unlike *Microfit* and *Cats*, *PcFiml* also allows users to run batch jobs where previous jobs can be edited and re-run.
14. It is also possible to graph the residuals of the VAR (or VECM if the model is estimated in error-correction form) as well as consider other graphical aids from an extensive menu (e.g., the residual density and distribution functions).
15. Note, the multivariate tests were developed in *PcFiml* first and then adopted in *Cats*. The normality tests were developed jointly by Doornik and Hansen.
16. The companion matrix which helps to verify the number of unit roots at or close to unity corresponding to the $I(1)$ common trends is available when choosing the 'dynamic analysis' option in the model menu.

Statistical appendix

Seaonally unadjusted data for UK money demand model (for sources see Hendry and Ericsson, 1991, and Ericsson, Hendry and Tran, 1992)

y_t	m_t	p_t	R
11.24249	8.923458	−2.199126	0.043125
11.30940	8.950517	−2.181253	0.043542
11.31434	8.963848	−2.182139	0.042083
11.35035	9.016422	−2.164564	0.043542
11.32181	8.992091	−2.168929	0.048958
11.36470	9.002809	−2.148149	0.050000
11.36434	9.023770	−2.143021	0.050746
11.39999	9.048013	−2.129472	0.067300
11.34351	9.021326	−2.119431	0.075200
11.38189	9.035228	−2.017018	0.067900
11.39172	9.046821	−2.099644	0.065033
11.41249	9.085797	−2.087474	0.062933
11.37748	9.075036	−2.081844	0.062317
11.40192	9.070388	−2.066723	0.063350
11.41333	9.080431	−2.059639	0.074800
11.42255	9.085287	−2.046394	0.073021
11.40622	0.076195	−2.047943	0.063646
11.43789	9.092274	−2.039452	0.056458
11.44467	9.132717	−2.034851	0.055833
11.46116	9.158758	−2.027229	0.072708
11.45502	9.130891	−2.009915	0.080104
11.46472	9.148518	−1.991431	0.082500
11.49327	9.161006	−1.977607	0.076771
11.52263	9.198470	−1.965399	0.074375
11.45767	9.146482	−1.954749	0.084896
11.49481	9.128208	−1.944911	0.092500
11.50790	9.143239	−1.933784	0.096042
11.54101	9.201653	−1.918684	0.089688
11.46955	9.166428	−1.899122	0.091042
11.52554	9.206182	−1.877971	0.080417

11.53734	9.226312	−1.857899	0.075104
11.57953	9.290941	−1.840110	0.071979
11.50149	9.296736	−1.819542	0.075104
11.55421	9.311079	−1.795767	0.065208
11.57429	9.348906	−1.775492	0.058021
11.60788	9.397040	−1.761424	0.047917
11.54471	9.409320	−1.746404	0.049583
11.59017	9.453241	−1.733302	0.056875
11.58717	9.470233	−1.707602	0.077500
11.66326	9.529387	−1.689022	0.080833
11.65699	9.503455	−1.665479	0.100833
11.66942	9.569498	−1.653913	0.089167
11.68661	9.547008	−1.611941	0.127292
11.70770	9.579166	−1.566857	0.147500
11.63317	9.538432	−1.520512	0.155625
11.66911	0.569498	−1.461880	0.133125
11.62954	9.594829	−1.413460	0.127708
11.70673	9.681674	−1.366492	0.126042
11.63186	9.681403	−1.300851	0.113750
11.64189	9.712169	−1.243060	0.097708
11.65736	9.765979	−1.196666	0.106042
11.69141	9.808451	−1.162831	0.114688
11.65829	9.824644	−1.124546	0.093021
11.67424	9.849699	−1.090049	0.109375
11.70458	9.900239	−1.058142	0.117187
11.74065	9.913141	−1.019154	0.151250
11.67640	9.917179	−0.979763	0.114167
11.69182	9.958089	−0.947265	0.078958
11.71070	10.03776	−0.926593	0.067396
11.74762	10.11013	−0.914542	0.061458
11.71093	10.13703	−0.885761	0.065937
11.73370	10.15654	−0.862276	0.090937
11.75159	10.20835	−0.839561	0.096667
11.76909	10.25991	−0.813960	0.118229
11.72591	10.26062	−0.787678	0.129167
11.78356	10.27470	−0.752473	0.126875
11.78988	10.31269	−0.701381	0.141979
11.80906	10.34401	−0.662424	0.162396
11.76507	10.31778	−0.618782	0.182083
11.73993	10.33932	−0.574298	0.172500
11.75840	10.33973	−0.542832	0.158750
11.75420	10.38259	−0.517011	0.153540
11.71160	10.39513	−0.500051	0.131042
11.71380	10.43479	−0.469844	0.124687
11.76178	10.45085	−0.448007	0.148229
11.77259	10.49002	−0.429092	0.157188
11.74381	10.48637	−0.415667	0.140417
11.74304	10.51263	−0.392746	0.133854

11.76609	10.54057	−0.379944	0.111667
11.78841	10.59751	−0.368314	0.100417
11.77779	10.62838	−0.349416	0.112708
11.77229	10.65573	−0.340520	0.100208
11.81789	10.66350	−0.328087	0.098333
11.84090	10.70414	−0.318278	0.092917
11.82017	10.74447	−0.306661	0.092083
11.80500	10.78932	−0.286749	0.093750
11.83675	10.81689	−0.274042	0.110457
11.88724	10.85048	−0.257217	0.096065
11.85927	10.88675	−0.236862	0.114193
11.84622	10.93218	−0.227403	0.084310
11.87596	10.97692	−0.228156	0.053998
11.91071	11.01794	−0.222518	0.042187
11.88705	11.06963	−0.220771	0.037409
11.89537	11.13270	−0.219899	0.026567
11.92995	11.20243	−0.216665	0.030419
11.96828	11.22117	−0.195650	0.038817
11.92837	11.27937	−0.185848	0.029188
11.93445	11.35025	−0.171382	0.027763
12.00155	11.39263	−0.165111	0.036876
12.02424	11.42810	−0.155835	0.026459
11.99932	11.46998	−0.150707	0.029792
12.00975	11.52171	−0.130678	0.029166
12.04889	11.55202	−0.114850	0.049266
12.08253	11.56216	−0.101147	0.050708
12.04665	11.59819	−0.084796	0.046375
12.04674	11.64730	−0.061237	0.054700

Table A.1 Empirical cumulative distribution of $\hat{\tau}$ for $\rho = 1$ (see Table 3.2)

Sample	Probability of a smaller value							
size T	0.01	0.025	0.05	0.10	0.90	0.95	0.975	0.99
				$\hat{\tau}$				
25	−2.66	−2.26	−1.95	−1.60	0.92	1.33	1.70	2.16
50	−2.62	−2.25	−1.95	−1.61	0.91	1.31	1.66	2.08
100	−2.60	−2.24	−1.95	−1.61	0.90	1.29	1.64	2.03
250	−2.58	−2.23	−1.95	−1.62	0.89	1.29	1.63	2.01
500	−2.58	−2.23	−1.95	−1.62	0.89	1.28	1.62	2.00
∞	−2.58	−2.23	−1.95	−1.62	0.89	1.28	1.62	2.00
				$\hat{\tau}_\mu$				
25	−3.75	−3.33	−3.00	−2.63	−0.37	0.00	0.34	0.72
50	−3.58	−3.22	−2.93	−2.60	−0.40	−0.03	0.29	0.66
100	−3.51	−3.17	−2.89	−2.58	−0.42	−0.05	0.26	0.63
250	−3.46	−3.14	−2.88	−2.57	−0.42	−0.06	0.24	0.62
500	−3.44	−3.13	−2.87	−2.57	−0.43	−0.07	0.24	0.61
∞	−3.43	−3.12	−2.86	−2.57	−0.44	−0.07	0.23	0.60
				$\hat{\tau}_\tau$				
25	−4.38	−3.95	−3.60	−3.24	−1.14	−0.80	−0.50	−0.15
50	−4.15	−3.80	−3.50	−3.18	−1.19	−0.87	−0.58	−0.24
100	−4.04	−3.73	−3.45	−3.15	−1.22	−0.90	−0.62	−0.28
250	−3.99	−3.69	−3.43	−3.13	−1.23	−0.92	−0.64	−0.31
500	−3.98	−3.68	−3.42	−3.13	−1.24	−0.93	−0.65	−0.32
∞	−3.96	−3.66	−3.41	−3.12	−1.25	−0.94	−0.66	−0.33

Standard errors of the estimates vary, but most are less than 0.02.
Source: Fuller (1976). Reprinted with the permission of John Wiley & Sons.

Table A.2 Empirical distribution of Φ_3 (see Table 3.2)

Sample	Probability of a smaller value							
size T	0.01	0.025	0.05	0.10	0.90	0.95	0.975	0.99
25	0.74	0.90	1.08	1.33	5.91	7.24	8.65	10.61
50	0.76	0.93	1.11	1.37	5.61	6.73	7.81	9.31
100	0.76	0.94	1.12	1.38	5.47	6.49	7.44	8.73
250	0.76	0.94	1.13	1.39	5.39	6.34	7.25	8.43
500	0.76	0.94	1.13	1.39	5.36	6.30	7.20	8.34
∞	0.77	0.94	1.13	1.39	5.34	6.25	7.16	8.27
se	0.004	0.004	0.003	0.004	0.015	0.020	0.032	0.058

Source: Dickey and Fuller (1981). Reprinted with the permission of the Econometric Sociey.

z(Φ₁)

Table A3 Empirical distribution of Φ_1 (see Table 3.2)

Sample size T	Probability of a smaller value 0.01	0.025	0.05	0.10	0.90	0.95	0.975	0.99
25	0.29	0.38	0.49	0.65	4.12	5.18	6.30	7.88
50	0.29	0.39	0.50	0.66	3.94	4.86	5.80	7.06
100	0.29	0.39	0.50	0.67	3.86	4.71	5.57	6.70
250	0.30	0.39	0.51	0.67	3.81	4.63	5.45	6.52
500	0.30	0.39	0.51	0.67	3.79	4.61	5.41	6.47
∞	0.30	0.40	0.51	0.67	3.78	4.59	5.38	6.43
se	0.002	0.002	0.002	0.002	0.01	0.02	0.03	0.05

Source: Dickey and Fuller (1981). Reprinted with the permission of the Econometric Society.

Table A.4 Recursive and rolling test statistics: critical values (see Table 3.4)

T	Percentile	τ_τ	Recursive min τ_τ	Rolling min τ_τ
100	.025	−3.73	−4.62	−5.29
	.050	−3.45	−4.33	−5.01
	.100	−3.15	−4.00	−4.71
250	.025	−3.69	−4.42	−5.07
	.050	−3.43	−4.18	−4.85
	.100	−3.13	−3.91	−4.59
500	.025	−3.68	−4.42	−5.00
	.050	−3.42	−4.18	−4.79
	.100	−3.13	−3.88	−4.55

Note: All critical values were computed using data generated as $\Delta y_t = \varepsilon_t$, ε_t iid $N(0, 1)$ and are based on 10 000 Monte Carlo replications for $T = 100$ and $T = 250$ and 5000 replications for $T = 500$.
Source: Banerjee, Lumsdaine and Stock (1992, Table 1). Reprinted with the permission of the American Statistical Association.

Table A.5 Sequential test statistics: critical values (see Table 3.4)

		Trend-shift statistics		Mean-shift statistics	
T	Percentile	max F	min τ_τ	max F	min τ_τ
100	.025	19.15	−4.76	20.83	−5.07
	.050	16.30	−4.48	18.62	−4.80
	.100	13.64	−4.20	16.20	−4.54
250	.025	18.36	−4.66	21.31	−5.06
	.050	15.94	−4.39	19.01	−4.80
	.100	13.32	−4.12	16.72	−4.51
500	.025	18.58	−4.69	21.26	−5.05
	.050	16.04	−4.39	18.99	−4.78
	.100	13.20	−4.13	16.78	−4.51

Source: Banerjee, Lumsdaine and Stock (1992, Table 2). Reprinted with the permission of the American Statistical Association.

Table A.6 Response surfaces for critical values of cointegration tests (see Table 4.1)

n	Model	Point (%)	ϕ_∞	SE	ϕ_1	ϕ_2
1	No constant, no trend	1	−2.5658	(0.0023)	−1.960	−10.04
		5	−1.9393	(0.0008)	−0.398	0.0
		10	−1.6156	(0.0007)	−0.181	0.0
1	Constant, no trend	1	−3.4336	(0.0024)	−5.999	−29.25
		5	−2.8621	(0.0011)	−2.738	−8.36
		10	−2.5671	(0.0009)	−1.438	−4.48
1	Constant + trend	1	−3.9638	(0.0019)	−8.353	−47.44
		5	−3.4126	(0.0012)	−4.039	−17.83
		10	−3.1279	(0.0009)	−2.418	−7.58
2	Constant, no trend	1	−3.9001	(0.0022)	−10.534	−30.03
		5	−3.3377	(0.0012)	−5.967	−8.98
		10	−3.0462	(0.0009)	−4.069	−5.73
2	Constant + trend	1	−4.3266	(0.0022)	−15.531	−34.03
		5	−3.7809	(0.0013)	−9.421	−15.06
		10	−3.4959	(0.0009)	−7.203	−4.01
3	Constant, no trend	1	−4.2981	(0.0023)	−13.790	−46.37
		5	−3.7429	(0.0012)	−8.352	−13.41
		10	−3.4518	(0.0010)	−6.241	−2.79
3	Constant + trend	1	−4.6676	(0.0022)	−18.492	−49.35
		5	−4.1193	(0.0011)	−12.024	−13.13
		10	−3.8344	(0.0009)	−9.188	−4.85
4	Constant, no trend	1	−4.6493	(0.0023)	−17.188	−59.20
		5	−4.1000	(0.0012)	−10.745	−21.57
		10	−3.8110	(0.0009)	−8.317	−5.19
4	Constant + trend	1	−4.9695	(0.0021)	−22.504	−50.22
		5	−4.4294	(0.0012)	−14.501	−19.54
		10	−4.1474	(0.0010)	−11.165	−9.88
5	Constant, no trend	1	−4.9587	(0.0026)	−22.140	−37.29
		5	−4.4185	(0.0013)	−13.641	−21.16
		10	−4.1327	(0.0009)	−10.638	−5.48
5	Constant + trend	1	−5.2497	(0.0024)	−26.606	−49.56
		5	−4.7154	(0.0013)	−17.432	−16.50
		10	−4.4345	(0.0010)	−13.654	−5.77
6	Constant, no trend	1	−5.2400	(0.0029)	−26.278	−41.65
		5	−4.7048	(0.0018)	−17.120	−11.17
		10	−4.4242	(0.0010)	−13.347	0.0
6	Constant + trend	1	−5.5127	(0.0033)	−30.735	−52.50
		5	−4.9767	(0.0017)	−20.883	−9.05
		10	−4.6999	(0.0011)	−16.445	0.0

Source: MacKinnon (1991). Reprinted with the permission of Oxford University Press.

Table A.7 Critical values for the cointegration ADF test (intercept included in the cointegration regression)

		Probability of a smaller value							
		$m_2 = 1$				$m_2 = 2$			
m_1	T	0.01	0.025	0.05	0.10	0.01	0.025	0.05	0.10
0	25	−4.45	−4.02	−3.68	−3.30	−5.21	−4.71	−4.32	−3.90
	50	−4.18	−3.82	−3.51	−3.16	−4.70	−4.34	−4.02	−3.70
	100	−4.09	−3.70	−3.42	−3.12	−4.51	−4.15	−3.86	−3.54
	250	−4.02	−3.65	−3.38	−3.08	−4.35	−4.06	−3.80	−3.49
	500	−3.99	−3.67	−3.38	−3.08	−4.42	−4.07	−3.79	−3.49
1	25	−5.10	−4.60	−4.21	−3.79	−5.73	−5.20	−4.79	−4.35
	50	−4.65	−4.25	−3.93	−3.60	−5.15	−4.72	−4.40	−4.06
	100	−4.51	−4.17	−3.89	−3.55	−4.85	−4.56	−4.26	−3.94
	250	−4.39	−4.06	−3.80	−3.49	−4.71	−4.45	−4.18	−3.88
	500	−4.40	−4.08	−3.80	−3.48	−4.70	−4.38	−4.09	−3.83
2	25	−5.50	−5.02	−4.64	−4.23	−6.15	−5.66	−5.22	−4.75
	50	−4.93	−4.64	−4.30	−3.99	−5.54	−5.14	−4.77	−4.42
	100	−4.81	−4.49	−4.25	−3.93	−5.29	−4.90	−4.59	−4.26
	250	−4.77	−4.41	−4.16	−3.88	−5.06	−4.76	−4.49	−4.19
	500	−4.73	−4.41	−4.15	−3.83	−4.99	−4.68	−4.44	−4.16
3	25	−6.02	−5.49	−5.09	−4.64	−6.68	−6.09	−5.60	−5.12
	50	−5.38	−5.04	−4.71	−4.36	−5.76	−5.38	−5.08	−4.75
	100	−5.20	−4.89	−4.56	−4.25	−5.58	−5.23	−4.92	−4.60
	250	−5.05	−4.75	−4.48	−4.16	−5.44	−5.12	−4.83	−4.52
	500	−5.05	−4.71	−4.48	−4.17	−5.37	−5.06	−4.80	−4.48
4	25	−6.50	−5.98	−5.49	−5.03	−6.99	−6.41	−6.01	−5.53
	50	−5.81	−5.41	−5.09	−4.72	−6.24	−5.82	−5.48	−5.10
	100	−5.58	−5.23	−4.93	−4.59	−5.88	−5.50	−5.20	−4.89
	250	−5.39	−5.05	−4.28	−4.48	−5.64	−5.33	−5.07	−4.77
	500	−5.36	−5.03	−4.75	−4.45	−5.60	−5.31	−5.03	−4.74

The standard errors of the fractiles vary, but generally they lie in the interval {0.01–0.03}. The simulations were based upon 10 000 replications. An intercept was included in the cointegration regression. m_1 and m_2 denote the number of I(1) and I(2) regressors respectively.
Source: Haldrup (1994, Table 1). Reprinted with the kind permission of Elsevier Science SA, Lausanne, Switzerland, publishers of *Journal of Econometrics*.

Table A8 Critical values of the (t-ratio) ECM test (different number of regressors)

	T	0.01	0.05	0.10	0.25
		A. (with constant)			
(k = 1)	25	−4.12	−3.35	−2.95	−2.36
	50	−3.94	−3.28	−2.93	−2.38
	100	−3.92	−3.27	−2.94	−2.40
	500	−3.82	−3.23	−2.90	−2.40
	5000	−3.78	−3.19	−2.89	−2.41
(2)	25	−4.53	−3.64	−3.24	−2.60
	50	−4.29	−3.57	−3.20	−2.63
	100	−4.22	−3.56	−3.22	−2.67
	500	−4.11	−3.50	−3.19	−2.66
	5000	−4.06	−3.48	−3.19	−2.65
(3)	25	−4.92	−3.91	−3.46	−2.76
	50	−4.59	−3.82	−3.45	−2.84
	100	−4.49	−3.82	−3.47	−2.90
	500	−4.47	−3.77	−3.45	−2.90
	5000	−4.46	−3.74	−3.42	−2.89
(4)	25	−5.27	−4.18	−3.68	−2.90
	50	−4.85	−4.05	−3.64	−3.03
	100	−4.71	−4.03	−3.67	−3.10
	500	−4.62	−3.99	−3.67	−3.11
	5000	−4.57	−3.97	−3.66	−3.10
(5)	25	−5.53	−4.46	−3.82	−2.99
	50	−5.04	−4.43	−3.82	−3.18
	100	−4.92	−4.30	−3.85	−3.28
	500	−4.81	−4.39	−3.86	−3.32
	5000	−4.70	−4.27	−3.82	−3.29

Table A8 *Continued*

	T	0.01	0.05	0.10	0.25
		B. (with constant and trend)			
$(k-1)$	25	−4.77	−3.89	−3.48	−2.88
	50	−4.48	−3.78	−3.44	−2.92
	100	−4.35	−3.75	−3.43	−2.91
	500	−4.30	−3.71	−3.41	−2.91
	5000	−4.27	−3.69	−3.39	−2.89
(2)	25	−5.12	−4.18	−3.72	−3.04
	50	−4.76	−4.04	−3.66	−3.09
	100	−4.60	−3.98	−3.66	−3.11
	500	−4.54	−3.94	−3.64	−3.11
	5000	−4.51	−3.91	−3.62	−3.10
(3)	25	−5.42	−4.39	−3.89	−3.16
	50	−5.04	−4.25	−3.86	−3.25
	100	−4.86	−4.19	−3.86	−3.30
	500	−4.76	−4.15	−3.84	−3.31
	5000	−4.72	−4.12	−3.82	−3.29
(4)	25	−5.79	−4.56	−4.04	−3.26
	50	−5.21	−4.43	−4.03	−3.39
	100	−5.07	−4.38	−4.02	−3.46
	500	−4.93	−4.34	−4.02	−3.47
	5000	−4.89	−4.30	−4.00	−3.45
(5)	25	−6.18	−4.76	−4.16	−3.31
	50	−5.37	−4.60	−4.19	−3.53
	100	−5.24	−4.55	−4.19	−3.66
	500	−5.15	−4.54	−4.20	−3.69
	5000	−5.11	−4.52	−4.18	−3.67

Source: Banerjee, Dolado and Mestre (1992, Table 4). Reprinted with the permission of the authors.

Table A.9 Critical values for the 't' and 'F' statistics on π_3 and π_4 (see Table 4.2)

Coint. regr. with Deter.	T	't' π_3 0.01	0.025	0.05	0.01	't' π_4 0.01	0.025	0.05	0.95	0.975	0.99	'F' $\pi_3 \cap \pi_4$ 0.50	0.90	0.95	0.975	0.99
–	48	−4.04	−3.66	−3.34	−3.00	−2.99	−2.46	−2.05	2.05	2.42	2.90	2.59	6.01	7.46	8.81	10.80
	100	−3.94	−3.59	−3.30	−3.00	−3.01	−2.54	−2.12	2.10	2.50	2.94	2.61	5.91	7.21	8.63	10.24
	136	−3.90	−3.57	−3.28	−2.98	−3.01	−2.53	−2.15	2.13	2.51	2.92	2.60	5.83	7.11	8.39	10.14
	200	−3.89	−3.56	−3.29	−2.98	−3.04	−2.56	−2.13	2.13	2.52	2.99	2.63	5.84	7.11	8.35	10.10
I	48	−3.96	−3.57	−3.27	−2.93	−2.93	−2.44	−2.03	2.12	2.54	2.96	2.59	5.96	7.35	8.77	10.51
	100	−3.86	−3.54	−3.27	−2.95	−2.95	−2.49	−2.08	2.12	2.52	2.95	2.59	5.83	7.10	8.42	10.15
	136	−3.84	−3.54	−3.26	−2.96	−2.99	−2.52	−2.10	2.14	2.52	2.98	2.60	5.83	7.13	8.40	10.09
	200	−3.86	−3.52	−3.26	−2.96	−2.95	−2.53	−2.13	2.15	2.55	3.00	2.61	5.79	7.01	8.26	10.02
I, SD	48	−4.87	−4.49	−4.18	−3.84	−2.97	−2.48	−2.07	2.08	2.47	2.95	4.71	9.00	10.65	12.18	14.11
	100	−4.77	−4.40	−4.12	−3.81	−3.02	−2.56	−2.14	2.10	2.50	2.98	4.70	8.66	10.12	11.48	13.26
	136	−4.77	−4.42	−4.14	−3.81	−2.99	−2.55	−2.14	2.13	2.50	2.97	4.71	8.57	9.99	11.41	13.25
	200	−4.76	−4.40	−4.12	−3.81	−2.96	−2.52	−2.13	2.12	2.52	2.97	4.71	8.57	9.99	11.41	13.25

Source: Engle, Granger, Hylleburg and Lee (1993, Table A.1). Reprinted with the kind permission of Elsevier Science SA, Lausanne, Switzerland, publishers of *Journal of Econometrics*.

Table A.10 Quantiles of the asymptotic distribution of the cointegration rank test statistics: Model 2 in text (see equation (5.6))

$n-r$	50%	80%	90%	95%	97.5%	99%	Mean	Var
				λ – max				
1	3.40	5.91	7.52	9.24	10.80	12.97	4.03	7.07
2	8.27	11.54	13.75	15.67	17.63	20.20	8.86	13.08
3	13.47	17.40	19.77	22.00	24.07	26.81	14.02	19.24
4	18.70	22.95	25.56	28.14	30.32	33.24	19.23	23.83
5	23.78	28.76	31.66	34.40	36.90	39.79	24.48	29.26
6	29.08	34.25	37.45	40.30	43.22	46.82	29.72	34.63
7	34.73	40.13	43.25	46.45	48.99	51.91	35.18	38.35
8	39.70	45.53	48.91	52.00	54.71	57.95	40.35	41.98
9	44.97	50.73	54.35	57.42	60.50	63.71	45.55	44.13
10	50.21	56.52	60.25	63.57	66.24	69.94	50.82	49.28
11	55.70	62.38	66.02	69.74	72.64	76.63	56.33	54.99
				Trace				
1	3.40	5.91	7.52	9.24	10.80	12.97	4.03	7.07
2	11.25	15.25	17.85	19.96	22.05	24.60	11.91	18.94
3	23.28	28.75	32.00	34.91	37.61	41.07	23.84	37.98
4	38.84	45.65	49.65	53.12	56.06	60.16	39.50	59.42
5	58.46	66.91	71.86	76.07	80.06	84.45	59.16	91.65
6	81.90	91.57	97.18	102.14	106.74	111.01	82.49	126.94
7	109.17	120.35	126.58	131.70	136.49	143.09	109.75	167.91
8	139.83	152.56	159.48	165.58	171.28	177.20	140.57	208.09
9	174.88	198.08	196.37	202.92	208.81	215.74	175.44	257.84
10	212.93	228.08	236.54	244.15	251.30	257.68	213.53	317.24
11	254.84	272.82	282.45	291.40	298.31	307.64	256.15	413.35

Source: Osterwald-Lenum (1992, Table 1*). Reprinted with the permission of Blackwell Publishers.

Table A.11 Quantiles of the asymptotic distribution of the cointegration rank test statistics: Model 3 in text (see equation (5.6))

$n-r$	50%	80%	90%	95%	97.5%	99%	Mean	Var
				$\lambda-$ max				
1	0.44	1.66	2.69	3.76	4.95	6.65	0.99	2.04
2	6.85	10.04	12.07	14.07	16.05	18.63	7.47	12.42
3	12.34	16.20	18.60	20.97	23.09	25.52	12.88	18.67
4	17.66	21.98	24.73	27.07	28.98	32.24	18.26	23.47
5	23.05	27.85	30.90	33.46	35.71	38.77	23.67	28.82
6	28.45	33.67	36.76	39.37	41.86	45.10	29.06	33.57
7	33.83	39.12	42.32	45.28	47.96	51.57	34.37	37.41
8	39.29	45.05	48.33	51.42	54.29	57.69	39.85	42.90
9	44.58	50.55	53.98	57.12	59.33	62.80	45.10	44.93
10	49.66	55.97	59.62	62.81	65.44	69.09	50.29	49.41
11	54.99	61.55	65.38	68.83	72.11	75.95	55.63	54.92
				Trace				
1	0.44	1.66	2.69	3.76	4.95	6.65	0.99	2.04
2	7.55	11.07	13.33	15.41	17.52	20.04	8.23	14.38
3	18.70	23.64	26.79	29.68	32.56	35.65	19.32	32.43
4	33.60	40.15	43.95	47.21	50.35	54.46	34.24	52.75
5	52.30	60.29	64.84	68.52	71.80	76.07	52.95	79.25
6	75.26	84.57	89.48	94.15	98.33	103.18	75.74	114.65
7	101.22	112.30	118.50	124.24	128.45	133.57	101.91	158.78
8	131.62	143.97	150.53	156.00	161.32	168.36	132.09	201.82
9	165.11	178.90	186.39	192.89	198.82	204.95	165.90	246.45
10	202.58	217.81	225.85	233.13	239.46	247.18	203.39	300.80
11	243.90	260.82	269.96	277.71	284.87	293.44	244.66	379.56

Source: Osterwald-Lenum (1992, Table 1). Reprinted with the permission of Blackwell Publishers.

Table A.12 Quantiles of the asymptotic distribution of the cointegration rank test statistics: Model 4 in text (see equation (5.6))

$n-r$	50%	80%	90%	95%	97.5%	99%	Mean	Var
				λ – max				
1	5.55	8.65	10.49	12.25	14.21	16.26	6.22	10.11
2	10.90	14.70	16.85	18.96	21.14	23.65	11.51	16.38
3	16.24	20.45	23.11	25.54	27.68	30.34	16.82	22.01
4	21.50	26.30	29.12	31.46	33.60	36.65	22.08	27.74
5	26.72	31.72	34.75	37.52	40.01	42.36	27.32	31.36
6	32.01	37.50	40.91	43.97	46.84	49.51	32.68	37.91
7	37.57	43.11	46.32	49.42	51.94	54.71	38.06	39.74
8	42.72	48.56	52.16	55.50	58.08	62.46	43.34	44.83
9	48.17	54.34	57.87	61.29	64.12	67.88	48.74	49.20
10	53.21	59.49	63.18	66.23	69.56	73.73	53.74	52.64
11	58.54	64.97	69.26	72.72	75.72	79.23	59.15	56.97
				Trace				
1	5.55	8.65	10.49	12.25	14.21	16.26	6.22	10.11
2	15.59	20.19	22.76	25.32	27.75	30.45	16.20	24.90
3	29.53	35.56	39.06	42.44	45.42	48.45	30.15	45.68
4	47.17	54.80	59.14	62.99	66.25	70.05	47.79	74.48
5	68.64	77.83	83.20	87.31	91.06	96.58	69.35	106.56
6	94.05	104.73	110.42	114.90	119.29	124.75	94.67	143.33
7	122.87	134.57	141.01	146.76	152.52	158.49	123.51	182.85
8	155.40	169.10	176.67	182.82	187.91	196.08	156.41	234.11
9	192.37	207.25	215.17	222.21	228.05	234.41	193.03	288.30
10	231.59	247.91	256.72	263.42	270.33	279.07	232.25	345.23
11	276.34	294.12	303.13	310.81	318.02	327.45	276.88	416.98

Source: Osterwald-Lenum (1992, Table 2*). Reprinted with the permission of Blackwell Publishers.

Table A.13 Sample size is 25; the data generating process contains no trend; and the constant term μ is unrestricted

Dim	50%	80%	90%	95%	97.5%	99%	Mean	Var
				(A) Maximal eigenvalue				
1	2.43	4.93	6.70	8.29	9.91	12.09	3.06	7.36
2	7.86	11.38	13.70	15.75	17.88	20.51	8.54	14.76
3	13.80	18.16	20.90	23.26	25.66	28.57	14.46	22.80
4	20.36	25.56	28.56	31.66	34.47	37.61	21.07	32.97
				(B) Trace				
1	2.43	4.93	6.70	8.29	9.91	12.09	3.06	7.36
2	9.78	13.99	16.56	18.90	21.26	23.70	10.45	20.64
3	21.79	27.69	31.22	34.37	37.44	40.98	22.54	42.57
4	39.32	47.10	51.59	55.92	59.60	64.33	40.09	77.08

Source: Franses (1994, Table A.1). Reprinted with the kind permission of Elsevier Science SA, Lausanne, Switzerland, publishers of *Journal of Econometrics*.

Table A.14 Sample size is 25; the data-generating process contains no trend; and the constant term μ is restricted by $\mu = \alpha\beta_0$

Dim	50%	80%	90%	95%	97.5%	99%	Mean	Var
				(A) Maximal eigenvalue				
1	3.55	6.01	7.72	9.35	10.97	12.09	4.14	7.08
2	8.82	12.15	14.40	16.51	18.36	20.56	9.36	14.33
3	14.56	18.89	21.56	23.90	26.21	29.44	15.24	22.84
4	21.01	26.15	29.26	32.18	34.74	38.12	21.69	32.79
				(B) Trace				
1	3.55	6.01	7.72	9.35	10.97	12.90	4.14	7.08
2	11.95	16.09	18.63	20.96	22.78	25.71	12.55	20.81
3	25.01	31.01	34.44	37.85	40.56	44.60	25.74	44.16
4	43.40	51.38	55.78	59.98	63.51	67.74	44.20	78.19

Source: Franses (1994, Table A.2). Reprinted with the kind permission of Elsevier Science SA, Lausanne, Switzerland, publishers of *Journal of Econometrics*.

Table A.15 Sample size is 50; the data-generating process contains no trend; and the constant term μ is unrestricted

Dim	50%	80%	90%	95%	97.5%	99%	Mean	Var
				(A) Maximal eigenvalue				
1	2.44	4.89	6.40	8.09	9.54	11.39	3.02	6.73
2	7.71	11.09	13.15	15.18	16.98	19.18	8.30	13.42
3	13.34	17.44	19.94	22.29	24.31	26.98	13.92	20.61
4	19.00	23.78	26.63	29.15	31.93	35.20	19.64	28.05
				(B) Trace				
1	2.44	4.89	6.40	8.09	9.54	11.39	3.02	6.73
2	9.51	13.57	16.06	18.25	20.13	22.81	10.18	19.02
3	21.07	26.78	30.07	32.94	35.59	39.10	21.75	38.87
4	36.86	44.10	48.25	51.98	55.88	59.94	37.59	65.89

Source: Franses (1994, Table A.3). Reprinted with the kind permission of Elsevier Science SA, Lausanne, Switzerland, publishers of *Journal of Econometrics*.

Table A.16 Sample size is 50; the data-generating process contains no trend; and the constant term μ is restricted by $\mu = \alpha\beta_0$

Dim	50%	80%	90%	95%	97.5%	99%	Mean	Var
				(A) Maximal eigenvalue				
1	3.49	5.91	7.59	9.22	10.93	13.06	4.10	7.05
2	8.58	12.05	14.05	15.99	17.92	20.60	9.19	13.94
3	13.99	18.01	20.57	23.01	25.24	27.95	14.59	20.88
4	19.63	24.44	27.23	29.79	32.47	35.33	20.32	27.78
				(B) Trace				
1	3.49	5.91	7.59	9.22	10.93	13.06	4.10	7.05
2	11.74	15.79	18.25	20.61	22.85	25.49	12.32	20.40
3	24.16	29.91	33.08	36.33	39.28	45.58	24.79	40.81
4	40.88	48.44	52.71	56.62	60.00	64.29	41.73	69.24

Source: Franses (1994, Table A.4). Reprinted with the kind permission of Elsevier Science SA, Lausanne, Switzerland, publishers of *Journal of Econometrics*.

References

Banerjee, A., Hendry, D.F. and G.W. Smith (1986) Exploring equilibrium relationships in econometrics through static models: Some Monte Carlo evidence, *Oxford Bulletin of Economics and Statistics*, **52**, 95–104.

Banerjee, A., Dolado, J.J. and R. Mestre (1992) On some simple tests for cointegration: The cost of simplicity, Bank of Spain Working Paper, No. 9302.

Banerjee, A., Lumsdaine, R.L. and J.H. Stock (1992) Recursive and sequential tests of the unit-root and trend-break hypotheses: Theory and international evidence, *Journal of Business & Economic Statistics*, **10**, 271–87.

Banerjee, A., Dolado, J.J., Galbraith, J.W. and D.F. Hendry (1993) *Co-integration, Error-Correction, and the Econometric Analysis of Non-Stationary Data*, Advanced Texts in Econometrics, Oxford University Press.

Baumol, W.J. (1952) The transactions demand for cash: An inventory theoretic approach, *Quarterly Journal of Economics*, **66**, 545–56.

Blough, S.R. (1992) The relationship between power and level for generic unit root tests in finite samples, *Journal of Applied Econometrics*, **7**, 295–308.

Campbell, J.Y. and P. Perron (1991) Pitfalls and opportunities: What macroeconomists should know about unit roots, in Blanchard, O.J. and Fischer, S. (eds.) *NBER Economics Annual 1991*, MIT Press.

Cheung, Y.-W. and K.S. Lai (1993) Finite-sample sizes of Johansen's likelihood ratio tests for cointegration, *Oxford Bulletin of Economics and Statistics*, **55**, 313–28.

Clements, M.P. and G.E. Mizon (1991) Empirical analysis of macroeconomic time series: VAR and structural models, *European Review*, **35**, 887–932.

Davidson, R. and J.G. MacKinnon (1993) *Estimation and Inference in Econometrics*, Oxford University Press, Oxford.

DeJong, D.N., Nankervis, J.C. and N.E. Savin (1992) Integration versus trend stationarity in time series, *Econometrica*, **60**, 423–33.

Dickey, D.A. (1976) Estimation and Hypothesis Testing for Nonstationary Times Series, PhD dissertation, Iowa State University.

Dickey, D.A. and W.A. Fuller (1979) Distribution of the estimators for autoregressive time series with a unit root, *Journal of the American Statistical Association*, **74**, 427–31.

Dickey, D.A. and W.A. Fuller (1981) Likelihood ratio statistics for autoregressive time series with a unit root, *Econometrica*, **49**, 1057–72.

Dickey, D.A. and S.G. Pantula (1987) Determining the order of differencing in autoregressive processes, *Journal of Business and Economic Statistics*, **15**, 455–61.

Doornik, J. and H. Hansen (1993) A Practical Test of Multivariate Normality, Nuffield College, University of Oxford.

Doornik, J. and D.F. Hendry (1992) *PcGive (Version 7): An Interactive Econometric Modelling System*, Institute of Economics and Statistics, University of Oxford.

Doornik, J. and D.F. Hendry (1994) *PcFiml version 8: Interactive Econometric Modelling of Dynamic Systems*, Institute of Economics and Statistics, University of Oxford.

Engle, R.F., Hendry, D.F. and J.-F. Richard (1983) Exogeneity, *Econometrica*, **51**, 277–304.

Engle, R.F. and C.W.J. Granger (1987) Cointegration and error correction: Representation, estimation and testing, *Econometrica*, **55**, 251–76.

Engle, R.F. and B.S. Yoo (1991) Cointegrated economic time series: An overview with new results, in R.F. Engle and C.W.J. Granger (eds.) *Long-Run Economic Relationships*, Oxford University Press, 237–66.

Engle, R.F., Granger, C.W.J., Hylleburg, S. and H.S. Lee (1993) Seasonal co-integration: The Japanese consumption function, *Journal of Econometrics*, **55**, 275–98.

Ericsson, N.R., Hendry, D.F. and H.-A. Tran (1992) Cointegration, Seasonality, Encompassing, and the Demand for Money in the United Kingdom, Discussion Paper, Board of Governors of the Federal Reserve System, Washington, DC.

Fischer, A.M. (1993) Weak exogeneity and dynamic stability in cointegrated VARs, *Economic Letters*, **43**, 167–70.

Franses, P.H. (1993) A method to select between periodic cointegration and seasonal cointegration, *Economic Letters*, **41**, 7–10.

Franses, P.H. (1994) A multivariate approach to modeling univariate seasonal time series, *Journal of Econometrics*, **63**, 133–51.

Friedman, M. and A.J. Schwartz (1982) *Monetary Trends in the United States and the United Kingdom: Their Relation to Income, Prices, and Interest Rates, 1867–1975*, University of Chicago Press, Chicago.

Fuller, W.A. (1976) *Introduction to Statistical Time Series*, John Wiley, New York.

Ghysels, E. and P. Perron (1993) The effect of seasonal adjustment filters on tests for a unit root, *Journal of Econometrics*, **55**, 57–98.

Ghysels, E., Lee, H.S. and J. Noh (1994) Testing for unit roots in seasonal time series, *Journal of Econometrics*, **62**, 415–42.

Haldrup, N. (1994) The asymptotics of single-equation cointegration regressions with I(1) and I(2) variables, *Journal of Econometrics*, **63**, 153–81.

Hansen, B.E. (1992) Efficient estimation and testing of cointegrating vectors in the presence of deterministic trends, *Journal of Econometrics*, **53**, 87–121.

Hansen, H. and K. Juselius (1994) *Manual to Cointegration Analysis of Time Series CATS in RATS*, Institute of Economics, University of Copenhagen.

Harris, R.I.D. (1985) Interrelated demand for factors of production in the UK engineering industry, 1968–81, *Economic Journal*, **95**, 1049–68 (reprinted in G. Galeazzi and D.S. Hamermesh (eds.) (1993) *Dynamic Labor Demand and Adjustment Costs*, Edward Elgar, Aldershot).

Harris, R.I.D. (1992a) Testing for unit roots using the augmented Dickey–Fuller test: Some issues relating to the size, power and the lag structure of the test, *Economic Letters*, **38**, 381–6.

Harris, R.I.D. (1992b) Small sample testing for unit roots, *Oxford Bulletin of Economics and Statistics*, **54**, 615–25.

Harris, R.I.D. (1994) Cointegration analysis using the Johansen technique: A practitioner's guide to the software, *Economic Journal*, **104**, 1227–38.

Harvey, A.C. (1990) *The Econometric Analysis of Time Series*, 2nd Edition, Philip Allan.

Hendry, D.F., Pagan, A.R. and J.D. Sargan (1984) Dynamic specification, in Z. Griliches and M.D. Intriligator (eds.) *Handbook of Econometrics, vol. II*, North-Holland, Amsterdam.

Hendry, D.F. and N.R. Ericsson (1991) Modelling the demand for narrow money in the United Kingdom and the United States, *European Economic Review*, **35**, 833–81.

Hendry, D.F. and J.A. Doornik (1994) Modelling linear dynamic econometric systems, *Scottish Journal of Political Economy*, **41**, 1–33.

Hendry, D.F. and G.E. Mizon (1993) Evaluating dynamic econometric models by encompassing the VAR, in P.C.P. Phillips (ed.) *Models, Methods and Applications of Econometrics*, Basil Blackwell, Oxford.

Hylleburg, S., Engle, R.F., Granger, C.W.J. and B.S. Yoo (1990) Seasonal integration and co-integration, *Journal of Econometrics*, **44**, 215–28.

Inder, B. (1993) Estimating long-run relationships in economics: A comparison of different approaches, *Journal of Econometrics*, **57**, 53–68.

Johansen, S. (1988) Statistical analysis of cointegration vectors, *Journal of Economic Dynamics and Control*, **12**, 231–54.

Johansen, S. (1991) A Statistical Analysis of Cointegration for $I(2)$ Variables, University of Copenhagen.

Johansen, S. (1992a) Cointegration in partial systems and the efficiency of single equations analysis, *Journal of Econometrics*, **52**, 389–402.

Johansen, S. (1992b) Testing weak exogeneity and the order of cointegration in UK money demand, *Journal of Policy Modeling*, **14**, 313–34.

Johansen, S. (1992c) Determination of cointegration rank in the presence of a linear trend, *Oxford Bulletin of Economics and Statistics*, **54**, 383–97.

Johansen, S. (1992d) Identifying Restrictions of Linear Equations, Institute of Mathematical Statistics, University of Copenhagen.

Johansen, S. (1994) A statistical analysis of I(2) variables, *Econometric Theory*, forthcoming.

Johansen, S. and K. Juselius (1992) Testing structural hypotheses in a multivariate cointegration analysis of the PPP and the UIP for UK, *Journal of Econometrics*, **53**, 211–44.

Johansen, S. and K. Juselius (1994) Identification of the long-run and the short-run structure: An application to the ISLM model, *Journal of Econometrics*, **63**, 7–36.

Johansen, S. and B. Nielsen (1993) *Asymptotics for Cointegration Rank Tests in the Presence of Intervention Dummies – Manual for the Simulation Program DisCo*, Institute of Mathematical Statistics, University of Copenhagen.

Johnston, J. (1984) *Econometric Methods*, 3rd edition, McGraw-Hill International Student Edition, London.

Juselius, K. (1994) Do purchasing power parity and uncovered interest rate parity hold in the long-run? – An example of likelihood inference in a multivariate times-series model, *Journal of Econometrics*, forthcoming.

Kahn, J.A. and M. Ogaki (1992) A consistent test for the null of stationarity against the alternative of a unit root, *Economic Letters*, **39**, 7–11.

Kiviet, J. and G.D.A. Phillips (1992) Exact similar tests for unit roots and cointegration, *Oxford Bulletin of Economics and Statistics*, **54**, 349–67.

Kleibergen, F. and H.K. van Dijk (1994) Direct cointegration testing in error correction models, *Journal of Econometrics*, **63**, 61–103.

Kremers, J.J.M., Ericsson, N.R. and J. Dolado (1992) The power of co-integration tests, *Oxford Bulletin of Economics and Statistics*, **54**, 325–48.

Laidler, D.E.W. (1984) The 'buffer stock' notion in monetary economics, *Economic Journal*, **94**, suppl., 17–94.

Leybourne, S.J. (1994) Testing for unit roots: A simple alternative to Dickey–Fuller, *Applied Economics*, **26**, 721–9.

MacKinnon, J. (1991) Critical values for co-integration tests, in R.F. Engle and C.W.J. Granger (eds.) *Long-Run Economic Relationships*, Oxford University Press, pp. 267–76.

Maekawa, K. (1994) Prewhitened unit root test, *Economic Letters*, **45**, 145–53.

McAleer, M. and L. Oxley (1993) Software review of Microfit 3.0, *Economic Journal*, **103**, 767–74.

Muscatelli, V.A. and S. Hurn (1991) Cointegration and dynamic time series models, *Journal of Economic Surveys*, 6, pp. 1–43.

Nankervis, J.C. and N.E. Savin (1985) Testing the autoregressive parameter with the *t*-statistic, *Journal of Econometrics*, **27**, 143–61.

Osborn, D.R., Chui, A.P.L., Smith, J.P. and C.R. Birchenhall (1988) Seasonality and the order of integration for consumption, *Oxford Bulletin of Economics and Statistics*, **50**, 361–77.

Osborn, D.R. (1990) A survey of seasonality in UK macroeconomic variables, *International Journal of Forecasting*, **6**, 327–36.

Osborn, D.R. (1993) Comments on Engle *et al.*, *Journal of Econometrics*, **55**, 299–302.

Osterwald-Lenum, M. (1992) A note with quantiles of the asymptotic distribution of the ML cointegration rank test statistics, *Oxford Bulletin of Economics and Statistics*, **54**, pp. 461–72.

Pagan, A.R. and M.R. Wickens (1989) A survey of some recent econometric methods, *Economic Journal*, **99**, 962–1025.

Paruolo, P. (1993) On the Determination of Integration Indices in I(2) Systems, Discussion Paper, University of Bologna.

Perron, P. (1988) Trends and random walks in macroeconomic time series: Further evidence from a new approach, *Journal of Economic Dynamics and Control*, **12**, 297–332.

Perron, P. (1989) The Great Crash, the oil shock and the unit root hypothesis, *Econometrica*, **57**, 1361–402.

Perron, P. (1990) Testing for a unit root in a time series with a changing mean, *Journal of Business and Economic Statistics*, **8**, 153–62.

Phillips, P.C.B. (1986) Understanding spurious regressions in econometrics, *Journal of Econometrics*, **33**, 311–40.

Phillips, P.C.B. (1987) Time series regression with a unit root, *Econometrica*, **55**, 277–301.

Phillips, P.C.B. and S.N. Durlauf (1986) Multiple time series regression with integrated processes, *Review of Economic Studies*, **53**, 473–95.

Phillips, P.C.B. and P. Perron (1988) Testing for a unit root in times series regression, *Biometrica*, **75**, 335–46.

Phillips, P.C.B. and B.E. Hansen (1990) Statistical inference in instrumental variables regression with I(1) processes, *Review of Economic Studies*, **57**, 99–125.

Podivinsky, J.M. (1992) Small sample properties of tests of linear restrictions on cointegrating vectors and their weights, *Economic Letters*, **39**, 13–18.

Psaradakis, Z. (1994) A comparison of tests of linear hypotheses in cointegrated vector autoregressive models, *Economic Letters*, **45**, 137–44.

Reimers, H.-E. (1992) Comparisons of tests for multivariate cointegration, *Statistical Papers*, **33**, 335–59.

Said, S.E. and D.A. Dickey (1984) Testing for unit roots in autoregressive–moving average models of unknown order, *Biometrika*, **71**, 599–607.

Sargan, J.D. (1964) Wages and prices in the United Kingdom: A study in econometric methodology, in P.E. Hart, G. Mills and J.K. Whitaker (eds.) *Econometric Analysis for National Economic Planning*, Butterworths, London, pp. 25–63.

Sargan, J.D. and A. Bhargava (1983) Testing residuals from least squares regression for being generated by the Gaussian random walk, *Econometrica*, **51**, 153–74.

Schwert, G.W. (1989) Tests for unit roots: A Monte Carlo investigation, *Journal of Business and Economic Statistics*, **7**, 147–59.

Sims, C.A. (1980) Macroeconomics and reality, *Econometrica*, **48**, 1–48.

Stock, J.H. (1987) Asymptotic properties of least-squares estimators of co-integrating vectors, *Econometrica*, **55**, 1035–56.

Thomas, R.L. (1993) *Introductory Econometrics: Theory and Applications*, Longman, London.

Tobin, J. (1956) The interest-elasticity of transactions demand for cash, *Review of Economics and Statistics*, **38**, 241–7.

Tobin, J. (1958) Liquidity preference as behavior towards risk, *Review of Economic Studies*, **25**, 65–86.

Urbain, J.-P. (1992) On weak exogeneity in error correction models, *Oxford Bulletin of Economics and Statistics*, **54**, 187–207.

West, K.D. (1988) Asymptotic normality, when regressors have a unit root, *Econometrica*, **56**, 1397–418

Index